Earthbound

Earthbound

The Aesthetics of Sovereignty in the Anthropocene

Daniel Matthews

EDINBURGH
University Press

Edinburgh University Press is one of the leading university presses in the UK. We publish academic books and journals in our selected subject areas across the humanities and social sciences, combining cutting-edge scholarship with high editorial and production values to produce academic works of lasting importance. For more information visit our website: edinburghuniversitypress.com

Edinburgh University Press Ltd
The Tun – Holyrood Road
12(2f) Jackson's Entry
Edinburgh EH8 8PJ

First published in hardback by Edinburgh University Press 2021

Typeset in 11/13pt Adobe Garamond Pro by
Servis Filmsetting Ltd, Stockport, Cheshire

A CIP record for this book is available from the British Library

ISBN 978 1 4744 5530 5 (hardback)
ISBN 978 1 4744 5531 2 (paperback)
ISBN 978 1 4744 5532 9 (webready PDF)
ISBN 978 1 4744 5533 6 (epub)

Contents

Acknowledgements

The French philosopher Jean-Luc Nancy reminds us that 'one never writes alone'. This is particularly true of a project such as this, which has had the support of a number of people and institutions, to whom I would like to record my gratitude. The research that led to this publication was generously funded by the Research Grants Council of Hong Kong, General Research Fund (Early Career Scheme). This allowed for a semester of teaching relief which gave me the time needed to lay the foundations for the project. Two subsequent visiting research fellowships, first at the University of Glasgow and then at the Birkbeck Institute for the Humanities, provided excellent opportunities to bury myself in the library and occasionally emerge to test my nascent ideas on engaged, critical but always friendly audiences. Many thanks to Emilios Christodoulidis and Lindsay Farmer for supporting my time with the Glasgow Legal Theory group; and to Lou Miller and Stewart Motha for helping set me up in London and for facilitating a highly productive workshop whilst I was there.

My erstwhile colleagues at the Faculty of Law at the University of Hong Kong encouraged and assisted throughout the research and writing process. Particular thanks to my fellow travellers in the world of law and the humanities: Marco Wan, Janny Leung, Anya Adair, Michael Ng and Christopher Hutton. It has been a great privilege, and a source of enduring inspiration, to be part of a research and teaching community dedicated to interdisciplinary, critical and creative approaches to the study of law; long may it continue! Students taking my 'Sovereignty in Law, Theory and Culture' course invariably provided keen insight into many of the themes that animate these pages and always encouraged me to think harder (and be clearer) wherever possible. Thanks to Dihraj Nainani who was a diligent research assistant at various junctures as the project unfolded. My new colleagues at the University of Warwick have generously welcomed me into their ranks.

The Law, Literature and Humanities Association of Australasia and the Critical Legal Conference have both provided collegiate and thought-provoking forums in which to present my work and learn from others. Laura

Williamson and Sarah Foyle at Edinburgh University Press were mercifully patient as I finalised the manuscript; and many thanks to Bill MacNeil, Shaun McVeigh and the broader editorial team for supporting publication in this innovative series. Jasper Sutherland was immensely generous in providing assistance with the cover image; many thanks for this, and more besides.

Some aspects of this book draw on material published elsewhere. Some parts of Chapters 1 and 5 were published as 'Law and Aesthetics in the Anthropocene: From the Rights of Nature to the Aesthesis of Obligations', *Law, Culture and the Humanities*, DOI: 10.1177/1743872119871830 (2019, forthcoming in print); and elements of Chapters 1 and 3 were published in 'From Global to Anthropocenic Assemblages: Re-thinking Territory, Authority, Rights in the New Climatic Regime', *Modern Law Review*, 82:4, 665–91 (2019). This material has been reworked and expanded for the present publication.

This project benefited immeasurably from conversations with the following people: Stewart Motha, Illan rua Wall, Kathleen Birrell, Alex Schwartz, Lilian Moncrieff, Connal Parsley, Colin Perrin, Alistair Fraser, Peter Goodrich, Shaun McVeigh, Alessandro Pelizzon, Tara Mulqueen, Gray Kochhar-Lindgren, Nayanika Mathur, Anastasia Tataryn, Lindsay Farmer, Stacy Douglas, Kyle McGee, Costas Douzinas, Ari Hirvonen, Alain Pottage, Karen van Marle, Mark Maslin, Alison Young, Julen Etxabe, Marcelo Thompson, Rory Rowan, Vito De Lucia, Andreas Kotsakis, Tim Peters and Panu Minkkinen. My sincere thanks to all for their comments and advice, whether they knew they were giving any or not. I owe a particular debt of gratitude to Scott Veitch, without whose encouragement and support this project would never have been possible. Scott read early drafts of chapters, in various states of disrepair and auto-deconstruction, with characteristic generosity, rigour and care. A great teacher and friend, Scott continues to provide the best exemplar I know of what it means to be a scholar.

My parents, Beryl and Paul, continue to be a bountiful and deeply appreciated source of humour, wisdom and warmth. Too many friends to mention here have kept me smiling in all weathers, and for their love and comradeship I am forever grateful. Lastly, none of it would ever have happened without the support of my wife Naomi and our daughter Theodora; my admiration and love for them, though earthbound, remains boundless. That they agree to put up with me, I find joyful and humbling in equal measure. It is with heartfelt thanks that I dedicate this book to them both.

Introduction

Use your head, can't you, use your head, you're on earth and there's no cure for that!

– Samuel Beckett, *Endgame*[1]

In just four days in May 2016 the Slims River in northwest Canada ran dry. Spanning 150 metres at its widest point, this 24km waterway, originating in the Kaskawulsh Glacier, carried glacial meltwater north into Kluane Lake before joining the Yukon River and eventually heading out to the Bering Sea. Water levels in the Slims had been slowly diminishing for some years as the Glacier retreated in step with a warming climate, but a significant increase in average temperatures from January to April 2016 led to the sudden quickening of this course. The toe of the Glacier sits at a drainage divide where meltwater heads either north through the Slims or south through the Alsek River out to the Pacific Ocean. As the Glacier withdrew to a higher altitude a new channel was carved in the ice that redirected the meltwater into the Alsek. Only a reversal of the Glacier's retreat will return water to the Slims; and this will not be happening any time soon. The Kluane Lake, Yukon's largest, has seen a substantial reduction in volume and the lake basin may well become closed in the coming years; its chemical composition will change as nutrients once provided by the Slims will no longer reach its waters. The flow of the Alsek River has greatly increased, and its own course is likely to divert as the river valley accommodates the glacial runoff. All of these changes will affect habitats and ecosystems, particularly fish stocks, as the entire drainage system of the area is rewritten. Riverbed sediment, buried beneath the Slims' fast-flowing waters for hundreds of years, now regularly forms dust clouds that loom ominously over this dramatically altered landscape.[2]

Such reordering of freshwater systems, a process known as 'river piracy', is usually caused by purely 'natural phenomena': tectonic shifts, landslides or erosion. In this instance, the piracy was caused by anthropogenic climatic warming, with the transformative changes to the landscape all happening in a 'geological instant'.[3] The demise of the Slims River powerfully illustrates that the contemporary climate crisis is already reshaping landscapes and ecosystems, transforming the materiality of an earth that we so often like to think of as largely immobile. The material fabric of the planet is becoming increasingly dynamic, with its rhythms, processes and appearances liable to dramatic change. We can see these unsettling mutations, now featuring in newspaper headlines with an ominous regularity, in a range of places: the mass bleaching of corals; species extinctions; desertification and crop failures; heatwaves; flooding and coastal erosion; and the increasing ferocity of seasonal hurricanes and cyclones. The fate of the Slims also confirms how quickly the 'natural world' can be fundamentally reformed, challenging presumptions about nature's sloth-like rhythms. In the context of today's climate crisis the earth, its landscape and ecosystems, can change form with alacrity. Since the 1990s, climate scientists have become increasingly concerned about the precipitous changes that can unfold as the planetary climate system passes through 'thresholds' or 'tipping points' that can trigger large-scale changes in a matter of decades.[4] The Slims River stands as a miniature representation of precisely the kind of abrupt change that can affect the earth system as a whole. If, for instance, there continues to be a rapid loss of Arctic sea ice alongside a collapse of ice sheets and glaciers in Greenland, we will witness not only huge sea level rises – threatening some of the world's largest cities – but also the replacement of the largely reflective cover of snow and ice with a much darker ocean surface that absorbs more heat, further amplifying warming. Such a chain of events could trigger further feedback mechanisms that propel the climate system very quickly into a much hotter state.[5] It is becoming increasingly likely that in the course of this century the planetary climate system will undergo a set of significant alterations, perhaps passing through sudden transitions and reformations, that will make our astonishment at the vanishing of the Slims River pale in comparison.

Human activity, primarily through the burning of fossil fuels, is altering the chemical composition of the atmosphere and oceans in a way unprecedented for millions of years. The atmospheric CO_2 'parts per million' (ppm) count recently passed the 400ppm mark that many climatologists take to be a signal of irreversible change beyond the nominally 'safe limit' of a 2°C increase above pre-industrial averages. The last time atmospheric CO_2 ppm was at this level was during the Pliocene epoch, 4 million years ago, when humans did not exist and sea levels were 25 metres higher than today. The speed of reductions in CO_2 emissions needed to reach the 2°C target is so extreme that many consider the goal itself unachievable. Global temperatures are already 1.1°C above the pre-industrial average and the speed of change required to restrain emissions in an effort to keep warming at that level is almost unthinkable. Nicholas Stern's 2006 report into the economic costs associated with climate change argued that stabilisation of CO_2 levels at 550ppm was the best we could expect, as any sharper reductions would be unattainable with current and achievable technologies.[6] But even meeting the 550ppm target seems unlikely. Even if we assume that emissions peaked at the time of writing (in 2020) and global emissions reduce by 3 per cent every year, with rich countries meeting very high reduction rates of 6–7 per cent, we would most likely surpass the upper limit of 550ppm and reach a level of 650ppm by the end of the century.[7] The Intergovernmental Panel on Climate Change (IPCC) predicts with near 100 per cent certainty that CO_2 levels of this magnitude would surpass the 2°C stabilisation point,[8] with some estimates suggesting we are heading for 4°C of warming as soon as 2060.[9]

Leading climate scientists paint a bleak picture of our current and expected climatic conditions. Let me provide a brief snapshot, mainly drawn from the two most recent IPCC reports, which, it is worth recalling, are generally conservative as they synthesise vast amounts of published material, moderating more extreme forecasts.[10] Based on current and expected emissions, we can make the following predictions for the coming century.

Biodiversity, already in steep decline, is likely to drop off dramatically as most species cannot naturally shift their range of habitability sufficiently fast to keep up with current rates of climatic change. We can expect a warming planet to present up to 39 per cent of the earth's organisms with conditions with which they have never before faced, with up to 48 per cent of existing climatic and meteorological conditions around the world set to be fundamentally altered.[11] We are already seeing widespread extinctions with some claiming that we have begun the sixth 'mass extinction event' in planetary history, comparable to the period of change that killed off the dinosaurs.[12] Wheat, rice and maize production are all likely to be adversely affected if warming trends continue, producing global pressures on food supply. Rising global temperatures will also mean that agricultural labourers face even less hospitable conditions, further decreasing productivity at the very moment that human population reaches its peak. The globe's geography will be redrawn: productive land will be exposed beneath melting snow and ice in the Arctic regions and desertification is likely to take hold in some currently temperate areas; rising sea levels threaten low-lying countries and some of the globe's most populous coastal cities; many islands are likely to become uninhabitable. In developing countries in particular, underlying human health issues will be exacerbated, with malaria and yellow fever expected to reach new regions. Terrestrial water cycles are being affected as river water is intercepted by dams and irrigation systems which alter the flow of water and water vapour from the land to the oceans and atmosphere. Africa and Asia, in particular, are likely to see unprecedented pressure on freshwater supplies, with large-scale shortages possible by 2050.

Though global warming and CO_2 emissions tend to command most attention, human activities are altering a range of biogeochemical cycles and systems. The phosphorous and nitrogen cycles, essential for the production of fertilisers, are under unprecedented pressure. Phosphate mines extract millions of tons of phosphorous each year with production likely to peak in 2030. A greater scarcity of phosphorous will have severe consequences for global food production and security as the demand for fertiliser continues to grow in step with population increases. As phosphates are absorbed by the oceans, human intervention within the natural flow of phosphorus through the earth system also has the effect of decreasing marine oxygen levels. This, coupled with increasing acidification of the oceans and rampant overfishing (up to 75 per cent of all fish stocks are currently overfished), is producing increasingly large areas of the ocean referred to as 'dead zones' that lack sufficient oxygen to support marine life.[13] A major study has argued that through a combination of ocean acidification and overfishing, there is a possibility that almost all marine fish species will be extinct by the middle of this century.[14]

If these physical alterations to the earth system are disturbing, reflecting on their social and political consequences should give us pause. If we accept Harald Welzer's assessment, detailed in his unsettling book *Climate Wars: Why People Will be Killed in the 21st Century*, the prospect of widespread human conflict in the coming decades is highly likely. Projections suggest that by 2070 the mean global temperature will be higher than it has been since the human species evolved.[15] Clearly this presents unprecedented strain on the conditions for continued human habitability in many parts of the planet. Competition for natural resources, mass migration towards more temperate regions, and the adverse effects of efforts to mitigate the losses associated with climate change will all lead to a dramatic increase in the likelihood of militarised interstate conflict.[16] The civil war that has raged in Syria since 2011 is arguably the first of many climate change conflicts to come. In the years leading up to the outbreak of violence, Syria suffered the worst droughts on record, and grain prices spiked in 2010–11 at the same time that many were leaving the arid, Sunni-majority countryside for Alawite-majority cities. Tensions flared only to be exacerbated by the Assad regime's draconian response to dissent.[17] Of course, no war is reducible to a single cause but increased pressure on natural resources at the very same time that energy and food security becomes less certain will only deepen existing tensions in a number of locations, most notably in the Middle East, central Africa, the South China Sea and the Indian sub-continent. Increased pressure on soil, water and air will lead to the jealous protection of resources in climatically benign regions. The increasingly brutal modes of processing and interning migrants, within and at the peripheries of Europe, USA and Australia, is a grim indication of the kinds of state responses that we can expect as eco-migration adds to today's already vast flows of people worldwide.

Since beginning the research that has led to this book, the scale of scholarly, political and litigious engagement with the climate crisis has dramatically increased, and as this brief survey indicates, this trend will only continue in the coming years. Perhaps like many who have recently been drawn into thinking more deeply about this topic, I do not consider myself a great environmentalist and I certainly do not claim to possess the strongest 'green' credentials in terms of political action or even lifestyle choices, though this is now changing. Until relatively recently, I considered climate change to be a serious if rather diffuse and complicated social and political issue that was but one amongst a number of contemporary challenges. But recent research and writing in the sciences, social sciences and the humanities have made it clear, to me at least, that the planet's ensuing climatological and ecological transformation is the most pressing and perhaps the most intractable challenge of our time. Not only are all other social, legal and political concerns – from migration to automation; global inequality to rising nationalisms; from the enduring legacies of empire, and their contemporary manifestations; to xenophobia, patriarchy and others forms of domination – ultimately grounded on the relative stability and predictability of the earth's systematic functioning (which is becoming more unstable by the day) but each of these unique challenges will only be exacerbated in the context of a warming world which will put unprecedented pressure on the essential resources on which human habitation depends. We are, as our epigraph reminds us, irredeemably *earthbound* beings. The climate crisis recalls this fact, which for too long we moderns somehow thought we had managed to obviate or overcome.

Notwithstanding a slow coming to consciousness about these issues, inspired in part by political action associated with what have now become household names – Greta Thunberg, Extinction Rebellion, Standing Rock – it is hard to avoid the sense that this situation remains strangely unreal, as if somehow the claims of the climatologists did not apply to us; as if it were not *this land, this sea, this atmosphere* that is under threat and, indeed, is already undergoing dramatic mutation. The opening of new wells, pipelines, power plants and airport runways carries on unabated; global elites continue to search for short-term profits by investing in waterfront property that is increasingly threatened by rising seas; and more extreme techniques of fossil fuel extraction have become *de rigueur*. That peculiar group of deluded and dangerous climate change deniers still have enormous power, particularly in the USA and Australia. And writing on climate change and the environment is still generally consigned to specialist publications, only surfacing in the mainstream news pages when dramatic new scientific results are published, and rarely featuring at all within so-called 'generalist' academic literature. The reality of human-induced climate change ought to be embedded within the fabric of our political and legal discourse, at the heart of all governance agendas and an essential element within our social imaginaries but it is still something of a fringe concern, associated with single-issue parties, specialist parliamentary committees and the discrete fields of environmental science, law and policy. As Simon Critchley puts it, 'we're fucked' and we 'know it' but only 'kind of'.[18] It is this 'kind of' that we have to confront.

So great has the human impact on the earth's natural systems become that stratigraphers and earth system scientists suggest that we have entered a new geological epoch: the Anthropocene (from *anthropos* meaning 'human' and *kainos*, meaning 'recent'). This postulated new 'human age' seeks to capture the dominant role that human activity – in the form of production, consumption and pollution – has within the planetary system. The vast scale of human activity is now thought to rival the 'great forces of nature in its imprint and functioning of the earth system',[19] and the trace of these activities will almost certainly be readable within the earth's deep history for millennia to come. Clive Hamilton points to a startling fact that, in my mind, encapsulates the extraordinary power that the Anthropocene thesis assigns to human agency. With reasonable accuracy earth scientists are able to predict the onset of the next ice age, largely based on the patterned eccentricity of the earth's orbit. Other things being equal, the next ice age is due to begin in 50,000 years' time. But because human activity has released such large quantities of CO_2 and other greenhouse gases (GHGs), thereby trapping more of the sun's heat within the earth's atmosphere, the onset of this ice age has been delayed. And it is quite likely that the ice age following that, due to begin in 130,000 years' time, will not come to pass.[20] The actions of 'modern man' – arguably over the course of as little as the last 200 years – have diverted the course of planetary history. The social forces that have produced high-pollution economies have acquired so much power within the earth's systemic functioning that the prevailing climatic conditions of the last 12,000 years have been displaced, with human societies now having assumed the extraordinary capacity to shape 'geohistory'. That this raises eminently legal and political questions about the nature of agency, responsibility, collective action and the prevailing ideologies that shape our sense of the *res publica* is clear. It is earth scientists themselves who have shown us this fact. Legal and political thought now needs to catch up.

Sovereignty and Aesthetics

If we are to move beyond a situation in which we can only 'kind of' recognise the awesome challenges heralded by global climatic change, we must grapple with what it means to live in the Anthropocene. I say 'grapple with' this idea because it is no easy task. The modern worldview tends to approach the natural world as little more than a backdrop against which human history is played out; we see natural cycles and rhythms as operating at timescales that have little relevance to human life. But the Anthropocene makes tremble the quintessentially modernist bifurcation between 'societal' and 'natural' forces that has animated aspirations for 'progress' and technological advancement, largely predicated on the notion that the natural world can – and indeed should – be 'harnessed' or 'tamed' by anthropic powers. The emergent mobility of a once-docile 'Nature' and the deep connections between human agency and environmental change demand new modes of perception that supersede what Peter Sloterdijk calls the 'backdrop ontology' that has largely defined modern ideologies.[21] Clearly, the Anthropocene is a creature of modernity but the concept names something that struggles to be comprehended within the very framework that has produced it.

A central component in the construction and maintenance of the modern worldview is the concept of, and practices associated with, sovereignty. In the course of modernity political life has largely come to be defined by reference to this concept and a set of concomitant principles and processes like territorial jurisdiction, individual rights, constitutionalism, citizenship and fiscal autonomy. Sovereignty is the defining principle of the modern nation state and provides the lexicon and conceptual schema through which so many political claims are mediated. Despite various challenges to the supremacy of the state in structuring contemporary social life – usually understood as aspects of 'globalisation' – sovereignty continues to be the predominant *frame* through which we perceive, order and give sense to forms of authority, human relations and indeed the earth itself; something to which the recent return of ethno-nationalism in Europe, the USA and elsewhere is an unhappy testament.

Understanding sovereignty as a *framing device* and a *mode of perception* is an essential aspect to the argument made in this book. In developing an account of the *aesthetics of sovereignty*, I demonstrate that sovereignty has the capacity to shape our sense perception, rendering us sensitive, attentive or attuned to certain phenomena, whilst bracketing or keeping 'offstage' a range of other seemingly 'non-political' forces, spaces and actors. The sense of aesthetics deployed here is a little unorthodox. We usually take aesthetics to refer to the nature of judgements about the beautiful; or else, more broadly, to the study of aesthetic objects: texts, images, films or other artistic media. The notion of aesthetics elaborated in the chapters that follow, whilst occasionally drawing on this orthodox approach, more readily turns to an older understanding of the term. Most fundamentally, as indicated by its etymological roots in the Greek *aesthesis*, aesthetics refers to our *sense percep-tion*, describing the way in which we both 'perceive' and 'give meaning to' the world around us. To study aesthetics is to be concerned with *the manner in which we are rendered sensitive to given phenomena*. The aesthetics of sovereignty, then, is concerned with how the practices, modes of thinking and forms of representation on which sovereignty depends render political subjects sensitive to the world in a given constellation, organising that which is seen and unseen, foregrounded or backgrounded, within the framing of social life. This goes further than an account of sovereignty's ability to inflect and shape our visual field but also calls for an attention to the operative power of sovereignty at multiple sensory and affective registers, often working in subtly occluded ways.

In order to give an initial sketch of the aesthetic power of sovereignty, let us return to the Yukon and the now-dry riverbed of the Slims. The shores of Kluane Lake, a key player in the geophysical drama of the Slims River, form part of the territory of the Kluane First Nation (KFN). The status of this indigenous community as a 'First Nation' implies that the Canadian state recognises the land rights of its people (including property and hunting rights) and guarantees a high degree of autonomy for the KFN governmental authorities that administer and manage its territory. The establishment of First Nations, undertaken throughout the 1980s, 1990s and early 2000s, in many important respects ameliorates conditions for the indigenous popula-tion in Canada. The previous legislative regime – largely conducted under the auspices of the federal Indian Act – controlled the conditions under which 'Indians' were to be recognised as such and the means through which Indian territories were to be administered. The establishment of First Nation status introduces a large degree of *self-government* that was previously lacking. Whilst the existence of First Nations opens some complex issues regarding the nature of Canadian state sovereignty – which, since the establishment of First Nations, must include an account of how the 'state-like' authority of these nested territorial units sits within the greater Canadian state[22] – we can better approach the *aesthetic* power of sovereignty by attending to the effects that the mobilisation and deployment of sovereignty has had within the indigenous communities themselves.

As Paul Nadasdy has detailed in a study based on extensive ethnographic work in the region, the formation of First Nations in the Yukon involved translating indigenous knowledges, forms of association and ways of living into the rubric of sovereignty and its various 'entailments': territorial jurisdiction, citizenship, nationhood, and a linear and 'progressive' temporality.[23] Clearly, this schema is of European heritage and involves adopting of a range of boundary-drawing techniques that were largely alien to the indigenous community in the Yukon before European colonisation. In a move seen throughout the post-colonial world, Yukon Indians were forced to engage in a kind of 'looking glass war' in which they had to adopt the political forms and conceptual apparatuses of settler communities in order to register as a political body capable of recognition at all. Of course, by relying on the statist lexicon of sovereignty, territory, jurisdiction and citizenship, indigenous peoples have been able to lay legitimate claim to a set of rights that were denied them in the *ancien régime*. But, as Nadasdy shows, the translation of an indigenous way of life into the legal and political forms of modernity has come at a price. Most strikingly the scope of social and political life is dramatically narrowed. Indigenous practices of kinship and reciprocity involve actors from across the indigenous community – irrespective of any putative 'band' or 'national' identity[24] – as well as a range of non-human actors: both animals and abiotic elements within the environment. As Nadasdy explains, non-human actors play a crucial role in Yukon Indian social life, with human–animal relations providing essential knowledge of both the environment and interpersonal, human relations. And yet, 'there is no room for these . . . politically powerful beings in the (semi-)sovereign communities of the new Yukon First Nations'.[25]

The legal and political forms of modernity, orientated around sovereignty, hold that political community is attached to a *territory* (in which place, terrain, and the materiality of the earth are largely ignored); political power is ultimately vested in *the people* (to the exclusion of non-human actors like God or Nature), and legal competencies and political allegiances are ordered at *the scale of state* (to the detriment of sub- and supra-state forms of authority). These modes of organisation entail a particular way of ordering the world and giving value to a discretely *political* sphere of social existence. But, as Nadasdy claims, 'indigenous practices in the Yukon are rooted in a radically different way of being in the world and of organising relations among humans, animals and the land'[26] than that provided by modern sovereignty. In lieu of seeing themselves as 'part of the land, part of the water'[27] – embedded in complex kinship relationships across human and non-human forms of life – First Nations represent and order social life through the register of popular sovereignty, territory, and those rights which are enforceable by national governmental authorities. In this process of translation *that to which the community is rendered sensitive* is radically altered. Nadasdy's account of the transformative effects of sovereignty on indigenous ways of life in the Yukon takes us into the heart of the aesthetic dimensions of sovereignty because it attunes us to the historically, geographically and epistemically contingent ways in which human agents are *sensitised* to the world and its inhabitants through the installation of a given political and legal form. Indeed, the deployment of the sovereignty schema in the context of indigenous land claims in the Yukon shows that sovereignty is itself implicated in a *world-forming* exercise, creating a social morphology quite distinct from non- or a-modern understandings of collective life.

When it comes to the drying of the Slims River, this has important consequences. If we wish to see this event – and others like it – not simply as part of a *geophysical* drama but as a properly *political* event, the question of *whether, and how, we are rendered sensitive or insensitive* to it is paramount. As we will explore in what follows, it is the manner in which sovereignty orders the sensible domain that is at the heart of understanding the nature of such political sensitivities. Viewed through the optics of sovereignty, an event like the drying of the Slims River struggles to register politically because it fails to stimulate the relevant receptors: it fails to trouble *territory*, *people* or *state authority*. Indeed, sovereignty and its various 'entailments' have the capacity to render us strangely *insensitive* to such an event.

What is at stake here, then, is the aesthetic force of legal and political form. As James Scott makes clear in his celebrated account of the rise of modern governance, 'the premodern state was, in many crucial respects, *partially blind*'[28] because it knew remarkably little of the spatial extent, wealth and health of the nation. The political and infrastructural technologies of modernity – urban planning, cartography, bureaucracy, the penal system, legal codification, surveillance and so forth – provide a new optics for power which allows for a new political–aesthetic configuration to emerge. In this shift from pre-modern to expressly modern social forms a *partial blindness* nonetheless remains. In order for the Yukon Indians to become legible as political actors, capable of recognition by the state, an aesthetic disposition that seems strikingly apposite for our times – a disposition in which non-human actors are understood to have political agency, in which obligations are seen to traverse state borders, in which non-national forms of community are championed – had to be disavowed in favour of a distinctly modern aesthetics that keeps these concerns largely 'offstage'.[29] If in the course of modernity political power began to 'see like a state', in the prevailing conditions of the Anthropocene we are perhaps coming to realise the *blindnesses* that inhere this prevailing condition.

Earthbound: A Political Aesthetics beyond Modern Sovereignty

The changes to political form within indigenous communities in the Yukon speaks to a set of challenges which, I argue in this book, are writ large globally: the aesthetics of sovereignty and an anaesthetised sensibility to Anthropocenic climate change are inextricably related. This is not a book about indigenous sovereignty, nor is it concerned with elaborating how indigenous knowledge and jurisprudence might guide contemporary responses to the climate crisis. I turn to these changes and challenges in the Yukon only to indicate how powerful a device sovereignty is in organising a prevailing 'distribution of the sensible'[30] within contemporary political life. As we turn to face the climate crisis, it becomes clear that there is no simple choice between 'going back to the old ways', on the one hand, or 'embracing modernity', on the other. If modernising involves shedding all our attachments to the earth in an effort to become 'enlightened' political beings (this, of course, is the central theme of contractarian accounts of sovereignty), then 'modernising' offers us little hope. But neither can we burden indigenous knowledges and ways of life with guiding contemporary social, political and economic forces away from climate catastrophe. Given that understanding the gravity of the current situation – not to mention any hope for mitigating or adapting to climate change – can only be done by engaging with cutting-edge scientific knowledge, to jettison modern epistemologies *in toto* would clearly be extremely dangerous. To suggest that the answers to our current predicament lie in somehow simply returning to pre- or non-modern ways of life is to deny the irredeemably modern social and epistemic forms that prevail across the globe, and indeed, continue to inform the aspirations of many millions worldwide.[31]

As Bruno Latour has suggested, what is needed in this context is some 'philosophical trigonometry' which might articulate a 'third attractor' that pulls us away from the false binaries of modernisation/nostalgia; progressivism/conservatism; localism/globalism.[32] If we are to properly apprehend the precariousness of the human condition in the time of the Anthropocene, and begin to develop viable legal and political alternatives to the destructive status quo, we must shed our attachments to both the dream of a fully modernised 'globality' *and* a return to a pre-modern, autochthonous 'land of old'.[33] The task lies in articulating what it might mean to *be bound*, to place and in community, in a way that is radically different from either of these two attractors. Latour describes this emergent condition, in which the human is conceived neither as *rising above* nor as *situated against* an othered 'Nature' but as intricately enfolded *within* the earth's dynamic systems and processes, as a matter of becoming *earthbound*.[34]

For Latour, *the earthbound* names a nascent political subject that supersedes the various binaries and exceptionalisms associated with a putatively rational and isolated Enlightenment 'Man'. To reimagine the human as earthbound is to respond to the altered ontological conditions that the Anthropocene brings into view, pointing to networks of agency and cycles of action/reaction that traverse supposed divisions between the human and the non-human. In what follows I draw on and expand Latour's evocation of 'the earthbound' as a key concept with which to assess the legal and political implications of the Anthropocene, paying particular attention to the forms of *attachment* or *binding* that exceed the modes of association that modern sovereignty installs and polices. This does not deny the important contribution that indigenous knowledge and jurisprudence can make to these ongoing efforts to reimagine human sociality in the Anthropocene; and I take the task of developing the requisite forms of conduct that can facilitate meaningful dialogue between indigenous and non-indigenous traditions to be imperative.[35] This, however, is not my focus in the present project, which develops its argument by drawing on Western, largely European, traditions of critical thinking about law, ecology and political form.

The main thesis of the project can be stated quite simply: sovereignty, the quintessentially modern mode of organising and theorising law and politics, contrives to keep the reality of our entry into a new climatic regime 'offstage' through its deployment of a distinctive aesthetics that makes us see, feel and order the world in a way that inures us to the forces and relations that, the Anthropocene tells us, are increasingly shaping the contours of social life. I argue that the great, and often under-appreciated, achievement of sovereignty is precisely an aesthetic one in that it attunes us to the world, sensitising and desensitising us in a unique configuration. In this way, sovereignty is engaged in ordering the sensible domain.[36] In seeking to understand the aesthetics of sovereignty I pay particular attention to the 'jurisdictional technologies' that produce and represent the distribution of agencies and attachments on which sovereignty relies. Jurisdictional technologies represent sovereign power, give it voice as well as material, institutional and symbolic form. Through an attention to these technologies, I focus on the ways in which sovereignty *enframes*, *distributes* and *orders* our sensibilities, underscoring how this aesthetic ordering alienates legal and political life from the earthly forces that ought to be at the very heart of our concerns as we begin to think through the consequences and challenges of living in the Anthropocene.

In sum, if we are to address the challenges that the Anthropocene presents to law and politics, we have to begin to think beyond the aesthetics of modern sovereignty and embrace a political aesthetics that attends to our earthbound condition. In this way, the book has two distinct goals: firstly, to examine how sovereignty constitutively *anaesthetises* us to the realities of the new climatic regime; secondly, and in a more speculative mode, to explore what an alternative political aesthetics for the Anthropocene might consist of, opening avenues for further research and exploration. As recent political events have only underscored, sovereignty remains a deeply important concept for contemporary law and politics. As I argue in what follows, the enduring power of sovereignty to provide a 'frame' for political life lies in its aesthetic power, which works at somatic and affective registers, constituting a background ordering to a dominant rendering of the political.[37] In this sense, the task of somehow transcending the sovereignty schema remains deeply challenging, especially if our legal and political theorising is to maintain some meaningful connection to the widely held beliefs, instincts and practices shared by existing political communities. Rather than vainly hope for some final supersession of sovereignty, I follow Donna Haraway's advice and aim to 'stay with the trouble'[38] that our prevailing modes of thinking have themselves provoked. This involves developing new critical perspectives that draw attention to the earthly forces and relations which are constitutively ignored by the 'sovereignty frame'. Climate mutation is an eminently political problem but as I aim to demonstrate, the *form* that the political has taken in modernity – and the specific aesthetics on which this depends – is very much part of the problem. In this sense, adequate institutional or policy-orientated responses to climatic change and the implications of the Anthropocene can only be achieved on the basis of an aesthetic transformation in which we *see, feel and order the world* in a new way. *Earthbound: The Aesthetics of Sovereignty in the Anthropocene* outlines the meaning of such an aesthetic shift through an engagement with a range of texts spanning legal, political and cultural theory; ecology; and literary fiction.

Outline of the Chapters

The first chapter assesses the broad implications of the Anthropocene thesis for law and politics, engaging with stratigraphic, geological and sociological debates on the concept. In finding a path through the ongoing disputations around the meaning and usefulness of the Anthropocene concept, I draw out how the Anthropocene can be understood as a direct challenge to some of the co-ordinates that have defined modern accounts of legal and political life. The reorientation that the Anthropocene prompts has both prospective and retrospective dimensions, forcing us to reread the history of modernity in light of the radical climatic disturbance that civilisation's 'progress' has precipitated at the same time that it signals an opening onto an uncertain future that will require modes of thinking that are purposively *a-modern*. In terms of jurisprudential thought, I argue that one way of approaching this challenge is to move away from discourses of *right* and examine instead the

theoretical, ethical and political purchase to be found within an account of
obligation. In this respect, the chapter develops an argument against aspects of
the 'Earth Jurisprudence' literature, one of the few strands of contemporary
legal theory that has engaged with questions of climatic change and ecological
degradation. Where Earth Jurisprudence develops a novel account of the
'rights of nature', I turn instead to the language of *obligation, binding* and
attachment, drawing together Latour's reading of Lovelock's Gaia hypothesis
and Simone Weil's insistence on the *priority of obligation* ahead of right
in an effort to begin to articulate what it means to be *earthbound* in the
Anthropocene. Underscoring Weil's themes of *attention* (understood here
as a form of aesthetic attunement or sensitivity) and the *impersonal* (evoking
those forces that transcend the human but nonetheless work in concert with
situated human actors), the chapter concludes by establishing lines of inquiry
into the aesthetic and existential dimensions of the nature of our *being-bound,*
prior to those rights that are installed and enforced by modern sovereignty.

Chapter 2 develops an account of the aesthetics of sovereignty, expanding
on some of the themes already alluded to in this Introduction, in order to
establish the mode through which we will assess this concept in the chapters
that follow. I contend that paying attention to the aesthetic dimensions
of sovereignty is particularly apposite in the current conjuncture, which is
marked by both the threats associated with climatic change and a resurgence of the rhetoric of sovereignty in forms of neo-nationalism. An aesthetic
approach to sovereignty opens avenues of inquiry that remain foreclosed
if we remain tied to the 'sovereignty and biopolitics' or 'sovereignty and
globalisation' frames that have dominated scholarship on the topic in recent
years. I approach the aesthetics of sovereignty from two directions. Firstly, in
relation to sovereignty's *mode of appearance*; that is, its forms of representation
and expression which, I argue, rely on a range of artistic and literary devices.
Secondly, in terms of sovereignty's *mode of perception*; that is, as a shared
imaginary through which social and earthly relations are ordered and given
sense. Drawing on scholarship on affect – a dimension of human experience
akin to but distinct from the emotions – as well Castoriadis's account of the
social imaginary and Rancière's assessment of the inherently aesthetic dimensions to the political, I suggest that the collective imaginary that sovereignty
installs needs to be understood in *somatic* and *affective,* not simply cognitive
terms. Key to this account of sovereignty's aesthetic dimensions are what
I call 'technologies of jurisdiction', understood to refer to the techniques
through which lawful relations are expressed or announced. In this way,
jurisdiction is not simply the means through which a given distribution of
power is achieved through the courts, but is also integral to understanding
sovereignty's aesthetic and affective purchase within social life.

The next three chapters each assess one aspect of modern sovereignty. In traditional state theory, and within international law, it is generally accepted that sovereignty has three components: (1) a clearly delineated and largely uncontested territory over which state powers are effective; (2) a stable population which is bound to, and in most cases is understood to legitimate, state authority; (3) an apparatus of government with administrative and coercive powers, operative at the scale of the state.[39] Each of these three elements is often associated with a particular aspect or form of sovereignty: *territorial sovereignty*, *popular sovereignty*, and *parliamentary* or *constitutional sovereignty*. Broadly following this schema, we look first at the aesthetics of 'territory' (Chapter 3), then 'people' (Chapter 4) and finally 'scale' (Chapter 5). This latter designation represents a slight departure from the traditional 'three-element' approach to sovereignty, which focuses on the existence of administrative and coercive institutions which allow for the passage, promulgation and enforcement of laws, amongst other things. By approaching this third element of sovereignty as a matter of 'scale' I am less concerned with the coercive capacities of state institutions than I am in how the organisation of institutional competencies itself *produces* or *enframes* our sense of the political at the scale of the state to the detriment of (or at least in a hierarchical relation with) global, regional or sub-national scales. The question of scale is one of the key challenges that besets legal and political thought in the context of the new climatic regime, with the meaning of and tensions between *national, local, global* and *planetary* scales at the heart of contemporary debates on this topic.

Chapter 3 gives an account of the aesthetics of territory, drawing on Stuart Elden's seminal work on the history and theory of the concept in order to show how territory names a highly contingent means through which the relation between place and power is articulated. With a particular attention to the jurisdictional technology of mapping, I seek to show how the polygonal and abstract forms on which territory depends constitutively inure us to the complex, dynamic, *earthly* scene that the Anthropocene situates at the heart of social life. The chapter assesses the tension between the aesthetics of territory and the possibilities of an altered political aesthetics that I develop through the concept of *terrain*. Terrain is a term used in geophysical, meteorological and strategic studies but rarely in legal and political theory. What I call the 'terrain prospect', a unique mode of apperception appropriate to the concept, offers a markedly different aesthetic framing and attunement to space, power and questions of political belonging to those installed and policed under the auspices of territory. The terrain prospect aims to resituate legal and political agencies *within* a lively, dynamic and processual geophysical environment rather than *set against* an abstract and conceptually empty territory. This movement from territory to terrain involves a shift from an *aesthetics of representation* and *abstraction* to an *immersive aesthesis* which seeks to bring to the fore the material, legal and political entanglements between human life and dynamic geophysical forces and relations.

Chapter 4 is focused on the 'the people', understood as the constitutional principle central to the birth of a properly modern conception of the political. In order to examine the aesthetic dimensions of 'the people', I turn to the prototypical event which captures the transfer from monarchical to popular sovereignty: *the declaration* in which the people appear for the first time as the legitimate authority that grounds the political and legal order. Drawing on Costas Douzinas and others, I approach this founding moment as a specifically 'juris-dictional' act, a moment when the law is spoken and, through the 'magic' of a performative speech act, a new civic order and subject of power are created. If in the previous chapter we foregrounded the visual regime that modern mapping installs, here I am more concerned with the *fictions* that help give shape to popular sovereignty. In this sense, it is the *as if*, the fictional or the consciously false, that lies at the heart of modern articulations of popular sovereignty. However, in keeping with our approach to the aesthetics of sovereignty already outlined, the fictions that animate political power are understood to be operative at somatic and affective registers that foreground the embodied reality of political actors. In this way, the fictional and aesthetic dimensions of power are played out within what Eric Santner calls the 'flesh' of political subjects. This effort to connect the fictional and the fabulous with the corporeal and the affective offers some guidance for the kind of shift in our political aesthetics that, I suggest, the Anthropocene demands. This more speculative element is elaborated through an engagement with Judith Butler and Donna Haraway in order to outline the meaning of, and the aesthetic disposition associated with, a *sympoietic, earthbound people*.

Chapter 5 examines some of the dominant scalar units that structure our sense of the political in the contemporary moment. One of the chief achievements of modern sovereignty is to delimit our sense of the political at the scale of the nation state. In the context of global warming, many commentators have concluded that this scaling of authority is largely ineffective: rising seas, pollution and ecological collapse do not stop at national borders; we are dealing with a truly 'global' phenomenon that apparently requires 'global solutions'. But as I explore here, 'the global' scale remains deeply anthropocentric, focused on human-to-human networks of communication and trade, which work to keep the inhuman milieu within which social life is situated largely in the background of our legal and political thinking. Rather than an account of *the global*, I explore the possibility of returning to an older and apparently smaller scalar unit in an effort to rethink the political in the context of our contemporary ecological mutation: *the city*. Drawing on contemporary writing in urban studies and spatial theory, I approach the city as a discrete legal and political form which might allow us to sense our changing planetary conditions and attune us to the forces and relations that define our entry into the Anthropocene epoch. In this way I aim to outline how privileging the city scale, ahead of the national or the global, might form part of an altered political imaginary fit for our new climatic regime.

A final word on disciplinary orientation and style of argument. This book is transdisciplinary in approach, drawing on legal, political, literary and ecological resources in order to develop its key claims about sovereignty, aesthetics and the Anthropocene. The topic itself dictates this wide range of reference. Sovereignty has been widely debated across the disciplines – in law, philosophy, political theory, anthropology and beyond – and engaging with the concept in the context of the Anthropocene has necessitated venturing, however gingerly, into the earth sciences and ecology. The aesthetic dimension, which I argue is central to understanding the enduring force of sovereignty in the contemporary moment, has likewise called for an engagement with aspects of cultural theory. And my interest in territory, terrain, scale and the city drew me to work on spatial theory, political geography and urban studies. These forays across the disciplines have been at times exhilarating, at others daunting, and there is much in my approach that experts in relevant fields will doubtless wish to supplement or criticise. I nonetheless feel that we scholars are often too disciplined by our disciplines. The enormous challenges that our entry into the new climatic regime poses to every aspect of our social and intellectual lives require that we look beyond the narrow confines of our own academic fields, which are, after all, largely determined by funding bodies and research assessment exercises rather than the aspirations of creative intellectual inquiry.

The transdisciplinary approach that I take in this book has been championed within the satisfyingly nebulous field of 'law and the humanities', which embraces traditions of critical legal theory; cultural legal studies; progressive, creative and critical political and constitutional theory; legal history; legal geography; law and literature; and more besides. If the reader feels that the relevant field of inquiry to which this book contributes needs to be identified, I would happily situate my efforts here, with one important caveat. Despite being indebted to the interpretative strategies and styles of argumentation associated with the humanities, this book seeks to draw attention to the limits of the modern rendering of the human and concomitant traditions of humanism. The Anthropocene urges us to understand how human agency is entangled with various *inhuman* forces and relations, undoing many of the presuppositions which undergird the anthropic exceptionalism of modern, particularly post-Enlightenment, thought in law, politics and philosophy. In this sense, the argument here might be better understood as developing a *law and inhumanities* approach, in that it draws on law and humanities scholarship but aims to engage this tradition in new, more-than-human problematics, at the limits of the discourse.

There are two legal strands to the following discussions that are worth emphasising. The first is the role of *jurisdiction* in giving voice and form to sovereignty. The theoretical implications of jurisdiction within studies of sovereignty have been underexamined, with theorists tending to draw more readily on the traditional canons of political philosophy or constitutional theory. Drawing on the work of Shaunnagh Dorsett, Shaun McVeigh, Bradin Cormack and others, I approach jurisdiction as being less about the competency of judicial decision-making powers and more a question of how the lawful relations that sovereignty describes come to be known and have effects within social life. Taking a cue from the etymology of the term (*ius dictio* or 'law's speech'), I argue that we can reimagine jurisdiction as referring to law's expressive or enunciative register, and the various technologies of representation that allow for lawful authority to be seen, heard and felt. Understood in these terms jurisdiction helps attend to sovereignty's *worldforming* capacity and examine how the various technologies which express or declare lawful relations come to be deeply embedded in a taken for granted mode of perception associated with modern sovereignty. I argue that a focus on those jurisdictional technologies which present and represent sovereign power – the cartographic depictions of sovereign territory, the declarative acts which fashion a sovereign people, and the institutional orderings which give precedence to the nation-state scales of authority – allows us to examine the aesthetic dimensions of sovereignty, in terms of both *appearance* and *perception*.

The second legal strand concerns the privileging of *obligation* ahead of *right*. It is commonplace to associate modern law with the 'age of rights'. Individual rights have been central to the development of Western law since at least the eighteenth century and rearticulated as 'human rights' in the twentieth century. In this context, 'rights-talk' dominates almost all aspects of our social lives, with any number of moral or political claims being amenable to the rhetoric of rights.[40] This long-standing trajectory is today being given new impetus within emergent practices and theories of the 'rights of nature'. Recent legislative innovations in New Zealand/Aotearoa, India and Ecuador have all recognised the rights of aspects of the non-human world, in some cases ascribing legal personality to specific natural phenomena and ecosystems.[41] Similarly, litigation has been pursued on the basis of novel, environmentally conscious, interpretations of constitutional rights.[42]

Notwithstanding the generative possibilities that this extension of rights might hold, in this project I examine instead the purchase to be found in a thinking of and with *obligation*, ahead of rights. As indicated by its etymology in *ligare* obligations point to the themes of *attachment*, *binding* and *ligature* that have a significant resonance in the context of the ecological mutation, where it is the *entanglements* between the human and non-human that are at the heart of contemporary writing on the topic. Drawing on Simone Weil, I suggest that obligation evokes a set of ontological questions that turn on the nature of human *needs* and *dependencies*. If rights have become predominant in legal discourse, a focus on the theoretical possibilities implied within obligations constitutes something of a 'minor' theme within contemporary legal thinking. I aim to draw out some implications of this 'minor jurisprudence' of obligation as we explore how we might recast the legal and political subject as *earthbound*, that is, as irredeemably *dependent* on the inhuman forces and relations that constitute the earth system.

Lastly, readers will note the brief moments of personal reflection at the beginning of each of the subsequent chapters, which aim to serve as a route into the substantive analysis. Whilst some may find this off-putting, I have endeavoured to avoid the habit, common to much academic writing, of adopting 'a voice from nowhere' with its apparently disembodied, neutral and objective tone. One of the central insights of this book is that the Anthropocene forces us to reassess the bonds that tie human actors to particular places and within particular networks of human and non-human agency. It felt imperative to at least try to acknowledge how I am myself so bound by evoking, if only fleetingly, some of the memories, sites and scenes that have accompanied the writing of this book.

1

Earthbound in the Anthropocene

> When people face what nothing in their past has prepared them for they
> grope for words to name the unknown, even when they can neither define
> nor understand it.
>
> — Eric Hobsbawm, *The Age of Extremes*[1]

As a child I spent many happy hours – and some cold, wet and bored ones
– walking the heavy, clay-steeped land of my great-aunt's farm in East
Anglia. There the earth sticks to your boots, forming great curtains of mud
that need to be levered off with a stick or else laboriously scraped away on
the nearest patch of grass. The sense that the earth can have its own kind of
agency and force, that the land has a certain *pull* and *stickiness* that can moor
us in place, is something I learnt young and that has always stayed with me,
despite having long ago left the rurality of my upbringing in search of more
urban, more cosmopolitan, more 'modern' horizons. This trajectory away
from the earth, and the 'stickiness' of the land, towards a putative freedom
found elsewhere, is central to the ideologies of modernity, where the promise
of an escape from the trappings of place has animated so many desires for
'progress'. The moderns are not 'stick-in-the-muds' – as I once was, and
sometimes dream of going back to being – they are liberated beings and are
thereby able to rise above and marshal such natural attachments. Or so we
thought. The climate crisis and the onset of the Anthropocene urge us to
question this trajectory and return us to the stickiness of the earth, the bonds
of place and the intractability of our earthly conditions.

In this chapter I explore how our entry into the new climatic regime
prompts renewed reflection on these questions of attachment and binding,
and the obligations that this new sense of being-bound to – both shaped
by and shaping – the earth's systems and processes might entail. As we will
examine below, the Anthropocene interrupts many of the presuppositions
that structure modern accounts of law, politics and social life more generally.
But this characterisation is far from contested and part of the task taken up
in the following pages is to navigate the various disputations and debates

that have surrounded the Anthropocene thesis before we turn to think about how it challenges us to rethink some of the basic co-ordinates of modern legal and political thought. We begin by attending to the specific disciplinary context in which the Anthropocene concept was born (within Earth System Science) before we turn to assess how the concept has been interpreted within the social sciences, particularly in relation to the history of capitalism. The chapter concludes by arguing that the Anthropocene, and its various entailments as elaborated by Bruno Latour in his turn to 'face Gaia', prompt a move away from discourses of *rights* (including emergent assertions of the 'rights of nature') and instead give priority to *obligations* and the related themes of *boundedness* and *attachment*, which a prevailing 'rights-talk' too often occludes.

Setting the '-cene'

An important question to begin: what is *new* about the Anthropocene? For a start, the human capacity to alter the environment and shape ecosystems to their own ends clearly has a very long history, from clearing forests, to domesticating animals, from intervening in freshwater systems to provide irrigation, to vast transformations to landscapes through urbanisation projects. What, then, is novel about the situation today: by intervening in the earth's natural cycles and systems, are humans not simply doing what we have always done? Furthermore, the modernist myths of human exceptionalism and 'Man's' supposed autonomy from 'Nature', that the Anthropocene appears to challenge, have surely already been debunked and derided by post-modernists and post-humanists, by scholars of Science and Technology Studies (STS) and social constructivists. Have we not, as Bruno Latour counselled some twenty-five years ago, 'never been modern'?[2] The purported 'newness' of the Anthropocene, in this sense, might be viewed as little more than the latest fashion, the latest 'turn', within the humanities and social sciences, simply rehashing extant theoretical positions under the banner of a provocative new sobriquet. Or worse still, might the Anthropocene be associated with a dubious politics that postulates a faux-universalism that lets those responsible for climate change – the bourgeois, oil-guzzling producers and consumers of the West – off the hook?

Though the Anthropocene has been deployed and debated by arts, humanities and social science scholars,[3] it is important to foreground the disciplinary heritage of the concept and to understand the emerging account of the planetary climate system that the contemporary earth sciences present. Paul Crutzen, Nobel Prize winning atmospheric chemist, is often credited with coining the idea that we have entered a new geological epoch. Speaking at a conference of the International Geosphere-Biosphere Programme (IGBP) in Mexico in 2000, he claimed that the Holocene (spanning the last 12,000 years, beginning as the last glacial period ended) had been surpassed by a new geological epoch he designated 'The Anthropocene'. Of course, there is a pre-history to Crutzen's declaration[4] and, as we will see in what follows, obsessing over both the Anthropocene's nomenclature and its starting date (as both signifier and signified) is largely unhelpful outside the specialist domain of stratigraphy. What is more significant, however, is the disciplinary setting in which Crutzen's declaration was made. As Clive Hamilton has emphasised, the IGBP conference, at which Crutzen was speaking, 'is the institutional heart of Earth System Science'.[5] And it is grasping the significance of the new 'meta-discipline' of Earth System Science (ESS) that is key to understanding the meaning of the Anthropocene.

Emerging in the 1980s, ESS understands *all* components of the earth as forming an integrated system and takes as its object of study the interactions between the earth's various elements: water; ice; atmosphere; organic life; the earth's crust, its tectonic plates, and core; the moon's gravitational pull; and the flow of energy from the sun. As Hamilton stresses, this is most emphatically *not* the same as thinking of the earth as a collection of 'ecosystems' (which would only attend to the interaction between organisms and their local environments) but involves a scalar shift in which both biotic and abiotic elements are understood to be operating in a single, complex, integrated system.[6] John Lawton offers a helpful definition:

> ESS takes the main components of planet Earth . . . and seeks to under-stand major patterns and processes in their dynamics. To do this, we need to study not only the processes that go on within each component (tradi-tionally the realms of oceanography, atmospheric physics, and ecology, to name but three), but also interactions between these components. It is the need to study and understand these between-component interactions that defines ESS as a discipline in its own right.[7]

Some of the limitations of this 'system-view' of the earth are outlined in the sections that follow; at this stage, however, it is key to grasp the 'gestalt shift'[8] that ESS proposes. The postulated epochal transition away from the Holocene to the Anthropocene – advocated and debated by Crutzen and others – does not claim that human activities are or have been reshaping the earth's *landscape*, disturbing its *ecosystems*, or even simply polluting the *atmosphere*; though all this is clearly true. The key point is that a range of human actions have become a significant force within *the earth system as a whole*, thus affecting the earth's systemic functioning beyond the parameters established within the Holocene. And these parameters, it should be empha-sised, describe the climatic conditions in which human civilisation emerged.

The Anthropocene tells us that our species is entering climatically uncharted territory.

A variety of nomenclatures, histories and frames of reference have been developed through which this 'new climatic regime' can be understood. Some date the onset of the Anthropocene from the beginnings of agriculture over 10,000 years ago that cleared forests and domesticated animals, thereby increasing atmospheric carbon dioxide and methane. This approach effectively does away with the Holocene designation, arguing that human civilisation has from its earliest stages been a planetary force.[9] Others have tied the Anthropocene to the transformations set in motion by early modern colonialism that reordered the earth's biota, causing widespread changes to the global human population and mixing once discrete ecosystems in a process known as the 'Columbian Exchange'.[10] These changes, along with the near-total annihilation of the Amerindian population as a result of colonial expropriation, enslavement and disease, left a readable trace in the geological record as the reforestation of once cultivated lands caused a reduction in global atmospheric CO_2.[11] Alternative approaches argue that the Anthropocene is a much more recent phenomenon, traceable to either the early days of the industrial revolution in the late eighteenth century or even beginning as recently as the middle of the twentieth century as the so-called 'great acceleration' in human energy consumption took hold within a new age of globalisation.[12]

The definition that one favours lends itself to distinct political narratives and commitments. The 'early Anthropocene' thesis tends to naturalise our current condition, ascribing this new epoch to the 'incremental spread of human influence over the landscape' rather than a rupture associated with the widespread burning of fossil fuels.[13] The early modern Anthropocene explicitly ties the onset of a new climatic regime to colonialism, enslavement and plunder: the dark sides of 'modernity' and 'progress'. A later date of origin foregrounds the role of industrial capitalism, and a mid-twentieth-century start date grounds the Anthropocene in American economic, cultural and political dominance, the early days of globalisation and the birth of the nuclear age. Efforts to connect the prevailing social relations at each of these historical junctures has prompted a range of neologisms: terms like 'Capitalocene',[14] 'Technocene'[15] and 'Plantationocene'[16] all seek to underscore the material, political and economic conditions of the period in which the beginnings of our current climate crisis are thought to be found. But coining such terms, drawing attention to the historical conditions which caused a shift in the planet's climatic system, is to be engaged in a fundamentally different project to that which is pursued in geology and the earth sciences. Indeed, much confusion around the Anthropocene is attributable to a lack of care in understanding the disciplinary distinctions and modes of knowledge production that the sciences and social sciences deploy in the course of their analyses. The Anthropocene involves navigating a range of interdisciplinary encounters with what Bruno Latour has called a form of 'diplomacy'.[17] I take diplomacy, in this context, to refer to two things. Firstly, that there is no ultimate arbiter that can resolve the disputes that emerge between disciplinary traditions in defining the meaning and significance of the Anthropocene thesis. The various claims that are made regarding the Anthropocene cannot be mediated by *Scientific*, *Sociological* or *Political* readings alone. The Anthropocene, in describing the enfolding or entangling of the 'social' and the 'natural', cannot be resolved in favour of one or the other of these domains. Secondly, being 'diplomatic' involves a degree of sensitivity to the forms of knowledge production appropriate to the disciplines. In the same way that diplomatic blunders often occur in international relations when national etiquette or *sui generis* social mores are ignored or misunderstood, interdisciplinary diplomacy requires a sensitivity to the idiomatic concerns of the disciplines and the different research questions and methodologies that animate their inquiries.

Navigating the Disciplines

In order to take up this task, we can do worse than recall the etymology of our central concept. In keeping with the naming of other geological epochs, the Anthropocene comprises the '-cene' suffix, rooted in the Greek *kainos* meaning 'recent'. As Ian Angus explains, this usage was developed in the nineteenth century by the geologist Charles Lyell to discriminate between

> various layers of rock by determining the proportions of extinct and non-extinct fossils each contained. Thus the Miocene is from *meios – few* of the fossils are recent. *Pliocene* is from *pleios – more* of the fossils are recent. Pleistocene is from *pleistos – most* of the fossils are recent . . . [the Holocene, from the Greek *holos* designates the stratum in which] the fossils are *wholly or entirely* recent.[18]

The notion of an Anthropocene epoch therefore suggests the existence of a geological stratum which is dominated by recent human activity. Defining a geological epoch requires agreement between stratigraphers on a globally readable marker in stratigraphic material such as rock, sediment or glacier ice. This marker is known as the 'Global Stratotype Section and Point' (GSSP) or, more colloquially, as the 'golden spike'. Very often the GSSP will refer to a mass extinction event, the emergence of new species or widespread volcanic activity, all of which leave clearly observable traces in the strata. For the stratigraphers, what is crucial in determining a start date for the Anthropocene is the identification of a sufficiently clear, and globally readable, mark or trace in the earth's strata that will be discernible many years into the future. For instance, the urbanisation of the human population from 1945 is thought to contribute to such a globally significant marker: 'since ancient cities show up well in archaeological excavations, this spate of urbanisation [over the last fifty years] will be evident stratigraphically in the distant future'.[19]

It is worth underlining that what constitutes a relevant GSSP or 'golden spike' is largely arbitrary from a human-historical perspective. All that is relevant for the stratigrapher seeking to delineate the Anthropocene is whether certain forms of human activity leave a readable trace in the geological record. Given that the Anthropocene is such a recent epoch, any marker is liable to revision as events unfold; a stratigraphically significant trace could be made by human actions in the future, thereby superseding existing speculation about the most efficacious start date for the Anthropocene. To be clear, this in no way discredits the work that stratigraphers undertake. But it is worth being clear about the scope of their inquiry, which leaves untouched an enormous range of questions about the social relations that precipitated stratigraphically significant activities, the economic and political milieus in which these activities took place and so on. It is these issues that proponents of a various 'counter-cenes' seek to address. However, if postulated as a *corrective* to the stratigraphic notion of the Anthropocene, such terms clearly miss the mark; in fact, they commit something akin to a category mistake. For example, Andreas Malm suggests that the Anthropocene is 'analytically flawed' because it ignores the socio-cultural forces that have led to the climate crisis and argues that a 'more scientifically accurate designation . . . would be "the Capitalocene"'.[20] We turn to the 'Capitalocene' thesis in a moment, but at this stage we can simply point to the fact that Malm and other Capitalocene advocates emphasise the socio-techno-historical *causes of* and provide a political and economic *context to* our current climatic crisis. However, they say nothing about the *geological traces* that mark a qualitative shift from the climatic conditions of the Holocene. And it is only the latter that is of interest to the stratigraphers. To ignore the relevant scientific methodologies, in favour of social and economic analysis, in an effort to develop, in Malm's own words, '*a more scientifically accurate*' designation for this new epoch, muddles the distinct contributions that both the earth scientist and the social scientist can offer.

What, then, does the Anthropocene, understood as a technical matter of geological time, offer non-specialists? For Jeremy Davies – who published one of the first book-length studies of the Anthropocene – the stratigraphic understanding of this new epoch encourages us to see human history as having always been entwined with geological history. From the perspective of 'deep' or 'geological' time we can approach the Holocene, for instance, not as a 'backdrop to civilization but as a mode of life in which the evolution of human societies participated'.[21] We can trace the three geological epochs that human history has traversed (Pleistocene, Holocene and Anthropocene) and situate the current climate crisis against this expansive timeframe. It is a sensitivity to the relations between human agency, climatic systems and geological time that Davies urges for a new environmental politics that is cognisant of the enormous challenges posed as we transition from one geological epoch to another. In this sense, the date that marks this transition is, for Davies, key:

> The politically salient issue is *the time of transition into the Anthropocene, not the new epoch as such* . . . Stratigraphic science provides a model of earnest engagement with the particular characteristics of *singular moments in the history of the earth*. The stratigraphic Anthropocene places the present crisis in its deep time context only so as to let its distinctive features be seen more clearly and to help in assessing its significance. It has the potential *to foster a deeper sense of entanglement in immediate historical circumstances*, rather than an indifferent acceptance of the fact that nothing lasts forever.[22]

Whilst becoming sensitive to a new historical scale of human history that engages an understanding of species evolution, planetary climatic conditions and geological time is both provocative and illuminating, Davies's overreliance on stratigraphic thinking and methodologies leads to a number of confusions, evident in this short passage.

As we have seen, the stratigraphic method involves speculating about the historical traces of human activity that will be readable in the geological strata, hundreds of thousands (if not millions) of years into the future. As Davies himself suggests, the stratigraphic Anthropocene 'begins with a thought experiment'[23] in which we imagine an intelligent visitor to earth, thousands of years in the future when humankind has died out. Like their fictional, intelligent alien observer, the stratigrapher seeks to determine the discernible traces left by human life. How this methodology 'foster[s] a deeper sense of entanglement in immediate historical circumstances' is unclear. In fact, it appears to do precisely the opposite by abstracting us from our current condition and projecting ourselves into an imagined future in which humankind has long since left the earth. From the perspective of deep time, we are all dead. What such a postulation offers in grappling with our current condition remains highly uncertain.

In lieu of attention to the very recent history of the climate crisis, an emphasis on the 'time of transition into the Anthropocene' tends to engage not in the embrace of a vast new temporal horizon but in a return to the recent European and American past, tracing how the Anthropocene is the result of colonial exploitation and the perpetuation of an economic system that exploits, pollutes and degrades both human societies and the environment alike. Whilst a historical consciousness of these injustices is of course imperative, with the ongoing debates over whether the Anthropocene began in 1610, 1800 or in 1945 – those 'singular moments in the history of the earth' on which Davies urges us to focus – we fail to grasp the more immediate challenges at hand. Chief amongst these is the rise of China and India as mass polluters as they have become the industrial parks for the world. China is now the world's largest emitter of CO_2 and its total historic emissions will soon be larger than those of the United States. Strikingly, global CO_2 emissions since 1986 account for a staggering *half* of all emissions from 1751 to 2010; and this is largely attributable to China's economic boom.[24] With India's dependency on fossil capitalism secured, by the middle of the century the global south 'will be responsible, both contemporaneously and historically, for much more damage to the global climate system than the North'.[25] By forever turning to the moment of transition, inevitably located in a Western historiography, we lose sight of the new economic and political actors that are key players in the complex and messy networks of contemporary global fossil capitalism.

To suggest that the 'politically salient' issue is not grasping 'the epoch as such' but its moment of appearance, participates in what Clive Hamilton has called 'golden spike fetishism'.[26] By dwelling on the *marker* for the epoch, we ascribe it an undue importance: *the marker is just a marker*[27] and, as we have seen, from a socio-historical perspective it is a largely arbitrary one at that. It is not the mark in the strata but what this mark signifies that is important. A globally significant human 'signature' in the geological record tells us very little about the human, non-human, biotic and abiotic, relations to which we need to become sensitive as we negotiate living in the Anthropocene. For this we need to return to the present, to our current lived realities, and to understand why a reattunement to our earthly reality remains so difficult to effect. This entails confronting aesthetic, ideational and ontological challenges as much as historical ones.

Whether the stratigraphers agree over a 1945, 1800 or 1610 GSSP, social, political and economic analysis that traces the complex combination of factors that led to this epochal shift will not have been made redundant. The methodologies appropriate for these inquiries are clearly not the same as those deployed by the stratigraphers. By either leaning too heavily on the science (as Davies does) or by too readily dismissing it (as Malm does), we lose the specificity of the contribution that non-scientific disciplines and modes of analysis can make as we try to grapple with the broader consequences of the Anthropocene thesis. It is worth noting too that so much of this debate, conducted in rather febrile tones amongst groups of largely white men in the global north, frames the issue in terms of the question of the *inauguration*, *founding* and *naming* of a new epoch. This desire to *be first* in finding the *ultimate marker, cause* or *name* for our entry into a new climatic system itself carries with it, what Jacques Derrida would call, a *phallogocentrism* that has been central to the history of power and politics in the West. Indeed, this desire to *name the beginning* and to *found a new origin* has been one of the central motifs associated with the history of sovereignty. Given the orientation of the present book, I am naturally wary of these sovereign instincts and, as I suggest below, prefer a more nebulous rendering of the Anthropocene, one that is analogous with the less controversial fact of our arrival in a 'new climatic regime'.

As we have already suggested, the postulation of the 'Capitalocene' is unhelpful if understood as a direct critique of, or corrective to, the technical designation of the Anthropocene within stratigraphy. However, in focusing on the social relations and modes of production that prefigured huge increases in GHG emissions from the 1800s onwards, does the Capitalocene not do the work that is required in developing a historically, politically and economically sensitive account of the new climatic regime in which we live?

Anthropocene or Capitalocene?

To address the climate crisis through the language and conceptual scheme of the 'Capitalocene' has two apparent benefits. Firstly, it stresses that the current climate crisis is the result of the forms of social and economic relations that have dominated the West since the end of the fifteenth century. This long history of capital accumulation took on new dimensions in the 1800s with the birth of 'fossil capitalism' as huge untapped resources of energy were exploited through the burning of coal, and intensified again with the Great Acceleration of the post-1945 oil-powered, globalised economic system. By foregrounding the history of the social relations that have produced the contemporary globalised carbon economy, the Capitalocene thesis warns against a tendency, implied within the Anthropocene nomenclature, to ignore the differential responsibilities for climate change that attach to various social actors, classes and populations. As Andreas Malm and Alf Hornborg, the two social theorists credited with coining the term, suggest: 'a significant chunk of humanity is not party to fossil fuels at all . . . hundreds of millions rely on charcoal, firewood or organic waste such as dung' for energy production.[28] For advocates of the Capitalocene thesis, the language of the Anthropocene implies that responsibility attaches to 'humanity as an undifferentiated whole' (the *anthropos*) and ignores the inequities, both in terms of vulnerability to climatic change and responsibility for emissions, that defines the climate crisis.[29]

Secondly, the Capitalocene thesis seeks to explore the manner in which capitalism has depended on modes of thinking that work to externalise and neutralise 'Nature', constructing an ontological separation between environmental processes and human agency. As Jason Moore argues, throughout the early history of capitalism we see the emergence of

> A new law of value . . . expressed by two epoch-making movements. One was the proliferation of knowledges and symbolic regimes that constructed nature as external, space as flat and geometrical, and time as linear (the field of abstract social nature). The other was a new configuration of exploitation (within commodification) and appropriation (outside commodification but subservient to it).[30]

In this way, to think in terms of the Capitalocene we can understand not only how capitalist forms of production and consumption have become integrated within 'the web of life' but also how capitalism itself depends on a form of thinking that occludes this fact, posing 'Nature' as something radically distinct from the 'Human'. For Moore, this 'Cartesian dualism' continues to haunt the Anthropocene concept itself as it positions 'Human activity in one box; Nature in another' and wrongly understands the Anthropocene as nothing more than 'human activity plus biospheric change', ignoring the complex, constitutive relations between human and natural forces.[31]

The Capitalocene narrative is an important contribution to the ongoing effort to frame our understanding of the history and causes of the contemporary climate crisis. But our quest for 'disciplinary diplomacy' suggests that we must proceed with caution. The notion that geologists postulate a unified and homogenous *anthropos*, as the agent responsible for the birth of this new epoch, for example, appears to labour under two misapprehensions. Firstly, the Anthropocene signifies that it is human action *as opposed to non-biotic forces*, like the movement of tectonic plates, orbital eccentricity, or volcanic eruptions, that has shifted the earth system beyond the conditions observed in the Holocene. That it is only a small portion of the *anthropos* that is directly responsible for this does not detract from the novelty of the situation from a geological point of view. Secondly, advocates of the Anthropocene have themselves been at pains to point out that large-scale disturbance within the earth system is attributable to a very small fraction of humanity. One of the first published scientific papers on the Anthropocene, for instance, ascribes responsibility to a mere 25 per cent of the global population and this clear rejection of the notion that a 'unified *anthropos*' is responsible for large-scale climatic change is referred to in a number of other scientific publications.[32]

A related point turns on the kind of class analysis to which the Capitalocene approach remains wedded. It is undeniable that relatively poor workers are, in general terms, more vulnerable to climatic change than relatively rich

capitalists. And of course, the global, plutocratic elite will do everything in
their power to avoid suffering from the negative effects of global warming by
building iron-clad bunkers, buying up land in more temperate zones, and
defending their island homes with the latest in flood defence technology. But
remaining bound to the class dynamics of modernity is not necessarily apt
in the context of the new climatic regime. In assessing empirical data that
traces the risks associated with both coastal and river flooding in England,
Ulrich Beck underscores the various factors that produce vulnerability in
each case.[33] In the case of coastal flooding, increased risk falls largely along
existing social class lines, with the most socially and economically deprived
being most at risk of the negative effects of rising sea levels. In the case of river
flooding, however, the negative effects are almost entirely democratic in the
sense that there is minimal variation in terms of risk across social classes. The
vulnerabilities to climate change, and indeed the new solidarities that might
emerge as these vulnerabilities become known, do not necessarily fall across
extant class or even national divisions. A similar issue is raised by Dipesh
Chakrabarty in a widely derided, but largely misconstrued, claim that climate
change means that 'there will be no lifeboats for the rich and the privileged'.[34]
Chakrabarty's point here is not to deny the existence of social inequities but
to underscore his intuition that the climate crisis is *more than* a crisis of capitalism and that the modes of analysis and sorts of justice claims that might be
developed in this context transcend Marxist, and even modernist, categories
and ways of thinking.

A further issue lies with the 'enduring Cartesianism' that supposedly
besets the Anthropocene thesis. Moore's suggestion that proponents of the
Anthropocene equate the term to 'human activity plus biospheric change'
misrepresents the Earth System Science approach, dominant since the 1990s,
which associates the Anthropocene not just with disturbance in the biosphere
– that is, the aggregation of the earth's ecosystems – but with disturbances
within a range of abiotic systems like the carbon, phosphorous and nitrogen
cycles. Pursuing an Earth System Science approach involves an integrated
and systematic view of *all* the operative elements of the earth system (including, of course, humans), with the functioning of each element within the
system dependent on a range of other elements. The Anthropocene suggests
that human agency is so firmly integrated within these systems that human
actions are shaping geological history. To suggest that this relies on an unre-
constructed Cartesianism that maintains a stark Human/Nature division is
directly challenged by these contemporary approaches.

However satisfying it might be to place responsibility for the current climate crisis at capitalism's door by renaming our current epoch the
'Capitalocene', the animating logics of capital accumulation ought not to

be the *only* forces that draw our attention. It is worth recalling, for instance, that a fossil economy need not be capitalistic. The communist states of the twentieth century were no less committed to the burning of fossil fuels and the radical reordering of the natural world to human ends than their capitalist rivals. Arguably, they were even worse. Andreas Malm, one of the early critics of the Anthropocene rhetoric, raises this very point, only to dismiss it, suggesting that given the near total collapse of twentieth-century communism – with North Korea and Cuba left as the last remaining outposts – his study of the historical origins of global warming need not engage with this particular iteration of the fossil economy.[35] As he rightly suggests, the Soviet mode of production needs to be approached 'on its own terms';[36] but the fact that communist economies maintained modes of production that depended on massive CO_2 emissions and aspired to large-scale intervention within landscapes and ecosystems does imply that an economy's dependency on fossil fuel consumption is not wholly reducible to capitalist property relations, something that 'Capitalocene' rhetoric implies.

That the capitalist mode of production – especially since the fall of communism in Europe – has played an essential role in producing the current climate crisis is undeniable, but our analysis has to embrace a broader set of forces, institutions and modes of thinking than that acknowledged by Marxist political economy alone. Indeed, what is noticeable in the Marxist readings of the Anthropocene concept is an unwillingness to critique the broader project of modernity and the political and legal forms that it has produced. We can see this in the normative dimensions of Malm's project. As he convincingly shows, capitalist industrial production depends on the spatiotemporal orderings afforded by fossil fuels. This means that the transition to renewables works against the inner logics of capitalism; it is this, for Malm, that explains the painfully slow progress of switching to green (what Malm calls 'flow') energy. Malm's proposed solution is to install a centrally planned distribution of energy production via 'flow power'.[37] Malm finds a model for this form of top-down management in the Irwell Commission of 1832, a system that sought to administer the hydropower of the Irwell reservoirs through taxation and the distribution of shared liabilities for mill and land owners. It is a twenty-first-century Irwell Commission that today is required if 'flow power' is to be harnessed and energy production is to take a more benign form.

Malm's vision of a 'planned economy for power'[38] seems at odds with the very nature of 'flow power', which is 'inherently local, autonomous, in tune with the heterogeneous movement of nature'.[39] Furthermore, his proposal retains a centrally important role for existing state structures and the modes of governance associated with capitalism itself. It is only by vastly strengthening the power of the state that something like a contemporary Irwell Commission could be realised. In Malm's vision of planned flow power, 'Man' rises up above 'Nature' and tames it for just ends, reiterating the bifurcation between 'human' and 'natural' forces that has animated modern thought and the political structures that it has conceived. Malm's planned green economy will be administered by a centralised state, presumably undergirded by an ever stronger national sovereignty.

I remain unconvinced that the economic relations that have driven modernity can be jettisoned, whilst the legal and political structures that have developed in tandem with them remain untouched. My scepticism about the Capitalocene narrative in no way disregards the important historical and theoretical work done by Malm, Moore and others in seeking to situate the contemporary global warming crisis within the history of capitalism. One of the crucial contributions of this approach to debates within legal and political ecology has been to encourage a rereading of the history of capitalism, colonialism, and the extractive and exploitative practices on which human 'civilisation' and 'progress' have been built, precisely as a history of ecological disruption and degradation. In this way, the climate crisis becomes a structural condition of the dominant relations of production, rather than some unexpected 'externality' which market forces must now address. Nonetheless, the causes that lie behind the climate crisis cannot be reduced to an account of the history of capitalism alone. Advocates of the Capitalocene narrative are perfectly right to stress that our changing climatic conditions are the result of *sociogenic*, not anthropogenic forces. But the Capitalocene thesis offers a limited explanation of the very forms that the 'social' has taken throughout modernity, reducing an account of political community to an analysis of capitalist property relations. As we will see in the chapters that follow, the legal and political forms that have existed alongside, and have operated in conjunction with, the capitalist mode of production – most importantly the emergence of the modern state and the distribution of liabilities and agencies on which this depends – have played a crucial role in consigning the climate crisis to the background of our political imaginaries.

As we will argue in what follows, it is precisely the question of political and legal *form* that should command our attention; and on this point, Marxian analysis can take us only so far. The Anthropocene thesis contends that collective human action has become so potent that it is shaping the earth's systemic functioning, destabilising the climatic conditions in which human civilisation emerged. In this way, the Anthropocene reveals a new ontology or mode of being-in-the-world in which human agency is intimately bound up with the functioning of the earth's geochemical systems and cycles, situating human agency and our political formations *within* rather than *set against* the so-called 'natural environment'. The Anthropocene forces us to reflect on the fact that our 'being' traverses the presumed dualism between the biotic and abiotic, human and non-human. We find ourselves in *geosocial formations*,[40] inextricably attached to, shaped by and shaping a range of natural forces. It is this ontology that remains remarkably difficult to grasp and it can only be cursorily addressed if we obsess over the nomenclature or temporal scope of the Anthropocene concept.

Many commentators see inherent flaws in the Anthropocene terminology, particularly the implication that a unified *anthropos* is responsible for the present climate emergency; notwithstanding that earth scientists themselves are deeply sceptical of this point. In this book, I follow Latour in suggesting that 'the new climatic regime' can be taken as being largely synonymous with the Anthropocene thesis. The former term has the benefit of evoking the political, and not simply scientific, implication of *regime change* and the complexities and challenges that such transformations entail. I have no great investment in the designation of the 'Anthropocene' itself but the concept does remain useful if it can prompt critical reflection about the conceptual co-ordinates on which we regularly rely in order to explain social and political life. It is a term that, for better or worse, has circulated widely in recent years and it has the benefit of gathering together a range of scientific, political, historical and philosophical concerns that put in question the epistemological and ontological presuppositions frequently associated with modernity. And, as I have tried to suggest here, the thesis forces a negotiation between and amongst the disciplines, putting in question taken for granted frames of reference and modes of inquiry. For these reasons, the concept remains useful.

In relation to political and legal theory, the Anthropocene thesis points to the inadequacy of forms of knowledge that seek to isolate the human from the inorganic, the non-human or the environmental. That the aspirations of human civilisation depend on the postulation of an anthropogenic superiority in which a 'natural condition' ('the state of nature', as Hobbes, Locke, Kant, and so many others have evoked) is overcome in the pursuit of a truly 'political' life, is one of the mainstays of modernist political ideology. To think politically in the Anthropocene involves overturning assumptions of this kind. As Latour suggests, the new climatic regime ensures that we 'no longer have a stable and indifferent framework in which to lodge [our] desire for modernisation'.[41] The prospect of human survival in this new epoch is bound up with a range of non-human forces that our political thinking has approached as an uninteresting backdrop against which human political dramas are played out. In the relatively stable conditions of the Holocene this 'backdrop ontology' was perhaps understandable. But the Anthropocene tells us that the backdrop is beginning to move, the scenery and props have come to life. If our social and political theory is to remain useful, we have to grasp the significance of this reality.

Gaia and the 'Rights of Nature'

Bruno Latour has been at the forefront of addressing both the political and ontological questions that the Anthropocene poses, most recently through an extended reading of James Lovelock's Gaia hypothesis, a forerunner to contemporary Earth System Science.[42] Despite frequent mischaracterisation, 'Gaia' is a theory about biogeochemical processes, not a postulation about some new age Goddess or 'Mother Earth'. Lovelock does not posit any agency *in addition to* the interactions between various elements within the biosphere, lithosphere and so on; these interactions simply are what he calls 'Gaia'.[43] Working throughout the 1970s with biologist Lynn Margulis, Lovelock suggested that the totality of organisms (including, of course, humans), surface rocks, oceans and the atmosphere are bound up in a series of feedback loops that regulate the surface conditions on earth. One of the novelties in Lovelock's early account of Gaia was the role he assigned organic life in the functioning of geochemical processes, something that until the 1990s was rejected by mainstream geochemists who understood life as little more than a 'passenger' on earth and simply subject to the evolutionary pressures of the environment. Lovelock was amongst the first to argue that without the intervention of living organisms, the chemical composition of the atmosphere, lithosphere and oceans would be radically different. In this way organic life (the biota) is integrated into geochemical processes (the abiotic elements of the earth), making Gaia – in Bruce Clarke's terminology – 'metabiotic'.[44] Lovelock's thesis suggests that organic life has *the capacity to shape* geochemical forces, rather than simply be subject to them. As Latour puts it, Lovelock's key intervention is the refusal, common to prevailing scientific approach, to '*de-animate* the planet by *removing most of the actors* that intervene all along a causal chain'.[45] By rigorously following the connections, Lovelock is able to trace the agencies that moved across biotic and abiotic registers and describe a properly *lively* planet in which agencies are widely distributed.

In Latour's reading of Lovelock he consistently emphasises that Gaia ought not be understood as a totality or a unity; or, perhaps better, Gaia forces us to understand the notions of 'totality' or 'unity' in new ways. In particular, Gaia is non-systemic – it is, for Latour, the 'anti-system'[46] – because it is incommensurate with a thinking of 'parts' that aggregate into a 'whole'. In this way, Latour positions Gaia against the Earth System Science approach we introduced earlier. Latour's non-systemic and non-holistic account of the earth's functioning raises two related issues that help us begin to sketch some of the implications the Anthropocene has for political ontology.

Firstly, Latour stresses that in Gaia everything is *always already in relation*. In other words, all human and non-human, biotic and abiotic agents and forces can only be understood through their relations with others: each singularity (an organism or some other entity) can only be grasped through the existence of other singularities with which it is always already bound. Any effort to isolate or disentangle one agent or function – any effort to isolate a single 'part of the system' – is futile. To isolate a single element involves artificially circumscribing its borders, severing the constitutive relations it has with others. Crucial to this view is the innovation introduced by Margulis, who jettisons an understanding of 'environment' as a background *in which* an organism resides and *to which* it adapts. The 'outside' (environment) is also 'inside' (organism), with each actant *always in relation*. Margulis and Lovelock insist that we cannot start with the organism and work out how it fits with its environment; nor vice versa. The Gaia-view of the earth embraces a network of relations where there is no discernible centre or end, no easy division between the biotic and abiotic elements, and where each attempt at enclosure or isolation forces us back within an ongoing play of actants.

The second point flows from the first. If there are no clearly individuated 'parts', they cannot coalesce into a 'whole'. This point is borne out in Lovelock's own methodology, which slowly assembles the various agents within the biogeochemical scene. It is only by refusing to transcend the particular interactions he observed and making a claim about the functioning of *planetary life as a whole* that Lovelock is able to show the specific roles that given organisms and ecosystems play in the production of the geochemical conditions on earth. It is this that allows Lovelock to think in terms of a '*connectivity without holism*'.[47] As Latour argues, if we view the earth's functioning as a system in which *parts fulfil a function in relation to a whole*, we are 'inevitably bound to imagine, *also, an engineer* who proceeds to make them work together'.[48] Indeed, the 'systems analogy' views the earth's dynamic operations as being predictable and mechanistic, as if fulfilling the design of a blueprint or use-plan. Latour does not deny the allure of the metaphor but simply underscores its status *as a metaphor*. Though the earth might function *like* a system, a system it does not make. The technological metaphors to which systems-thinking will always return posits a set of rules (the so-called 'laws of nature') to which the various elements within the system submit. But this prematurely unifies the earth's functions rather than attending to its qualities of emergence and creativity. As Latour suggests,

> Those who accuse Lovelock of conceptualizing the Earth as a unified whole fail to say that they too use an extraordinarily powerful unifier, since they have attributed to the laws of nature – in practice, to equations – the task

of *compelling obedience* everywhere, on every point. The problem is how to dispense completely with the theme of obedience and mastery – that is, of government (the etymology of cybernetics).[49]

If the 'systems approach' urges a kind of *transcendence* where the particularity of the connections between singularities within the earth's functioning are overlooked in favour of a 'whole which is more than the sum of its parts', Gaia calls for a kind of *subscendence* in that it finds something greater, both more numerous and more significant, in the plurality of connections 'within' than we do in the apparent unity of the whole itself.[50]

The systems view encourages us to see the earth as something that is already unified and enclosed, something 'over there' from which a human observer can, through a movement of thought, detach themselves. Gaia insists on an earth that is irreducibly 'down here' in a mess of hybrid interactions with which we humans are always already engaged. This makes the pre-eminent political task for the Anthropocene one of *assembly* and *composition*:

> It is . . . [the] total lack of unity that makes Gaia *politically* interesting. She is not a sovereign power lording it over us. Actually, in keeping with what I see as a healthy Anthropocene philosophy, She is no more unified an agency than is the human race that is supposed to occupy the other side of the bridge . . . This is why Gaia-in-us or us-in-Gaia, that is, this strange Moebius strip, is so well suited to the task of composition. It has to be composed piece by piece, and so do we.[51]

The plurality of elements within Gaia only come to be known through careful composition, by tracing the relations and slowly assembling the networks. Likewise with the *geo-bio-political* formations of the future. The political task as we turn to 'face Gaia' lies in assembling and composing new allegiances and alliances across assumed divisions between human and non-human, biotic and abiotic life, bringing into the *polis* the very forces and relations that the modern political imaginary kept resolutely consigned to the stage wings.

The implications for legal and political thought are important to grasp. In order to do so, let me briefly compare Latour's emergent 'Gaia-politics' with the politics and ethical commitments that inform the Earth Jurisprudence movement, one of the few efforts within legal theory that has addressed the challenges of climatic change and environmental destruction. In bringing these two approaches into conversation, I am particularly keen to explore the *political aesthetics* that we can draw out of this discussion. As already indicated, the argument developed in this book aims to draw out how our legal and political categories and dispositions render us *sensitive* or *insensitive* to the world in a given constellation. As I understand it, one of the key limitations of the Earth Jurisprudence approach is in its *political aesthetics*, which advances themes of *harmony, integrity* and *wholeness* in a way that is utterly disconnected from the messy entanglements to which Latour's reading of Gaia attends.

Whilst encompassing a range of perspectives, Earth Jurisprudence aims to shift away from the anthropocentricism of Western law and legal theory in order to give value to the environment and non-human forms of life on which human communities ultimately depend.[52] In seeking to champion an 'eco-centric' worldview, Earth Jurisprudence situates human laws in relation to a set of ecological imperatives for sustainability and the diminution of environmental harm. A persistent reference in this growing literature is the work of theologian and historian Thomas Berry, whose *The Great Work* seeks to develop an integrated ecological, theological and cosmological view of the earth's history and the place of humankind within it.[53] At the cornerstone of Earth Jurisprudence is the notion of the 'great law' (borrowed from Berry), referring either to the 'laws and principles by which the universe functions' or to the more limited notion of 'ecological integrity'.[54] The task for human law – largely understood by the literature as state law – is to harmonise with these broader laws of nature. The ultimate goal of Earth Jurisprudence is to theorise and instantiate legal systems, and a corresponding account of legal validity, that ensure that laws act for the 'common good of the earth community', referring to the totality of living organisms and ecosystems. In effect this involves first 'revealing' the laws of nature[55] – by attending to a range of sources, from biology and quantum physics to indigenous knowledges – and then constructing human or positive laws that accord with them. The predominant themes in Earth Jurisprudence are *harmony* and *wholeness*: a harmony between the 'laws of nature' and 'human laws' in which the whole of the 'earth community' and the broader cosmological context are taken into account.[56]

Earth Jurisprudence scholars mobilise and extend the language and conceptual schema of 'rights' in order to realise these goals. It is hoped that in expanding the scope and meaning of rights to include the 'rights of nature', the very contours of the contemporary political imaginary might be enlarged. As articulated by Cormac Cullinan, the principles of Earth Jurisprudence contend that 'all beings that constitute [the earth's biosphere] have fundamental "rights", including the right to exist, to a habitat or a place to be and to participate in the evolution of the Earth community'.[57] The notion of 'wild law', developed by Cullinan, refers to those laws that respect these fundamental rights of nature. Such 'wild laws' need to be developed that recognise the various qualities of all aspects of the natural environment and provide for their flourishing. Cullinan has been involved in the formalisation of these rights, helping draft the 'Universal Declaration of the Rights of Mother Earth', adopted by the World People's Conference on Climate Change and the Rights of Mother Earth in April 2010. Some of the impetus behind the Earth Jurisprudence movement has been reflected in recent legal developments, particularly on the question of legal personality. In New Zealand/ Aotearoa, for instance, the legal personality of Te Awa Tupua (Whanganui River) has recently been recognised and a statutory framework established by which the rights of the river can be represented and defended.[58]

Let me reiterate the two central tenets of Earth Jurisprudence: (1) the postulation of certain 'natural laws' to which human laws ought to conform; and (2) the extension of rights to the natural environment and all members of the 'earth community'. In both these aspects I argue that Earth Jurisprudence makes fundamental errors that fail to address the radicality of the challenge posed by the Anthropocene thesis. Let me address each of these points in turn.

Leaving aside the dubious understanding of scientific knowledge as depending on the 'revelation of nature',[59] let us focus instead on the political aesthetics that this approach implies. We can see the power of the 'system analogy' that Latour wants to avoid at work in the contention, made by Earth Jurisprudence scholars, that a seemingly unified set of 'natural laws' ought to dictate the shape of human legislative ambitions. There is in this view a code that dictates obedience from all parts of the natural system. And it is us unruly humans who need to get in line. As Helena Howe has recently argued, insights from Earth Jurisprudence encourage a fundamental reassessment of basic Western legal principles, particularly in property relations. In light of this thinking, Howe suggests, 'property would be given content and form by reference to the common good of human and non-human nature',[60] effectively harmonising extant property regimes with a superordinate ecological law. The point that Latour powerfully draws out of Lovelock is that this view prematurely unifies the natural order and imports a series of governmental metaphors into an account of 'natural life'. In lieu of a deductive approach that moves from a 'natural code' to questions of human normativity, Latour foregrounds an *inductive* attitude that dispenses completely 'with the theme of obedience and mastery – that is, of government'.[61]

Through Lovelock's Gaia hypothesis Latour articulates not a transcendent 'Nature', constituted by a unified code, but a messy and emergent set of relations that lack final closure. This establishes an important point of both political and aesthetic distinction between Latour's emergent Gaia-politics and the ambitions of Earth Jurisprudence. Where Latour emphasises the overwhelming urgency for a *creative* politics, in which new assemblies, new networks, and new sensitivities are fashioned, Earth Jurisprudence offers nothing but a politics of *submission*. It tells us nothing but that *we must obey*, by submitting human law – which can apparently achieve the unlikely task of facilitating both human flourishing and the flourishing of the *entire earth community* – to the 'laws of nature', as defined by the scientific-priests of contemporary ecology. Latour offers us a sense of what political agency might entail in the messy, heterogeneous and refractory, terrestrial world that the Anthropocene brings into view; Earth Jurisprudence simply hands the discrete capacities of political and legal knowledge production over to a 'higher law' encased in the 'laws of nature' to which it claims to have easy access.

In this way, Earth Jurisprudence remains wedded to the staid binaries that have always animated theories of Natural Law. Latour offers a very different scenography, and thereby a distinct aesthetic distribution, in which the 'natural forces' that constitute our lively planet are understood to be an emergent network within which human agency is always in negotiation. The Gaia hypothesis reimagines the natural world as something 'down here', approachable through an unfolding set of complex relations, not something 'out there' to which we owe obedience. The aesthetics of *harmony, wholeness* and *unity* are well-known and enduring tropes of modern legal and political thought.[62] One way of understanding the force of Latour's work on the new climatic regime is to read it as an *aesthetic* project which seeks to move beyond these figures of systemic closure and harmonic integrity. In Gaia, everything turns on an *attunement* or *sensitivity* to the multifarious relations that constitute the thin pellicle or 'Critical Zone' in which all life is found. This aesthetic sensitivity is common to both the natural and social scientist: both are concerned with the matter of *rendering oneself sensitive to a given set of phenomena*. And this is the question that we examine in this book: what are the legal and political concepts, theories and fictions that render us sensitive to the forces and relations that are shaping the political in the Anthropocene?

Earth Jurisprudence relies on 'rights' to do this work. But again this returns us to a distribution of the sensible – individuated and juridified – that has been central to a modern ethos and worldview. As Cullinan argues, all members of the 'earth community' have distinctive, inalienable and incommensurable rights: human rights are for humans; river rights, for rivers; aardvark rights, for aardvarks and so on. Cullinan argues that 'the rights of each being are limited by the rights of other beings to the extent necessary to maintain the integrity, balance and health of the communities within which it exists'.[63] This view isolates each actant within a given environmental scene and holds that a balance or harmony of conflicting 'rights to life and habitat' can be maintained. Recent work in biological science radically questions this view, with Lynn Margulis (Lovelock's sometime collaborator) demonstrating the highly complex relations that exist between an organism and its environment, with organisms continually shaping as well as being shaped by their given environment. This symbiotic view of the organism–environment assemblage leaves no room for an individuated 'right to habitat' because the flourishing of any one organism will necessarily affect the flourishing of others in a constantly unfolding matrix of relations.[64]

Irrespective of the science, the political aesthetics of this rights-based approach is itself problematic. Firstly, it does not *begin* with relations between actants but foregrounds instead the individuated rights that supposedly attach to discrete ecological monads. Secondly, it presupposes a theory of law that necessitates the state or some state-like authority that can adjudicate on the conflict between rights claims. This speaks to the broader desire within the Earth Jurisprudence scholarship to remain within the framework provided by state regulation. Whilst clearly indebted to the Natural Law tradition that posits a superordinate legality, transcending the particular provisions of positive law, Earth Jurisprudence continually orientates its theory of law towards the state. Indeed, state law is the privileged object of critique because it is this form of law that so clearly fails to align with the higher 'laws of nature' to which Earth Jurisprudence has apparent access. Rights make sense only in relation to some adjudicative 'third' that is able to resolve conflicts between competing rights claims. The history of rights, in this sense, is unthinkable apart from the history and theory of the modern state, with the 'age of rights' progressing hand in glove with the celebrated accounts of sovereignty in early modernity. Rights, therefore, are inextricably tied to modern law and its various entailments. In expanding the scope of rights – to include non-human actors – we therefore tacitly acknowledge that such claims ought to be recognised and enforced through existing state structures, juridifying any claims made in their name and presupposing a set of adjudicatory mechanisms that serve as the ultimate arbiter of their meaning and application. Given the critical orientation of this book with respect to sovereignty, this tacit acceptance of extant state power is impossible to endorse; it is, I argue, sovereignty – as a distinct legal and political form – that anaesthetises us to the challenges that the Anthropocene names.

The Earth Jurisprudence literature presents a starkly bifurcated view of lawful relations. The 'natural laws' of ecological integrity, with its aesthetic of harmony and wholeness, occupy one plane; and state law, which is largely deficient and in need of being properly aligned with the former, occupies another. This ordering of normative life is profoundly at odds with the complex, contested and overlapping matters of concern that define contemporary climate science and politics. As Latour has made clear, the Anthropocene thesis has brought into view a messy, conflictual and disordered 'natural world', one with which human agency is deeply entwined and that existing epistemological tools are frantically trying to decipher. This terrestrial, discordant meshwork of forces could not be, aesthetically or politically, further removed from the aspirations of harmony, unity and order that permeate the Earth Jurisprudence.

The Priority of Obligation

An alternative approach can be developed by shifting our attention away from *rights* and focusing instead on *obligations.* The language and conceptual schema associated with obligation opens a set of ontological concerns about the nature of our *being-bound* in place, in community and to a range of biotic and abiotic forces that exceed the human. It is these broader questions of the nature of our *attachment* and our *being-bound*, understood at both aesthetic and existential registers, that I want to foreground here in an effort to begin to reimagine how lawful relations can be understood in the context of the messy imbrications of the Anthropocene.

In foregrounding the role of obligation in our account of lawful relations I aim to supplement and extend Latour's claim that the 'human of the Holocene' needs to give way to an altered political subjectivity in the Anthropocene that he names *the earthbound*:

> Every conception of the new geopolitics has to take into account the fact that the way the Earthbound are attached to Gaia is totally different from the way Humans were attached to Nature. Gaia is no longer *indifferent* to our actions. Unlike the Humans in Nature, the Earthbound know that they are contending with Gaia. They can neither treat it as an inert and mute object nor as supreme judge and final arbiter . . . The Earthbound and the Earth . . . Both parties share the same fragility, the same cruelty, the same uncertainty about their fate.[65]

The earthbound grasp what it means to be living in the Anthropocene. They know that the most basic legal and political questions need to be re-posed: *To whom are we bound? To what are we attached? How are we assembled?* The Humans of the Holocene presume that the answers to such questions have long been settled; following Latour, my contention is that the earthbound can only hope to *compose* and *assemble* some fragile responses along the way. This involves outlining new forms of attachment to place and the forces and relations that sustain the habitability of place. Indeed, to think of ourselves as 'earthbound' reimagines subjects as primarily *bound*, rather than *free*, beings, urging an attention to the various bonds that constitute – and thereby limit – the scope of social life.

To approach the bonds that constitute our 'earthbound' condition in terms of obligation explicitly engages the law. The challenge, in this context,

is to reimagine the *vincula juris* – those ligaments or bonds of law that provide the basis for the assignation of duties, burdens and responsibilities[66] – in
a way that is sensitive to the geological and ecological entanglements at the
heart of the Anthropocene problematic. In the course of modernity we have
come to understand these *vincula* as taking shape within a field of individuated rights, largely dependent on an atomised subjectivity and situated within
a modern, oppositional rendering of nature/culture. With Michel Serres,
the first major philosopher to tackle the implications of climate change in a
strikingly prescient publication of 1990, we might want to evoke a new set of
vincula through the creation of a 'natural contract' that reattaches 'us humans'
to 'earth', superseding the social contracts of early modernity.[67] But it is
precisely the stability of any subject capable of signing such a contract – with
we Humans on one side and *Nature* on the other – that the Anthropocene
puts in question. There is an unavoidable asymmetry to our relation with the
earth that Serres's 'natural contract' cannot address.[68] As the Gaia hypothesis contends, we are *already* bound to the earth, primordially immersed
within its complex and emergent functions. There can be no *re*attachment to
something to which we have always been tied. It is this sense of the *priority*
of our boundedness – taking hold in a deep ontological sense – that I draw
out here, relying specifically on Simone Weil, who, perhaps more than any
other twentieth-century philosopher, was keenly aware of the inadequacies of
modernity's obsession with *rights* and who insisted on recognising the *priority
of obligation*. 'The notion of obligations', she reminds us, 'comes before that
of right which is relative and subordinate to it.'[69]

Weil argues that modern political life is mediated through a set of
institutions – courts, tribunals, legislatures – that she describes as a 'middle
region': they are neither sacred nor profane and are marked by a studied
'mediocrity'. These institutions are implicated in a generalised 'uprootedness' within the human condition, something Weil felt most acutely in the
proliferation of 'rights', which, she says, 'hang in the middle air, and for this
very reason they cannot root themselves in the earth'.[70] Rights are tied to
questions of measurement and exchange, the judicial economy of claim and
counter-claim that distorts the demands for justice made by the afflicted and
oppressed. Weil found in *obligation* an antidote to the prevailing conditions
of modern uprootedness as it spoke to the 'rootedness' of place and community.[71] Weil's privileging of obligation ahead of right, and the 'taking root'
(*enracinement*) that obligations express and facilitate, works within a radically
different political aesthetics to that offered by rights, mediating social relations in a distinct configuration. Most strikingly, Weil ties obligation directly
to questions of *need*, thereby suggesting an inherent connection between
obligations and the vital processes that sustain the human habitation of the

earth; as Weil puts it, 'for each need there is a corresponding obligation; for each obligation a corresponding need'.[72] In this way, an attention to obligation foregrounds the conditions of possibility for rights, calling to mind those *needs* and *dependencies* which precede the work associated with the institutions of the middle region and the language of contemporary 'rights-talk'.

Weil emphasises that contemporary 'rights-talk' is subtended by a deeper, *existential* register of obligation which both precedes and exceeds the jural correlate of 'right-and-obligation'. There is, as Weil reminds us, a categorical difference between an obligation owed at law and those obligations, grounded in *needs* and *dependencies*, which are immanent to communal life, prior to any question of institutionalisation or codification. And it is this prior sense of obligation, woven into the very ontology of associative life, to which we need to attend in the context of our Anthropocenic present. Weil contends that this more radical sense of obligation is revealed when we confront the prototypical cry of injustice: 'why am I being hurt?' Such an exclamation, Weil argues, is *infallible* and reveals a fundamental and unquestionable *fragility* to the human condition that demands our response, assistance, care and attention simply by virtue of our *being-in-community* and the forms of *reciprocity* and *solidarity* that this must entail. As she says,

> if someone tries to browbeat a farmer to sell his eggs at a moderate price, the farmer can say: 'I have the right to keep my eggs if I don't get a good enough price.' But if a young girl is being forced into a brothel she will not talk about her rights. In such a situation the word would sound ludicrously inadequate.[73]

For Weil, the 'infallible cry' can never simply be *resolved* through its translation into the regime of rights;[74] indeed, *solving* such a claim of injustice – which carries the implication of a calculability and the balancing of interests – always runs the risk of *dis-solving* those more primary obligations that bind actors in community.[75]

Prioritising obligation shifts the ontological foundations that we commonly associate with modernity. As Alasdair MacIntyre reminds us, 'there is no expression in any ancient or medieval language correctly translated by our expression "a right" until near the close of the middle ages'.[76] The foundational thinkers of modern law and politics – Hobbes, Locke and Rousseau – all prioritise *rights* in a way that situates the state, understood as the ultimate guarantor of rights, at the heart public life, and, in the liberal mode at least, seeks to liberate the individual from oppressive forms of community that circumscribe the creative capacity of subjects. The modern theorists of natural rights rearticulated the political not as a matter of *obedience* and *obligation*, the prevailing language of late medieval law, but in terms of *inalienable rights*, attached to individuated subjects and justified by reason alone. As Locke famously suggests, we have an originary property relation with ourselves: *we own ourselves* and this originary propriety right serves as the basis for the entire edifice of his account of legal and political power. Weil, in contrast, reanimates a notion of *originary solidarity* and of the constitutive limitations that are imposed on individual subjects by virtue of their living in community. Instead of *owning* ourselves, Weil insists that *we owe ourselves* to the network of forces and relations that exceed us. Rather than being born in *credit*, as Locke and his neoliberal heirs will insist, and therefore free to capture the world and dispose of it as we see fit, the *priority of obligation* implies that we are primordially *indebted* (in an ontological rather than financial sense) and that our putative freedom is always circumscribed by this fact. In this way, Weil's work is more closely aligned with pre-modern approaches to the nature of law and its relation to political community. As Sir Edward Coke articulates in *Calvin's Case* (1608), the law's capacity to bind subjects emerges from the '*ligaments* that connect minds and souls to one another' that are prior to the positive law.[77] It is, for Coke and for Weil alike, those ligaments that bind us to place and in social relations which both *precede and exceed* the language of right.

How, then, should we understand the relation between this prior sense of 'obligation' and the practices of the 'middle region'? For Emilios Christodoulidis, Weil's insight here is that 'rights' should be understood as the imperfect and partial mechanism by which the fundamental values of reciprocity, community and solidarity are translated into a jural form.[78] Weil's central concern is that in this movement from obligation to right something inevitably gets lost along the way. As she suggests, a fundamental cry of injustice 'spoken from the depth of the heart' is transformed into 'a shrill nagging of claims and counter-claims'.[79] The languages of the middle region tend to become self-referential, entirely unmoored or 'uprooted', as Weil would put it, from the more basic obligations that rights seek to reflect. In this way, the imperfection and partiality of the movement from obligation to right introduces a '*faultline within* the institutional language of law'.[80] For Christodoulidis this structure indicates that there are resources *within* juridical language that can articulate the very values of reciprocity, community and solidarity to which this prior sense of obligation speaks.

As Christodoulidis makes clear, Weil ties obligation to fundamental *human* qualities (solidarity and reciprocity) that bind actors in community. But in the context of the unfolding climate crisis and the onset of the Anthropocene, it is hard to endorse Weil's humanistic outlook as it is precisely the *inhuman* – the abiotic, the geophysical and the environmental – with which we have to contend as we seek to rearticulate the meaning and trajectory of associative life. There is, nonetheless, something both *infallible* and decidedly *fragile* about the climatic crisis, indicating an enduring resonance to Weil's thinking in this context. As Latour describes it, 'Gaia' or the 'Critical Zone' is constituted by innumerable loops and connections between biotic and abiotic, human and inhuman actants that unfold in a complex and dynamic set of relations; these relations are the very stuff of an expanded sense of communal being. The provocation that I take from Weil's thinking is that in order to grapple with the 'infallibility' of climatic transformation and the 'fragility' of the relations that it illuminates, we need to get *behind* or *beneath* the apparent 'solutions' proffered by rights and attend to those forces that bind us in forms of *bio-geo-social* association.

In Weil's language – highly apposite in the context of the Anthropocene – by moving away from a discourse of *rights*, we begin to think in terms of the *impersonal*. Rights always attach to the person, the *persona* or *mask* that is the mark of juridical subjectivity. Obligations for Weil are *unconditional* and therefore engage an *impersonal* register which persists beneath and beyond any particular personality trait or individual capacity. As Weil suggests, 'if a child is doing a sum and does it wrong, the mistake bears the stamp of his personality. If he does the sum exactly right, his personality does not enter into it at all.'[81] In the same way, obligation, because it responds to an *unconditional need*, does not engage the question of *personality*. As Roberto Esposito comments, glossing Weil, 'our person is something that in the final analysis we *possess*, like a trait, a character, an ability – all nonessential things that we may hold onto, but also lose'.[82] *Obligation* and the *impersonal* subtend the realm of *rights* and *(legal) personality* and insist on some essential and unconditional commitments that cannot be traded, exchanged or given up in the to-and-fro of the practices of the middle region.

In the context of the Anthropocene this insistence that our most fundamental obligations are grounded in something *impersonal*, something beyond a mere *possession*, is highly instructive. As Latour's rendering of Gaia helps us see, the nature of the bonds and forms of attachment that define our entry into the new climatic regime speak precisely to this register. We are bound to a set of forces – biotic and abiotic – that clearly transcend the rights and duties that can be defined by reference to any legal *persona*; they are what our very being, unconditionally, depends on.

This view allows us to inquire into the *inhuman* forces and relations that traverse human life and ponder the role that they might play in constituting lawful relations. As Margaret Davies has asked, 'if an object, say, or a place, is related in multidimensional ways in the human world, in what sense can we say that it also participates *in the generation of law*?'[83] Here Weil's insistence that obligations have a priority with respect to rights, and are grounded in human *needs* rather than human *privileges* or *freedoms*, helps formulate a response. For Weil, our communal dependencies will always imply obligations: if we depend on our families or our neighbours for care; freshwater systems for potable water; global supply chains for food and medicine; state institutions for our security and so forth, then we owe obligations by virtue of these facts. These might include obligations of reciprocity and solidarity to family or neighbours; obligations not to pollute or otherwise degrade water supplies; obligations to sustain international co-operation or strive for self-sufficiency; obligations to change or support existing governmental structures or to simply pay one's taxes. And undergirding all of these particular dependencies is a common concern to maintain a climatic system that can sustain continued habitability of the earth, something on which all of us ultimately depend. Such a view calls on subjects and communities to articulate their dependencies. Which ecological, infrastructural or communal relations sustain your continued habitability of a given place? For how long can these networks of dependence be maintained and reproduced? How do these networks conflict with the dependencies of others? Who or what shares the same relations of dependence as you, and who or what threatens or undermines these relations?

In thinking through the implications of such questions, Weil stresses the importance of one quality above all: *attention*. The nature of our obligations, for Weil, is born out of our ability to dedicate our *attention* to human needs. Attention is not a matter of careful scrutiny or concentration but refers instead to a form of suspension or hesitation; something more readily discerned in the French where the resonance between *l'attention* ('attention') and *attendre* ('waiting') is clear. Attention involves 'stepping back from all roles, including that of the observer'[84] in order to open oneself to a given object in a way that is not determined in advance. Attention, in this sense, entails a particular kind of *attunement* and *sensitivity* in which thought is simultaneously opened up and emptied out, where a kind of 'void' is created which allows a matter of concern to affect a sensate subject. This entails an enlivening of the senses, a pause in which an actor becomes sensitised to a given set of social relations and the demands that such relations might make. As an ethical orientation, attention wards against premature or ready-made solutions; as Christodoulidis suggests, 'the most incisive way to capture the function of attention is as a resistance to (what Heidegger would call) the *readiness to hand* (*Zuhandenheit*) of the meaning construction afforded by the [institutions of the] middle range'.[85] In this way attention urges forms of *creativity* in the context of our emerging climatic condition, particularly by holding in suspense many of the deep-seated assumptions that structure a distinctly *modern* ethos and worldview. But so too does Weil's language of attention suggest that obligations are born out of a particular form of sensitivity or *aesthesia*. In this way it is only through a form of *aesthetic sensitivity*, which takes seriously the immersion of a sensate body within the elemental forces that provide the continued conditions of habitability in a given place, that the nature of obligations which that place generates can be discerned.[86]

Weil insists, then, that the register of obligation implies both an *ontological* and an *aesthetic* transformation vis-à-vis rights. As we have suggested, the aesthetics of the Anthropocene are *messy* and *pluralistic*, defined by the multiple and contested forces which struggle to maintain habitability in a given place. The sense of the aesthetic for which this account of the earth system calls, however, is less concerned with *form* or *order* than it is with *aesthesis*: the sensory and affective dimensions of human life that allow for one's *attention* to be directed to those relations of dependence and need that sustain a community's existence. The ontological transformation to which Weil points foregrounds the human's originary indebtedness to the impersonal (abiotic, geological, ecological) forces that are the condition of possibility for human life and flourishing. This imagines the human as a primarily *bound* – or *earthbound* – being. In what follows we examine the existential and aesthetic dimensions of our *being-bound* as we seek to unpack the implications that embracing our earthbound has on the meaning of sovereignty in the current conjuncture.

Frustrating though it may be, I am deliberately holding in abeyance the question of the *content* of our obligations and dependencies in this context and though they may take some inspiration from the themes of 'solidarity, reciprocity and community' that Christodoulidis sees animating Weil's account of obligation, they clearly must go beyond this humanistic (and decidedly anthropocentric) heritage. As Latour says of the ligaments that enmesh us within Gaia, the existential obligations that bind us to the earth cannot be posited in advance but must be *assembled* in an ongoing effort to trace the contours of an expanded sense of political community. In this way, these obligations must be understood in specific contexts that deal with particular matters of concern for situated actors rather than posited – as Earth Jurisprudence does – as universalised 'laws of nature' to which human communities must submit. My contention is that the important work of *composition* and *assembly* needs to work at this register, *prior to* the practices of the 'middle region' and the language of 'rights'. If, in Latourian terms, the obligations that emerge out of our social and ecological dependencies must be *composed* rather than *presupposed*,[87] we can nonetheless reflect, at a metatheoretical level, on the co-ordinates that might structure a new sense of *attention* appropriate for the new climatic regime. We will examine this in subsequent chapters as we speculate about how we might think outwith the theoretical co-ordinates that define modern sovereignty.

The End of the World

If we are to navigate a new age of attachments, bonds and obligations, then we have to see that the Anthropocene heralds *the end of the world*. Not that the functioning of the earth system itself will collapse, and not that humankind, or even a recognisable human civilisation, will be destroyed; though, of course, these things are possible. The Anthropocene means *the end of the world* in the sense that the predominant modes by which we organise and represent reality are becoming undone, the distribution of background, foreground and horizon that constitutes a believable world is being disturbed. Not only is the backdrop shifting around but the very distinction between the scenery and actors onstage has become fundamentally uncertain. The analogy with the theatre is apt because it reminds us that the efficacy of a given 'world' simply depends on the investment of an audience and the immersive power of the artistry. If the modern world insists that the earth is immobile, that 'Nature' is simply 'out there', and something over which we can take appropriative and instrumental control, an event like the drying of the Slims River with which we opened this book ought to make that world somewhat unbelievable. There are, of course, many more jolts or interruptions of this sort, all of which evidence the unwelcome arrival of the Anthropocene. These interruptions – from the bleaching of coral to the rising of sea levels, from mass extinctions to smog-filled skies – would seem to suggest that the artistry on which the modern world depends has become suspect; as if the whole set shook or a painting fell as an actor closed a door onstage, as if the lighting rig suddenly dropped into view or the fire alarm in the theatre began to ring. Such interruptions would destroy the world created by the drama; they would break the spell cast by the art.

The strange thing about the world that the moderns have created is that despite numerous jolts and interruptions we remain, by and large, immersed in the cosy atmosphere created by the dramaturgy. The fire alarm is ringing, and the set is falling to bits, but we still remain strangely transfixed by the anthropocentric dramas being played out under the auspices of modern law and politics. If we are to understand how this world is given shape, what is so convincing about its artistry, and why we struggle to get a handle on the fact that things are going horribly wrong, we have to understand the *political aesthetics* that modernity installs and maintains. It is this that we pick up in the next chapter as we start to think in more detail about the aesthetics of sovereignty.

2

The Aesthetics of Sovereignty

Change would be impossible if we could not mentally remove ourselves
from where we physically are located and *imagine* that things might as well
be different from what they actually are.
                                    – Hannah Arendt, 'Lying in Politics'[1]

In early 2018 I took up two research fellowships, first visiting the University
of Glasgow and then the Birkbeck Institute for the Humanities in London.
I arrived in Scotland at the end of February to be greeted by what the media
dubbed 'the beast from the east' – not, as I initially thought, a veiled reference
to Xi Jinping's ensuing power grab in Beijing – but a cold weather event that
affected large swathes of northern Europe. The severe weather in the British
Isles coincided with record high temperatures in the Arctic as the polar vortex
– a system of low pressure that corrals cold air towards the pole – undertook
an unprecedented migration south. Heavy snowfall the day of my arrival
meant that my scheduled visit with family in Edinburgh had to be extended:
trains were cancelled, the university in Glasgow was closed. Though remaining bitterly cold well into March, regular weather patterns soon returned.
In early May I left Scotland to begin the second phase of my research leave
in London only to find a city once again in the grip of exceptional weather.
Record temperatures were set across the northern hemisphere as the earth
dried, cracked and then smouldered with wildfires taking hold in Greece,
Portugal, California and even in the characteristically drizzly northwest of
England. As the thermostat settled at 34.5°C in London, air-condition-less
travel to an air-condition-less office in Bloomsbury was about as uncomfortable as it sounds.

   In the scorching summer heat the parched earth revealed strange mark-
ings in fields and gardens, tracing the outline of ancient settlements, long
abandoned, buried and forgotten. Prehistoric villages, ditches, monuments,
cemeteries and farms became suddenly visible in the landscape, revealing
a patchwork of earthly hieroglyphs, witnesses to extinct forms of life that
returned to haunt our present. I could not help but read these scars in the

earth – ruins of ancient societies, unceremoniously brought into the light of the summer sun – as timely harbingers of the possible future that awaits our own increasingly frangible modes of existence in the Anthropocene.

Against the backdrop of the Anthropocene and the 'earthbound' existence which it heralds, these uncanny encounters with traces of past civilisations invite a reckoning with the *earthliness* of the human. Indeed, the Anthropocene prompts reflection on what we might call *earthly life*: the uncanny and decidedly human encounter and imbrication with planetary biogeochemical forces and relations. If the material traces of long razed villages, fortifications and burial sites speak to the anxieties of our present, it is because our contemporary forms of life, modes of habitation, production and consumption are not simply *symbolic* forms or 'second natures', the traces of which might lose their significance or potency sometime in the future, but are expressly *material forces* that are instrumental in shaping the very possibility that extant forms of life may themselves wither and crumble. In this sense, we can think of *earthly life* as entailing a mode of self-reflection in which we see ourselves – and the collective force of human action – as taking on a planetary significance, comparable to shifting tectonic plates, meteor strikes or massive volcanic eruptions. It is the human *becoming-earthly*, to adapt Deleuze, with which we have to contend as we face the prospect of living in the Anthropocene. Timothy Morton captures this peculiar condition when he reminds us:

> Every time I start my car . . . I don't *mean* to harm Earth, let alone cause the Sixth Mass Extinction Event in the four-and-a-half billion-year history of life on this planet . . . [But] harm to Earth is precisely what is happening.[2]

It is the uncanniness of *earthly life* that Morton draws out here, highlighting how the most quotidian of acts is enmeshed with a set of biogeochemical relations, underscoring that everyday life in the Anthropocene, strange though it may seem, takes on a planetary and geological significance.

Unsurprisingly, the challenges that *earthly life* brings into view did not dominate the news agenda during my visit in London. Instead, the seemingly interminable fall-out from the recent Brexit vote wore on implacably. As the earth boiled, the disputed but ever desired shibboleth of sovereignty made a return to mainstream political discourse. The desire to 'take back control', as the Brexit campaign had it, animated a resurgence of nationalist sentiment that continually circled around rival claims to sovereignty. The apparently 'sovereign will' of the people expressed in the 2016 referendum was now in the hands of the executive and Parliament, the latter itself claiming sovereignty, much to the chagrin of the former, whose powers were themselves being carefully delimited by the UK Supreme Court, which claimed for itself a form of legal sovereignty, as both ultimate arbiter and interpreter of the constitution.[3] This reflux of sovereignty has of course been felt throughout the world as a range of neo-nationalisms have taken hold in Europe and beyond. As Steve Bannon – Donald Trump's former chief strategist – has commented, this new wave of neo-nationalists and right-wing populists are all 'sovereigntists',[4] united in their desire to reaffirm the nation state – and an ethnically coded national identity – as the anchor point for political life.

If, as Kyle McGee has argued, polities are today suffering from the 'twin vertigoes' of *placelessness*, provoked by the globalisation of economic and political power in which the established co-ordinates of social life have been deterritorialised, and *landlessness*, as climatic mutation renders uninhabitable or unproductive the very earth on which people depend, then a return to the trope of sovereignty, which aims to 'take back control', is perhaps eminently understandable.[5] But of course, back-to-the-nation instincts offer nothing but a dreary utopianism in the context of our present climatological and ecological upheavals. As the very land beneath our feet is reformed, as coastlines are rewritten, as drought desiccates productive soil, the postulation of an enisled community, supposedly secure in its sovereign solitude, rings as hollow as the empty promises plastered across Boris Johnson's Brexit bus. And yet it was such promises that so animated a majority of the UK populace who sought to reassert a seemingly waning national sovereignty. In this chapter I explore the enduring power of sovereignty and its ability to frame our most fundamental sense of the political. If, as I have intimated, a return to the sovereignty-of-old offers nothing but illusions in an age of planetary climatic change, how can we begin to think beyond this rendering of sovereignty or at least weaken the powerful grip it continues to have on our sense of the shape and purpose of associative life?

The Trap of Sovereignty

Let me begin by evoking some of the frequently used definitions of sovereignty. Sovereignty, we are told, is perpetual, indivisible and absolute, a supposedly supreme source of state power;[6] alternatively, we are told that sovereignty is marked by decisionism, describing the notion that the sovereign is unbound by legal norms;[7] sovereignty is supposedly transcendent, sacred or otherwise theological in nature;[8] it is both *grounded* by being tied to a particular territory and *ephemeral*, associated with affective qualities like awe, majesty and glory.[9] To this we can add some further qualificatory terms: sovereignty is described as being 'popular' or 'parliamentary', 'nation-state' or 'juridical', 'individualistic' or 'epistemic'; as well as having mutually reinforcing 'internal' and 'external' dimensions. These various attributes bear witness to the essentially hybrid nature of sovereignty, marking it out as a 'contested concept',[10] mobilised by a range of often contradictory interests and concerns, as well as raising issues for a number of fields of study: public international law, constitutional law, international relations, political philosophy and jurisprudence.

These competing, and often contradictory, characterisations of sovereignty have been augmented by radically changing factual dynamics, particularly in the West. The end of the Cold War and the institution of a new 'global order' has challenged classical conceptualisations of sovereignty. The increasingly free flow of capital, people, goods, services and information across state borders; the constitution of supra-state legal and political institutions; technological innovation, particularly in telecommunications; and the near-total dominance of corporate power within advanced economies, all suggest that classical, juridico-political conceptions of sovereignty have been fundamentally disrupted. And yet, sovereignty remains a potent and affectively charged concept. The rise of new nationalisms throughout Europe; demands for the building of new 'walled' frontiers, racial and religious profiling, and a return to protectionism in the USA; along with the emergence of new independence movements in China, Africa and beyond, have all mobilised the language of sovereignty, attesting to its enduring force in mediating and expressing political claims and desires. Whilst we might dismiss some of these movements as being motivated by atavistic fears of difference or as nostalgic yearnings for a lost sense of 'community' in the face of ever increasing economic precarity, the truth is that sovereignty today finds itself on the lips of left-wing radicals and little-Englanders alike. It was the call of 'we the people' that animated the global Occupy! phenomenon in 2011 and in Europe similar appeals were made by popular movements seeking to resist the technocratic impositions made by the 'Troika', that latter-day Cerberus intent on restructuring the economies and polities of supposedly 'sovereign' states in Europe. And, of course, as nation-state sovereignty has been transfigured in the era of globalisation, in Australia, Canada, the USA and beyond, 'sovereign' indigenous nations have been afforded increasing, and long overdue, recognition. Sovereignty, in this sense, has been mobilised in efforts to resist the vestiges of imperial power; though, of course, myriad difficulties and injustices endure.

If the premise of this project is that modern sovereignty deserves renewed critical pressure in the context of the Anthropocene, the concept's multiple forms and implications present some stark difficulties. Even if we wanted to somehow do away with sovereignty – which, given the fortunes of the concept in the context of democratisation and popular resistance to arbitrary power, we should treat with some scepticism – from what ground could we resist it? As James Martel has argued, resistance to sovereignty reveals a 'trap'.[11] The cry, 'Down with sovereignty!' requires a quintessentially sovereign decision to resist the current form it takes. And such a cry will invariably seek succour and support from some 'inalienable', 'transcendent' or 'timeless' (read, *sovereign*) set of values or beliefs.

Yet, the aspiration to think the political without continually spinning around the maypole of sovereignty is central to much contemporary political and legal thought. There is a widespread disquiet with the nineteenth- and early twentieth-century consensus that political life can only be cogently understood through the sovereign state and the system of states that constitute the international plane. Aspirations for a cosmopolitanism or global humanism that transcends the parochialism of the nation abound as theorists seek to find an escape from the clutches of the modern inheritance which situates political life, its modus operandi and range of possibilities, irredeemably *within* the framework of statehood. But getting away from sovereignty is not easy. As R. B. J. Walker has noted, the very ambition of *escape* from one political condition to another relies on a set of distinctly modernist assumptions, particularly regarding a progressive, linear temporality and some notion of autonomous, rational human action, that themselves are fundamental to the modern articulation of sovereignty:

> Any claim to a normative vision of escape from the modern state and system of states will be caught within accounts of what it means to be a visionary, to effect an escape, to imagine the possibilities of being otherwise that are *already* produced by modern accounts of political necessity, possibility and subjectivity.[12]

The trap of sovereignty redoubles itself. Even the wish of getting to some new political pasture, shorn of the outmoded ligatures of the old regime, invariably ends up reproducing the very temporal dynamics and conceptual divisions on which sovereignty itself depends. We seem to lack the political imagination to genuinely move beyond the sovereign structures that have dominated our sense of the 'who-what-and-where' of political life for the last 500 years.

Are we really 'trapped' by sovereignty? There is, as I have tried to sketch here, a sense of the woods closing in whenever sovereignty is evoked. Multiple, deeply contested, and sometimes contradictory, understandings of the term seem to overburden the concept before we can even utter its name. The diversity of situations in which sovereignty is mobilised has the tendency to empty the concept of any stable content. And efforts to escape the clutches of sovereignty face the enormous challenge of doing so whilst not repeating the foundational logics of inclusion/exclusion; linear temporal progress; transcendental values; and the postulation of human exceptionalism which are

themselves the hallmarks of sovereignty. Part of the problem lies in the lines
of inquiry we undertake. If we ask, 'what is sovereignty' or 'who is sovereign',
we are immediately drawn into a debate about the predicates that might
correspond to some 'essence' or 'substance' that can be confidently appended
to the term or office holder. And it is at this point that the woods close in, the
paradoxes multiply and contestations abound; like some therianthropic deity,
sovereignty is constantly being remade and, in so being, seems to persistently
elude our grasp. Similarly, if we ask how we might get from our current
condition to another, non-sovereign political landscape, we have to account
for the underlying impulses that prompt such a desire; and here our claims
to have somehow left behind the prevailing political forms of modernity will
often be found wanting. Perhaps we can find a route out of the thicket by
privileging not, '*what is . . .*' but some '*how . . .*' questions of sovereignty.
How is sovereignty claimed? *How* is it given form? *How* is it represented and
expressed?

Jean Bodin, roundly celebrated as the first theorist of modern sovereignty,
poses the *how question* of sovereignty in the following terms:

> just as a ship is but timber lacking the form of a vessel without a keel to
> support the ribs, the prow, the poop and the tiller, neither can there be a
> state without a sovereign power to unite all its several members and parts,
> be they households or colleges, into a single body.[13]

Bodin insists that a sovereign authority is a necessary condition for the existence of the state. Without it, we are told, the state would be *formless*, like
timber in a boatyard before the shipbuilders have set to work. What is striking about Bodin's metaphor is the presupposition, that is then quickly passed
over, of the *craft* or *technique* that gives form to sovereignty; sovereignty,
Bodin intimates, has to be *assembled* or *composed*, it must be *given form*
through a technological practice. And is not the all-important question, *how*
is this composition achieved? How do we move from a *formless* collective to
a *formed* state? And does addressing *this* question, rather than seeking to give
an exhaustible list of attributes to some increasingly hollow signifier, not give
a clearer sense of the particular mode, form and tenor of both the state and
the sovereign authority that it supposedly requires?

Of course, these questions have been given rich elaboration in the social
contract tradition, from Hobbes to Rousseau, from Locke to Kant along
with twentieth-century heirs like John Rawls. In pursuing the question of
sovereignty's *form* and *formation*, I propose instead, to shift terrain by reading
sovereignty through an attention to its *aesthetics*. This involves attending to
the way in which sovereignty appears, is given form, expressed and represented, as well as the force it has in shaping a collective imaginary or mode

of perceiving the world. This approach, I contend, allows us to overcome the shortcomings that beset dominant approaches to theorising sovereignty in the context of the new climatic regime and offers a mode of inquiry that goes some way in neutralising the 'trap of sovereignty', as we have described it here.

Sovereignty in the New Climatic Regime

Against an account of the political built on the presupposition of a strong sovereign state, two critical approaches have predominated within the scholarship on sovereignty in recent years. Firstly, as we have already intimated, a range of studies have assessed the changing nature of legal and political authority under the prevailing conditions of neoliberal globalisation. These accounts have focused on alterations to governmental competencies, tracking the various powers that have been ceded to a range of non-state actors over the course of the last thirty years or so. Studies have traced the plurality of jurisdictions that have become more or less unmoored from state law; the rise of supra-national structures that 'pool' state sovereignty; and the increasing significance of private power in the administration of once 'public' services like education, health, prisons and security. The prevailing view within these approaches is that a 'classic' or 'high' period of sovereignty, apparently supreme from the eighteenth to mid-twentieth centuries, has come to an end. If classic conceptualisations of sovereignty (theorised by Bodin, Hobbes, Rousseau and company) claim that civic powers are clearly delineated within national borders and have a superordinate relation with respect to religious, private, familial, and moral domains, contemporary writers have sought to show that today's multi-scalar, overlapping forms of authority, alongside the massive expansion of market forces and rationalities, have fundamentally reconfigured the sovereign form. Today, sovereignty is variously described as being 'in transition',[14] 'sleeping',[15] 'waning',[16] 'late',[17] 'fractured',[18] in 'crisis'[19] or otherwise in some state of ever more perfect 'deconstruction'.[20] Whilst early proclamations of sovereignty's demise[21] were premature – the state, quite clearly, is yet to wither away – this literature has persuasively shown how, at the level of governmental competencies, statecraft and the distribution of power within Western polities, sovereignty has been reconfigured as new assemblages of the capacities and capabilities traditionally associated with a unitary state power have taken hold.

A second strand of scholarship has focused on the question of sovereign power and the legal, political and disciplinary techniques that it mobilises. Much of this literature follows in the wake of Michel Foucault's account of 'biopolitics' – referring to the techniques of power, emerging in the eighteenth and nineteenth centuries, that take the biological functions of the human body as their primary object – and the expansion of these themes in the influential work of Giorgio Agamben. Foucault distinguishes biopower from sovereign power, arguing that the latter was a facet of kingship in medieval Europe, taking shape in the capacity to 'take life or let live' and dramatised in highly choreographed moments of punishment and pardon. Biopower, in contrast, came to replace the simple binaries and spectacular staging of sovereign power and was concerned with 'fostering life or disallowing it to the point of death'.[22] Following Agamben's efforts to trace the history of biopower through ancient Greek political thought, Roman law, and the more recent history of the deployment of emergency powers as a means of safeguarding the integrity of the state,[23] many studies have examined the intersections, rather than the differences, between sovereignty and biopolitical governance. One of the dominant concerns in this literature turns on the *forms of life* that sovereign power produces and depends upon. As Stewart Motha has described it, sovereign power increasingly treats 'the body' as its 'most basic elemental category, albeit one that can take many *forms*'[24] including 'citizen', 'refugee', 'enemy combatant' and so on. Efforts to describe the *forms of life* that sovereign power produces have given rise to a number of studies: Agamben's infamous figures of *homo sacer* and *bare life*; Judith Butler's *precarious life*; and Eric Santner's *creaturely life* all seek to describe the distinct forms of human subjectivity that sovereign power produces.[25] These forms of life are best understood as the abject surplus created through the operations of biopower, the living residue that is left through the formation and policing of a sovereign political sphere. These themes have been explored in a range of contexts, not least in relation to the systematised violence and expropriation of eighteenth- and nineteenth-century European colonialism which instrumentalised and brutalised human life to such an extent that, as Achille Mbembe has powerfully argued, the subject of colonial power became akin to the *living dead*.[26] In this way nineteenth-century colonialism can be understood as a nightmarish harbinger of the 'necropolitical' exterminations within the European death camps of the twentieth century.

These dominant approaches to sovereignty, despite their hugely important insights in tracing the changing dynamics of governmental power, the forms of life and systems of oppression that these changes have produced, nonetheless fail to grasp two of the most striking features of contemporary legal and political life: the return of sovereignty in new forms of civic and ethno-nationalisms on the one hand, and the emergence of the new climatic regime in which a range of biogeochemical forces have intruded into the social domain, on the other. Of course, we might point to the reordering of governmental competencies and the progressive weakening of the civic sphere as a contributor to the recent reaffirmation of nationhood, identity and the promise of a return to the bright lines of territorial integrity. But the ongoing efforts to describe, in ever greater detail, the reallocation of state powers to supra-national institutions, and within a range of private forums, offer few insights into the enduring force of sovereignty as an affective lure or mediating device for the meaning and scope of collective life. In this sense, by focusing on the reformation of sovereignty at the level of *governmental practice* and *raison d'état* alone scholars have ignored the passional, affective, sentimental and emotional aspects of sovereignty and the aesthetic scaffolding which has always buttressed the concept's material instantiations.

With respect to the challenges of climatic change, scholars who have detailed alterations to jurisdictional competencies and governmental form provide few relevant insights either. This is because they remain wedded to a modern political imaginary that remains deeply *sociocentric*,[27] and are therefore largely blind to the various transformations within the earth's climatic system that are the curse of our contemporary moment. Though offering an analysis of purportedly new developments in law and politics, these debates rely on a conceptual framing that continues to bear the distinctive hallmarks of modern political thought. Neil Walker makes this point explicit in his survey of 'global law',[28] arguing that postnational constitutionalism (with its emphasis on the constitutive, social and cultural forces that produce legitimacy) and postnational public law (with its emphasis on the forms of constituted regulatory schemes in new 'state-like' sub- and supra-national institutions) both remain committed to a modernist political and theoretical horizon. These globalist schemes champion individual autonomy and equality *and* seek to limit any encroachment on such freedom and equality through general norms and objective standards.[29] The enduring force of this modern heritage goes further still. As Walker comments,

> in the final analysis, the global division of the world into particular polities remains inevitable, but the particular form that such a division takes is not so; rather it is contingent upon shifts in the underlying circuits of social and economic power.[30]

This view retains the contention, distinctive to the legal and political presuppositions of modernity, that human actors have the capacity to break free from a range of 'natural attachments' in order to create new political forms that respond to the shifting sands of social and economic life. 'The world', in Walker's view, is something *on which* human communities live and something *over which* human polities of the future might claim control. In this sense, Walker continues to work within what Peter Sloterdijk has called the 'backdrop ontology'[31] that defines the moderns' worldview: the natural world is conceived as a largely immobile scenography that simply provides the staging for human political dramas. The Anthropocene brings a radically different set of forces into view as the terrestrial, biogeochemical systems and cycles that constitute the earth system make their presence felt within the social domain. In this sense, the tension between the *national* and *global* scales, which is the primary focus of the multifarious accounts of sovereignty's 'post-modern' reformation, provides an inadequate set of co-ordinates because it keeps the material, terrestrial, earthly forces that are increasingly shaping the parameters of collective life resolutely 'offstage'.

Similar problems haunt biopolitical readings of sovereignty. From the studies of internment camps at the peripheries of states, and the various modes of biometric surveillance used at the border, to the increasingly sophisticated theoretical work that seeks to reimagine the scope of biopower in an age of neural plasticity,[32] it is the politics of *human life* that remains an exclusive focus. These studies, which examine the ways in which contemporary governmental technologies regularly render indistinct *zoe* (biological or physiological life) and *bios* (political life), remain remarkably uninterested in how modes of governance interact with the geological, earthly and putatively inanimate 'natural' realm. As Elizabeth Povinelli has convincingly shown, biopolitics – understood as a politics concerned with the disciplining of bodies and the management of populations – has always been subtended by a more radical distinction between Life (*bios*/*zoe*) and Nonlife (*geos*).[33] In this way, Povinelli adds a *geontological* dimension to a theory of biopolitics and in so doing reveals the limited perspective afforded by approaches largely inspired by Foucault and Agamben.

The *anaesthetising* effects of such a limitation are evidenced within colonial governmental practices in Australia where, Povinelli argues, the division between Life (*bios*/*zoe*) and Nonlife (*geos*) has been central to the management of indigenous populations. In a striking example, Povinelli shows how sacred indigenous sites, understood to be *living members* of the indigenous community, with agency and distinct histories, were understood by colonial officials to be nothing but *inanimate rocks* that could be exploited at will. Povinelli argues that such divisions between the Living and the Nonliving constitute a 'common sense' backdrop to the modern imaginary that shaped the techniques of colonial governance and exploitation. In the context of the Anthropocene, however, these taken for granted divisions no longer hold: a seemingly inanimate *geos* has been revealed to be distinctly *lively*, both in contemporary ESS which describes the 'metabiotic' relations between ecosystems and their environments and within the Anthropocene thesis itself which troubles easy distinctions between 'societal' and 'natural' forces. As Povinelli sees it, modernity has always striven for the ever clearer distinctions between Life and Nonlife, characterising as decidedly non-modern (backward or archaic) any society that 'confuses' these two registers.[34] Discourses of biopolitics, however, continue to labour within this modern framework by retaining an exclusive focus on the *forms of human life* that bear no apparent relation to any *earthly, geontological* forces at all.

In this sense, the dominant accounts of sovereignty have failed to articulate the central problematics of our contemporary political situation, offering minimal guidance on how we might unpack both the enduring force of sovereignty in the contemporary moment as an affective, imaginary and emotional phenomenon *and* the unique challenges associated with the new climatic regime which urges an engagement with the geological, earthly forces routinely ignored by modern political thought. My contention is that by shifting our attention to the register of *aesthetics* we can better grasp these challenges. An aesthetic approach to sovereignty helps us reorganise some of the constituent elements of the concept and brings to the fore a set of tensions, contestations, divisions and relations that remain largely occluded within the predominant approaches to the concept. This offers a way of reading sovereignty that is particularly sensitive to the challenges associated with the new climatic regime in which the twin vertigoes of placelessness and landlessness characterise our increasingly disorientating contemporary political scene.

As we will elaborate below, the aesthetics of sovereignty has something of a double life. On the one hand, this refers to sovereignty's mode of appearance; that is, the forms representation, modes of expression and range of artistic and literary devices and techniques on which sovereignty depends. On the other hand, sovereignty's aesthetics (or what I call here sovereignty's *aesthesis*) refers to its mode of perception; that is, the shared imaginary through which social and earthly relations are ordered and given sense.

The Aesthetics of Sovereignty

Aesthetics is often understood as the study of the beautiful and the elaboration of the methods appropriate for the interpretation of art. The *aesthetics of sovereignty*, in this sense, might be taken to be interested in the beauty – or ugliness – of the sovereign form or the technologies of power which it exercises. We need not be confined in this way. We can expand the scope of inquiry to encompass the images, symbols, rituals, garbs and accoutrements that sustain sovereignty; the myths, narratives and fictions that undergird sovereignty's claim to plenary power; and to the semiotic, architectural and ceremonial dimensions of statecraft, kingship and popular authority. We might also attend to the *form* of sovereignty, inquiring into the matter of sovereignty's appearance, of how it stages, dramatises or theatricalises its power. In this context, the aesthetics of sovereignty would take as its object of study a range of aesthetic objects, from monumental or civic architecture, to artistic depictions of monarchs, presidents and judges; from cartographic techniques that represent the extent of a sovereign territory, to the emblems and visual motifs associated with the nation.

There is a long tradition of research into these topics: from the reflections of King James I of England on the 'theatre of power' in which he compares himself to an actor onstage, 'whose smallest actions and gestures, all the people gazingly doe behold';[35] to the numerous studies of the frontispiece to the *Leviathan* which powerfully visualised Hobbes's account of civic power in early modernity;[36] from Peter Goodrich's expansive studies of legal images and emblems and the central role they play in instituting the legal subject;[37] to Walter Bagehot's account of the 'dignified' aspect of the British consti-tution, associated primarily with monarchical pomp and ceremony, which 'excite and preserve the reverence of the population'.[38] These studies – and many others in this vein[39] – have taken as their primary focus, not the nature of sovereign force *per se* but the aesthetic dimension that allows such force to appear justified and reasonable, or otherwise be naturalised or dissimulated. These approaches constitute something of a 'minor' tradition within theories of sovereignty, tackling a set of supposedly second order issues in relation to the 'major' questions of political philosophy: the nature of the social contract or the principles and procedures that legitimate constitutional authority. As Jason Frank rightly argues, the relative lack of interest in the images, symbols and ceremonies that constitute political power within orthodox political theory is a reflection of the rationalising impulses of the Enlightenment that have sought to emphasise 'epistemic transparency and consensus over dazzling aesthetic display as the basis of legitimacy'.[40] In this sense, studies in the aesthetics of sovereignty very often champion the enduring force of *non-modern* modes by which the social domain is ordered, emphasising the enduring importance of the images, myths and rituals that continue to shape the political. Importantly, an emphasis on the aesthetic dimensions of sov-ereignty underscores that the political sphere cannot be reduced to a single, foundational moment – as the contractarian theories would have us believe – but is constantly being remade and reperformed through situated practices that both express and give form to the scope of law and politics.

This approach brings an important point of tension into view. There is, of course, an all-important distinction to be made between the modes through which sovereignty *appears* in imagistic or symbolic representations which depict a plenary, unified and homogenous power and the reality of sov-ereignty at the level governmental and juridical *practice*. As Lauren Benton has demonstrated in the context of European imperial sovereignty, the repre-sentations, theories and images of imperial plenitude were confronted by the reality of discontinuous, lumpy and fractured rule, in which legal authority and political power were often disconnected and where supposedly sovereign borders were often either mobile or highly porous. Imperial sovereignty, in Benton's reading, was more often than not a question of 'quasi-sovereignty', which created anomalous zones of authority within a variegated scene of enclaves and outposts with fragile corridors of legal authority constructed to allow the passage of imperial officers and subjects. As Benton makes clear, legal practice – the deciding and reporting of cases and the construction of regulatory regimes to deal with property, transactions, territorial delimitation and so forth – was central to the formation of this complex topography. In correcting the Schmittian view of a 'lawful' Europe set apart from a 'lawless' extra-European world, Benton shows how

> Imperial agents actively promoted the thrust of jurisdiction 'beyond the line', and no goal of empire could be achieved without the legitimization of subordinate legal authorities in distant locations. Complex plural legal orders included and even depended on indigenous sources and forums of law. As we find in declarations of martial law in colonial settings and in other moments of apparent legal rupture, even the suspension of law did not create legal voids, or spaces of lawlessness, but instead generated areas for novel procedural and doctrinal experiments that continued to reference imperial law.[41]

We will return to the role of law as a technology that mediates and catalogues sovereign power in a moment. At this stage, however, it is worth stressing how the heterogeneity at the level of juridical and political practice that characterised imperial sovereignty was masked by the prevailing images and representations of smooth spaces, conquered by a unified and homogenous political power. The great splashes of pink on so many schoolroom maps which sought to represent Britain's global dominance belied the messy and fragmented reality of imperial practice.

Benton's study speaks to a generalisable, and perhaps perfectly obvious, point in that any *theory*, *image* or *aesthetic representation* of sovereignty can only ever be a simplified systematisation of a complex reality; the promise of order and unity made by the great theorists of sovereignty – from Hobbes to Kant, Rousseau to Schmitt – will forever be beset by the compromises and complexities of governmental practice. A focus on the aesthetics of sovereignty, however, brings this tension to the fore and seeks to understand the unique force that the images and representations of sovereignty carry. The juridical and sociological accounts of the reordering of sovereign competencies under the conditions of globalisation, for instance, have failed to attend to this aesthetic dimension which, despite its apparent distance from the practical life of governmental authority, continues to give shape, sense and direction to the political.

Scholars who defend a traditional account of sovereignty are particularly ambivalent in their treatment of sovereignty's aesthetics, so understood. Martin Loughlin is perhaps the most forthright commentator on the enduring importance of sovereignty for contemporary law and politics, forcefully arguing against those who have sought to chart sovereignty's demise through an encroaching globalisation and pluralism in late modernity. For Loughlin, modern sovereignty is an expression of the autonomy of the political, which he characterises as being irreducible to religious, market or moral forms of reasoning. Sovereignty, for Loughlin, expresses neither an object that can be held by a sovereign actor (president, monarch, parliament or 'the people'), nor a set of governmental competencies distributed amongst the institutions of the state but is instead the *expression of a relationship between ruler and ruled*. In this sense, sovereignty is ultimately tied to a logic of representation, it is the representational form of a relationship between individuals who decide, through speech and action, to act in unison;[42] sovereignty underpins and guarantees the integrity of this sphere. Political power, for Loughlin, is a *symbolic power*[43] that is based on the *beliefs*, *opinions* and *trust* of a populace in the *idea* of the political – instantiated through the sovereignty relationship – to which the populace willingly submits.[44] It follows from this that sovereignty cannot be reduced to a purely formal, let alone a *legal*, principle but is the expression of a belief in the nature of the political community that the institutions of government supposedly represent; if sovereignty is (also) a legal principle, it must follow from a set of political commitments.[45]

Whilst affirming the capacity of politicians, civil servants and the judiciary to deploy a distinctive form of political reasoning in order to 'keep the ship on an even keel',[46] Loughlin is remarkably inattentive to the aesthetic forms that sustain the symbolic power of the political. As Stewart Motha has argued, Loughlin's account of the autonomy of the political cannot escape the logic of the *as if* that is one of the hallmarks of sovereignty's aesthetic aspect. Whilst Loughlin emphasises the practical life of political reason, locating political life in 'the expression of the immanent precepts of an autonomous [political] discourse',[47] everything turns on the *symbolic* and *imaginary* force of the *idea* of unity and coherence that undergirds that very autonomy. Loughlin disavows political metaphysics – drawing instead on a range of historicist, nominalist and pragmatic thinkers – in order to get 'closer to reality'. But political practice and the casuistry of *raison d'état* are unable to do all the work required to sustain Loughlin's cherished autonomy of the political; as Motha comments: 'the imaginary and symbolism of sovereignty assert a unity that is nowhere to be found'.[48] We might, as Motha does, reflect on the fiction or myth of unity that undergirds Loughlin's sense of the political – a fiction that is easily contested in the context of colonial states or in fragmented or bitterly divided polities – but so too does Loughlin's account beg the question of the aesthetic devices that mediate the discord, managing to perform or represent this fiction of political harmony. What are the symbols, images and modes of representation that manage to sustain this *idea* of an autonomous political space and the social unity it claims? In answering this question Loughlin continually returns to the celebrated theorists of early modernity – Hobbes, Montesquieu and Pufendorf – who take the foundation of the state as their primary object of concern, or otherwise he seeks solace in the rarefied realm of judicial practice and the niceties of *raison d'état*. It is here that an aesthetic approach to sovereignty provides a very different scenography, drawing attention to the technologies, images, myths and fictions that mediate the contestations that define collective life and are able to re-present the political as an autonomous sphere, however mythical or fictional that autonomy might be in practice. In this way, the nature of the tension between the *practice* of judicial and political reason and the *appearance* of the political, as a space in which political actors can appear as such, distinct from other aspects of social life, remains unaddressed in Loughlin's account of sovereignty. The aesthetics of sovereignty, as we have introduced it here, is able to bring this tension to the fore and point to a set of forces – architectural, monumental, cartographic, symbolic, imaginary, affective – that shape our understanding of the contours and meaning of political life.

Studying sovereignty in these expressly 'aesthetic' terms is particularly compelling in the context of the contemporary resurgence of nationalism in the West. It is here that the relation between the apparent weakening of state competencies, under the conditions of neoliberal globalisation, can be directly correlated to the resurgence of images, icons and symbols of sovereign integrity. Wendy Brown's nearly ten-year-old study of 'walled states and waning sovereignty' in which she examines the proliferation of walls, barriers and fences at state borders is, in this sense, remarkably prescient. As Brown argues, the border wall aims to satiate 'psychic fantasies, anxieties, and wishes . . . by generating visual effects and a national imaginary'[49] in which the state retains its hegemony in an increasingly uncertain and contested topography of global powers. Whilst the practical life of sovereignty is forever being reassembled in new configurations and the various threats to states are increasingly associated with non-state actors, seemingly confirming a sense of slowly vanishing power, the *aesthetics of sovereignty* – the modes of its appearance and the icons and symbols on which it relies – is remarkably enduring.

The prevailing conditions of the Anthropocene promise an enormous increase in eco-migration, rising sea levels, the desertification of land, the death of ecosystems and the reformation of networks of food production. Under such conditions, the affective, emotional and psychic force of sovereignty's 'visual effects' is only likely to be augmented, despite sovereignty's practical insufficiency as means of guarding against the various challenges to come. In this way, the aesthetics of sovereignty allows us to attend to the power that sovereignty continues to exert as a visual and affective shorthand for security, protection, identity and stability, values that are increasingly threatened by the globalising forces of neoliberal capitalism and the planetary reach of climatic change.

The *Aesthesis* of Sovereignty

As a philosophical discipline, aesthetics was first named and elaborated by the eighteenth-century German philosopher Alexander Baumgarten and, whilst questions of defining the beautiful and the distinct power of art – particularly poetry – are some of his central concerns, aesthetics in this early formulation evokes a much broader canvas than we normally associate with the term. Baumgarten's delimitation of the discipline returns us to its most ancient meaning: aesthetics (derived from *aesthetikos* and *aisthesthai*) refers to the *conditions of sensory perception*. For Baumgarten, aesthetics is presented as a form of knowledge pertaining to the 'lower faculties' – that is, the senses – that run in parallel to reason.[50] In this sense, the aesthetic is primarily concerned with the body: the affective and felt reality of a sensible subject. As Terry Eagleton puts it, aesthetics refers to

> the whole of our sensate life together – the business of affections and aversions, of how the world strikes the body on its sensory surfaces, of that which takes root in the gaze and the guts and all that arises from our most banal, biological insertion in to the world.[51]

Aesthetics, in this sense, becomes a matter of the interestedness, engagement and attunement of the somatic and affective registers. As Eagleton suggests, modern aesthetics emerges in the eighteenth century as a kind of 'primitive proto-materialism'[52] that took form as a distinct register of knowledge, crucial to the mediation and control of social life.

This account of aesthetics has largely been eclipsed, following a Kantian inheritance that has confined aesthetics as a specialist domain of philosophical inquiry primarily concerned with a *rational* understanding of the beautiful. Via Baumgarten, Eagleton draws attention to another aspect of the aesthetic in which the *non-representational, affective, felt* realities of a sensate subject's immersion in social space is at issue. Aesthetics in this sense becomes the study of how the visive, affective and sensuous dimensions are animated through a given configuration of power relations that orders, distributes and enframes the world. If an *anaesthetic* deadens our body to pain, aesthetics describes the modes by which our senses become enlivened, accounting for how we feel, perceive and order reality. We can describe this as a matter of *aesthesis*, differentiating it from *aesthetics* (*in stricto sensu*) which is primarily concerned with form, representation, appearance, modes of expression and so on. What I am calling the *aesthesis of sovereignty*, then, is not primarily concerned with the study of *aesthetic objects* – artworks that represent sovereignty, the symbols or emblems of power and so forth – but is concerned instead with the configuration of the political subject and the power that sovereignty has in shaping the subject's capacities to be *rendered sensitive or insensitive* to a given set of phenomena.

Theoretical reflection on the material and sensate body's complex and overlapping perceptive faculties has been revived under auspices of 'affect theory' and work contributing to the so-called 'affective turn' in the humanities and social sciences.[53] Affect refers to that dark hinterland between instinct and emotion, the ungraspable 'feelings' associated with a beautiful place, a moment of terror, an atmosphere of joyful abandon or stoical defiance. Studies of affect invite an engagement with the non-cognitive, the non-representational and the non-rational, paying close attention to those forces that are 'beneath, alongside or generally *other than* conscious knowing'.[54] To be affected by an encounter, an artwork, place or event is to be 'gripped' or 'moved' in a way that we often struggle to explain. In this sense, affect studies returns us to a tradition of aesthetics that is not primarily concerned with artistic texts and practices but with *the conditions by which we are rendered sensitive* to a given set of phenomena in subtle and often oblique ways that rarely permit straightforward or direct access. If Kant's aesthetics ultimately returns us to an autonomous, rational and disembodied judge – 'enacted on a spiritualized plane, disembodied [and] "de-physicalized"'[55] – affect studies has greatly expanded the domain of study, examining how socialised sense perceptions become embedded within somatic dispositions and affective life.

To study the *aesthesis of sovereignty* is not to be concerned with the affective or sensible domain in or for itself. As Jacques Rancière rightly underscores, the political question at stake within the aesthetic is 'a certain *modality*, a certain *distribution* of the sensible'.[56] It is in the *distribution* that the political work gets done. To be concerned with the *aesthesis of sovereignty* does not involve enumerating our sensations and feelings, cataloguing the various dimensions of our sensate lives, but in understanding how these elements are *ordered* in a given constellation. Indeed, it is to see the inherent connection between the ordering of the political and the ordering of the sensible that is crucial. In Rancière's well-known phrase, there is a certain 'distribution of the sensible' which prevails within a given historical-political juncture, referring to the '*a priori* forms determining what presents itself to sense experience'.[57] This 'sharing out' (*partager*) of sense experience delimits what is seen and unseen; heard and unheard; felt and unfelt, in the most general terms. As Rancière elaborates,

> I call the distribution of the sensible the system of self-evident facts of sense perception that simultaneously discloses the existence of something in common and the delimitations that define the respective parts and positions within it . . . This apportionment of parts and positions is based on a distribution of spaces, times, and forms of activity that determines the very manner in which something in common lends itself to participation and in what way various individuals have a part in this distribution.[58]

As a delineation of a common world, the distribution of the sensible describes a radical interweaving of aesthetics and politics. As Rancière has explored, the sensible order is maintained by what he calls 'police power', which ensures the reproduction of a regime in which bodies are ordered in a given configuration. Truly 'political' action involves a fundamental disruption of this taken for granted distribution. Importantly, Rancière's political theory takes this simple but radical sense of aesthetics (qua aesthesis) as its primary reference. In his account of political struggle, one of the greatest challenges lies in intervening in the existing sensible order and challenging the ways in which some actors are *within the frame*, and understood as having the time and capacity for political life, and others resolutely kept *off-camera*, so to speak. When the 'part who has no part' in political life – the poor, the excluded, the oppressed – appears and makes a claim to speak for the *demos*, it is the political order, as an ordering of the sensible, that is fundamentally troubled. Actors to whom the populace was once rendered *insensitive* – those once considered mute, invisible, untouchable – suddenly appear in the public sphere and claim to speak on behalf of the totality. It is, indeed, this moment of disruption that brings the existing ordering of the sensible itself into view which, in the normal course, is rendered as a kind of neutral 'backdrop' to social life.

   As Rancière makes clear, it is the *conditions* of sensory perception and the *ordering* of the sensible domain that are at issue here, suggesting that our apprehension of a political reality and a political world depends on a set of forces, institutions and practices that are symbolically mediated. The distribution of the sensible, then, forms a shared and hegemonic *imaginary* in which social relations are articulated and given value within a network of significations, symbols and representations that are collectively apprehended. What is at stake here is the relationship between the aesthetics of sovereignty – the images, symbols and modes of representation on which it depends – and the power that these techniques have upon a sensate political subject, working at the level of *aesthesis*. The aesthetics of sovereignty, in this sense, *creates a world* in which a given distribution of the sensible appears 'self-evident', an *a priori* ordering the social domain which 'brings into existence a comprehensive way of seeing, understanding and acting'.[59]

The nature of this immersive *social imaginary* – an 'affective grammar' or 'way of seeing' – is constructed through a network of significations (symbols, images, icons and concepts) that allow for a social reality to grasped and articulated, giving voice to shared understandings, and allowing for ascriptions of value to be formalised and policed. Cornelius Castoriadis captures the force of this 'social imaginary' in the following wide-ranging terms:

> This element – which gives a specific orientation to every institutional system, which overdetermines the choice and the connection of symbolic networks, which is the creation of each historical period, its singular manner of living, of seeing and of conducting its own existence, its world, and its relations with the world, this originary structuring component, this central signifying-signified, the source of that which presents itself in every instance as an indisputable and undisputed meaning, the basis for articulating what does matter and what does not, the origin of the surplus of being of the objects of practice, affective and intellectual investment, whether individual or collective – is nothing other than the *imaginary* of the society or of the period considered.[60]

Two things are worth underscoring in this characterisation. Firstly, the *a priori* nature of the imaginary. It is the *originary structuring component* that holds together a myriad of individual acts, representations, objects and functions within a given social scene. The social imaginary is in this sense a *background ordering* of collective life, establishing the parameters of the thinkable, doable and sayable in a particular historical constellation. For Castoriadis, the imaginary is not concerned with individual acts of creativity or speculation but the prior conditions that structure such efforts, allowing for any such individual act to have meaning in the first place. Secondly, Castoriadis's account of the imaginary must be clearly differentiated from an understanding of the imaginary as a *reflection* or *re-presentation* of an underlying reality. As Castoriadis makes clear throughout *The Imaginary Institution of Society*, the imaginary is not an image or representation of a pre-existing *something* but the very means by which the apprehension of something (the world, rationality, reality and so forth) is itself possible. The imaginary is the means by which any notion of the 'real' – a 'real social need' or 'the reality of climatic change', for instance – can be grasped. In this sense, the imaginary is not a 'mere epiphenomena of "real" forces and relations of production . . . [but] the laces that tie a society together and the forms that define what, for a given society, is "real"'.[61]

As Castoriadis underscores, there is an *immersive quality* to imaginary significations that endows them with a *world-forming* capacity. A social imaginary depends upon a world in which everything is seemingly captured in advance by a given economy of signification, creating an all-encompassing sphere of meanings, giving rise to a veritable glasshouse for social life. This enclosure of the social imaginary operates at a deeply affective register, working alongside conscious knowing. As Castoriadis outlines, the techniques that produce a given social imaginary are largely obscure to the society in which they themselves have taken hold. The imaginary is in this sense operative at the background of social life, a kind of 'mood music' or 'atmosphere' that helps present our institutionally mediated forms of doing, saying and representing as perfectly natural. The atmospheric bubble of a given imaginary – working on 'pre-conscious emotional reactions that escape the reflexive subject'[62] – offers a sense of homeliness and comfort by ordering the sensible domain in such a way that everything appears to be in its right place.

Understanding the distinctive force that 'atmospheres' have to shape social life is a key element of recent work on affect and the emotions. Gernot Böhme describes the production of atmospheres as fundamental to the 'new aesthetics', which takes, not artistic representation but the sensible domain, broadly conceived, as its object of study.[63] The atmospheric force that attaches to sovereignty is worth dwelling on as it captures the multi-scalar nature of sovereignty and underscores its capacity to work at the background of social life, structuring our assumption about the political in often subtly occluded ways. As Anderson has described it, the language of atmosphere can apply equally well to vast geographic and temporal ranges – as in 'an age of anxiety in the West', or a 'culture of fear' in a given institution or nation – and to highly localised phenomena – the collective awkwardness felt at a dinner party gone wrong or the momentary elation of a sports ground in full voice.[64] To think of a sovereign imaginary as akin to an atmosphere is to understand the various affective spheres and bubbles that sovereignty forms, both as a generalised condition of modern political life but also in discrete and localised moments when sovereignty's affective force palpably grips or moves the subject in ways that we often struggle to rationalise or fully comprehend.

Where Castoriadis adopts an extraordinarily wide scope, examining the entirety of social life, I am more concerned with a narrower focus on the formation of a *political imaginary* through the technologies, practices, images and modes of representation that constitute modern sovereignty. This *sovereign imaginary*, through its own symbolic economy and distribution of the sensible, will produce both a political *reality* and a *non-political outside*. As Castoriadis argues, systems of representation do not *emerge out of* or *reflect* an underlying 'reality'. Instead, it is the force of significations themselves that produces a sense of the 'real' and the 'imaginary'; the 'valued' and the 'unvalued'; the 'political' and the 'non-political'. It is through the emergence of these distinctions that the imaginary has the capacity to *form a world*. As R. B. J. Walker has rightly suggested, 'the international marks not the promise of a single world, one carrying all potentialities of a modernizing universality, but the *regulative rift between the world of modernity and all other worlds*'.[65] The rupture of the Anthropocene brings this rift starkly into view, suddenly making us aware of a range of forces, concepts, practices and forms of life that the modern world constitutively abandons as archaic, non-modern, non-political, backward or simply irrelevant.

In the context of sovereignty, this insight is crucial as it brings into view another important point of tension between the symbolic forms that create a given political imaginary and a non-political excess, a constitutive outside to the political sphere. This is one of the widely commented on features of modern sovereignty: it expresses itself as the ultimate authority that can draw a line between the political and the non-political; friend and enemy; civilised and uncivilised and so on. The formation of a sovereign imaginary necessitates the production of a non-political other, an excess or remainder that is the constitutive outside to the political order.

We can approach this non-political other in a variety of ways. In classic accounts of sovereignty in early modernity, this is most commonly associated with the 'state of nature': a non-political condition that has to be overcome in order for a civic space to be formed. This condition, however, continues to haunt the political, taking shape in the threat of civil war, anarchy or disorder. In the context of biopolitics, we might point to a particular form of life – *bare life* or *creaturely life* – that is produced through the formation of the political sphere; a subjectivity that is the obscene obverse of citizenship, for example. In Povinelli's expanded reading of the biopolitical, in which the geological (or the division between Life and Nonlife) is included within ambit of the technologies of governmental power, this non-political residue or remainder is best understood as *geos*, the Nonlife that does not form part of the modern political imaginary.[66] In Rancière this seemingly non-political element – the 'part without a part' in the everyday domain of politics – is reimagined as the political actor *par excellence* who returns in moments of dissensus to challenge the prevailing distribution of the sensible. Latour, taking in a broad sweep of modern political thought, would perhaps suggest that this non-political other is Nature itself, produced through the formation a discreet Social domain in early modernity.[67] There are, of course, any number of approaches to this question.

The point I want to stress, however, is that an examination of the *sovereign imaginary* explores the role that a range of techniques have in giving shape to an affective, visive and sensible *world* of relations, within which political subjects are fully immersed and which itself produces a non-political outside to that world. I take this to be the key insight that underlies Castoriadis's *social imaginary* and Rancière's *distribution of the sensible*. As already suggested, the techniques which give rise to a given world of relations are immensely difficult to apprehend from within that very world because they operate at an *a priori* or 'background' register, quietly structuring the distribution of *seen*, *heard* and *felt* in a way that we so often take for granted. Indeed, it is this background ordering which gives sense to the various bonds and attachments which constitute social life; we routinely fail to be rendered sensitive to those 'non-political' modes of attachment which fall outside the modern, sovereign imaginary. Indeed, such a non-political remainder is precisely *imperceptible* from within the dominant imaginary. By focusing on some of the key divisions and demarcations that constitute the sovereign form, we are able to both account for sovereignty's world-forming power and begin to attend to the putatively 'non-political' forms of attachment, dependence and need which the Anthropocene starkly brings into view.

A Fourfold View of Sovereignty

We can systematise these reflections on the different aspects and implications of sovereignty's aesthetic functioning, and the various tensions and relations that this approach foregrounds, through a fourfold view of sovereignty. This approach is grounded in the doubled nature of aesthetics as both a matter of *appearance and representation*, on the one hand, and a matter of the *perception and the affective, somatic ordering of the sensible domain*, on the other. These two aspects of the aesthetics of sovereignty each reveal moments of tension. A focus on sovereignty's symbols and images, maps and myths, begs the question of the relation between these representational forms and the *practices of sovereignty* within the institutions of law and government. Likewise, the immersive quality of the *sovereign imaginary*, as a mode of perceiving and ordering social life, reveals a tension between the *political world* that a subject inhabits and a constitutively other, non-political domain that exceeds it. We can schematise this in the following way:

Appearance

(i.e. *the aesthetics of sovereignty*: maps, images, symbols, myths etc. that represent sovereignty)

Perception

(i.e. *the aesthesis of sovereignty*: the distribution of the sensible made in the name of sovereignty, operative at affective, visual and somatic registers)

Practice

(i.e. *raison d'état*, judicial decisions, the distribution of governmental competencies, the formation of anomalous legal zones etc.)

Remainder

(i.e. bare life or *geos*, the part without part etc. Whatever falls outside the 'properly' political order and is imperceptible within the dominant imaginary)

To be clear, this approach is intended to offer *analytic* clarity only. Sovereignty is a bundle of practices, processes, technologies, spaces, places, subjectivities, documents, institutions, beliefs, offices, officers, dispositions, symbols, theories, ideas *et cetera*. As we intimated at the outset, all of these elements are muddled up in a great assemblage that precludes any easy or straightforward definition. However, by schematising this fourfold view of sovereignty, we can both isolate some of the more prominent elements associated with the concept and identify some of the scholarly traditions that have focused on one or more these four aspects. Perhaps most importantly, however, this approach allows us to pose a number of questions about how these different elements are related and exist in moments of tension, compromise or complementarity. We can ask how, for instance, the *appearance of sovereignty* relates to the production of a *sovereign imaginary*; or how the *appearance of sovereignty* is contradicted or compromised by a study of the *practices of sovereignty*; or, indeed, how the *practices of sovereignty* are implicated in the production of a *non-political remainder* and so on and so forth.

This schema offers a means by which the constitutive elements of sovereignty can be analysed and the relations between these elements brought to the fore, addressing some of the *how questions* of sovereignty by examining the means by which these different elements give both material and symbolic effect to the sovereign form. In an effort to elaborate this point, I turn now to assess the role that *jurisdiction* plays in the articulation of sovereignty. As we suggested above in relation to Lauren Benton's work on imperial power, the law has always mediated the aspirations of sovereignty, outlining the precise limits and contours of the sovereign form and giving material effect to its claims. In this sense, we commonly associate jurisdictional questions with the *practices of sovereignty*, approaching jurisdiction as the means by which governmental and juridical competencies are organised within the administrative state, or else associate the term with those legal techniques that are deployed in an effort to safeguard the state's power and integrity. Though these aspects to jurisdiction are of course significant, I want to pursue a slightly different reading by suggesting that jurisdiction can be productively reimagined as being broadly concerned with law's *expression* and *mode of representation*; an approach implied by the concept's etymology, *juris dictio* or 'speaking the law'. In this way, jurisdiction is not only a matter of sovereignty's material enforcement or the means through which a given distribution of power is achieved through the courts but is also integral to sovereignty's aesthetic dimensions.

Technologies of Jurisdiction

Until a recent uptick in interest, jurisdiction has generally been understood as a purely technical matter of interest only to legal practitioners, their clerks, clients and the 'black letter' scholars trying to keep the profession honest. The renewed interest in jurisdiction, from critical and theoretical perspectives, has largely been led by jurists working in the Australian common law system. The recognition of indigenous land rights in the landmark 1992 *Mabo* decision, and the administrative regime concerning 'native title' that followed,[68] led a number of scholars to reassess the function of jurisdiction as a fundamental aspect of law's normative power. By approaching the colonial project through a jurisdictional lens, Shaun McVeigh, Shaunnagh Dorsett, Peter Rush, Olivia Barr and others have sought to counter the common law's persistent dismissal of indigenous law and its rich jurisprudences.[69] Stressing the jurist's responsibility to the practices that produce lawful relations and the forms of conduct appropriate to the meeting of legal traditions,[70] McVeigh et al. have resituated jurisdiction as the locus of an inquiry into nothing less than *how to live well with the law* in the context of a colonial inheritance.

The relation between jurisdiction and sovereignty is complex. A plurality of partly overlapping, partly conflictual but always procedurally distinct jurisdictional orders prevailed within Europe, well into the eighteenth century: from Manorial Courts applying customary and feudal laws, to the Courts of Stannary resolving disputes in the tin-mining industry; from the Courts of the Forest to a range of ecclesiastical jurisdictions, along with the better known Courts of Equity and Admiralty in England and Wales.[71] The gradual centralisation of legal authority in England, for instance, culminating in the expression of a modern nation-state sovereignty, was conducted within a jurisdictional register with rival claims to authority being assimilated or defenestrated as modern political forms took hold. A patchwork of legal authorities were gradually subsumed within an increasingly cost-effective and reliable common law that from the late sixteenth century onward served to administer the 'king's justice'. The emergence of theories of modern sovereignty in the seventeenth century was a testament to the effectiveness of this jurisdictional reordering. The ecclesiastical jurisdictions that dominated social life in the feudal period and persisted as rivals to the temporal power of the monarch throughout the sixteenth and seventeenth centuries was finally laid to rest as a modern conceptualisation of sovereignty took hold, defining a discrete and supposedly autonomous political sphere, expressed in, and policed by, a single legal order. In this sense, sovereignty emerges as a conceptual scheme by virtue of the shifting forms of jurisdictional authority in the early modern period.

Given the significance of these changes to jurisdictional competencies immediately preceding, and indeed commensurate with, the seminal theorisation of modern sovereignty, it is striking that accounts of jurisdiction have played such a limited role in existing scholarship on sovereignty. Agamben, Foucault and Derrida, all offering celebrated 'deconstructions' of sovereignty, pay no attention to the jurisdictional orderings that were deeply implicated in establishing sovereignty's form. And in the account of sovereignty offered by orthodox public law scholars like Loughlin, the role of jurisdiction, as a mode of instituting a set of lawful relations essential to the sovereign form, remains largely unexamined; instead, theories of sovereignty return either, all too predictably, to the nineteenth-century British constitutional tradition (Dicey, Jennings, Bagehot et al.) or to theories of the social contract. In this sense, the range of implications and the unique labours associated with jurisdiction have generally remained under-theorised in scholarship on sovereignty, which usually allows political and social theory, rather than expressly jurisprudential themes, to hold sway. It is my contention that jurisdiction is crucial to the articulation and staging of sovereignty. Indeed, we can think of jurisdiction as a handmaid to sovereignty: jurisdiction refers to a bundle of practices that do sovereignty's heavy lifting, tidying and organising, allowing sovereignty's aspirations for a plenary and unitary power to be both presented and given effect. In emphasising the importance of jurisdictional orderings, technologies and modes of representation, we are able to attend to the way in which sovereign power is not simply conceived at the level of theory but also *lived*, *felt*, *sensed* and *perceived* through a juridically mediated social reality.

As we have suggested, jurisdictional thinking today tends to be approached in technical terms either as a matter of trial or courtroom procedure or in the realm of private international law. But it is worth recalling that 'while in modernity sovereignty is the lens through which we conceptualise . . . authority for law, for much of the history of the last 1000 years it was jurisdiction that fulfilled that role'.[72] The question of which body of law applied to any given case was central to the administration of communal life well into the nineteenth century.[73] In a sense, then, one of the marks of modern sovereignty has been to make jurisdiction uninteresting. In place of legal subjects and practitioners navigating the choppy jurisdictional waters of plural and overlapping lawful forms came the unitary simplicity of a single legal order that was chief administrant of lawful relations. Jurisdiction, in such conditions, becomes a matter of process and procedure only. In lieu of exploring these procedural issues themselves, I want to focus on the *productive* role that jurisdiction plays in giving shape, voice and form to sovereignty.

If *juris-diction* is a matter of 'speaking the law', then we might reimagine jurisdiction in quite general terms to refer to the law's *expressive register*, the means by which lawful authority is *announced* or *visualised*. In this sense, a range of jurisdictional technologies come into view: modern cartography, which represents the plenary power of the nation state; the founding declaration which gives voice to 'the people' of popular sovereignty; or the jurisdictional ordering of life that distributes bodies and responsibilities within the social sphere at particular scales and within a given set of institutions, are all aspects of jurisdiction, so understood. Jurisdictional technologies, then, are not purely a matter of an esoteric juridical technicality but also refer to the means by which sovereignty is disseminated, proclaimed and represented; in this way, jurisdiction can be understood as pre-eminently exoteric.

Jurisdictional technologies return us to the *world-forming* capacity of sovereignty's aesthetics. Jurisdiction orders a 'world' through the determination of spheres of lawful competency and by representing, declaring or making visible lawful relations. This conception of jurisdiction, far from innovative, has a long heritage stretching back to the rediscovery of Roman law in the twelfth century. As Pietro Costa has illustrated, the medieval glossators, grappling with the newly discovered Roman Codex, understood jurisdiction (*iurisdictio*) as the means by which the law's normativity was ultimately grounded. Jurisdiction emerged as a distinct practice that fashions a formal order and distribution from an existing, but informal, set of practices, objects and relations of power. Jurisdiction produces what Costa calls a '*gathered* norm', reflected from the world's natural distribution: '*iurisdictio* is nothing other than the place in which an informal given comes to be formalised: not changed but expressed, not created [ex nihilo] but reflected back'.[74] So, in the gathering of an informal distribution or set of relations, authority is represented back to itself, as a formalised authority, that is nothing more than the effect of this very gathering. As Bradin Cormack points out, it is this which reveals the essential power of jurisdiction: at the very moment that it re-presents the world – enframing, delimiting and distributing the world in a given way – jurisdiction both elides the contingency of its representation and naturalises its force by presenting itself as nothing more than a 'neutral' or 'normal' reflection of the real. As Cormack explains,

> Jurisdiction is the principle, integral to the structure of the law, through which the law, as an expression of its order and limits, projects an authority that, whatever its origin, needs functionally no other ground. At the jurisdictional threshold, the law speaks to itself, and in a mirror *reproduces* as administration the juridical order that it simultaneously *produces*.[75]

This crucial insight presents jurisdiction as a quintessentially *creative* practice, a technology that at once enframes the world, transforming its sensible distribution, at the same moment it disavows that transformation. This ordering reveals the world in a particular form but at the very moment that this form is *created*, the craft at the heart of this endeavour is disavowed. Jurisdiction in this sense refers to a kind of perspectival device which transforms the real whilst seeking to remain hidden. If sovereignty is associated with the fundamental way in which we become able to perceive and order the political in modernity, then jurisdictional technologies describe the devices through which this perception is installed and reproduced.

Cormack helps us understand the expressive and creative dimensions to jurisdiction and the role it plays in ordering social life; and as we have insisted through Rancière, the ordering of the political sphere is always already an ordering of the sensible. The technologies of jurisdiction in *declaring, representing* and *expressing* state law's supreme authority are crucial to the production of sovereignty's aesthetics, in terms of both sovereignty's *appearance* and its mode of *perception*. We can see the technologies of jurisdiction at work within each element of the fourfold view of sovereignty. In its esoteric and technical aspect, jurisdiction is central to the *practices of sovereignty*, it is through the juridical ordering of states and colonies that sovereignty – as a mode of power that manages bodies and controls resources – is made effective. Jurisdiction too is implicated in the production of a *non-political remainder*: in the ultimate test of justiciability, the *sine qua non* of jurisdictional authority, courts regularly dismiss losses and grievances, claims and counter-claims as falling outside the proper domain of political life, thus drawing the line that defines the political sphere. In this way, jurisdiction is the register through which we can navigate the fourfold view of sovereignty, understand the complex relationalities that exist between each element and account for sovereignty's *world-forming* power.

Building a New Sensible World

The aesthetic approach to sovereignty developed here moves away from theories of globalisation, biopolitics and the traditional points of reference within political theory and contractarianism in order to focus on the *form* of sovereignty, in a somewhat 'disinterested' fashion. This kind of 'disinterestedness' allows us, I contend, to begin to imagine a political aesthetics beyond that which is installed and reproduced under the auspices of modern sovereignty. It is this disposition which might allow a new sensible world to come into view. And this, as we argued at the outset, is essential if we are to contend with the Anthropocene and the various challenges it presents to our understanding of social life.

Reworking Kant's well-known account of the 'disinterestedness' that informs aesthetic judgement, Rancière argues that aesthetic contemplation can have a radical political potential. To illustrate, Rancière draws on a biographical account of a carpenter's working day written for a worker's newspaper in 1848:

> Believing himself at home, he [the carpenter] loves the arrangement of the room so long as he has not finished laying the floor. If the window opens out onto a garden or commands a view of a picturesque horizon, he stops his arms a moment and glides in imagination towards the spacious view to enjoy it better than the possessors of the neighbouring residences.[76]

Rather than see this as an example of Bourdieu's 'aesthetic illusion' where taking in the room's form and proportions, its situation and the vistas it affords simply obscures the reality of the worker's class position,[77] Rancière reclaims this moment for deeply political ends. 'It is not by accident', Rancière suggest, 'that this text appears in a revolutionary workers' newspaper'[78] because it is precisely the possibility of separating one's gaze from one's labour that is at stake here; that is, the possibility of shedding the mode of perception apparently proper to one's sociologically determined status in order to see the world otherwise. Indeed, it is a kind of *neutralisation* of the class-bound self that is achieved by the aesthetic gaze. As Rancière puts it,

> This is what disinterestedness or indifference entails: the dismantling of a certain body of experience that was deemed appropriate to a specific ethos, the ethos of the artisan who knows that work does not wait and whose senses are geared to this lack of time. Ignoring to whom the palace actually belongs, the vanity of the nobles, and the sweat of the people incorporated in the palace, are the conditions of aesthetic judgment. This ignorance is by no means an illusion that conceals the reality of possession. Rather, *it is the means of building a new sensible world*, which is a world of equality within the world of possession and inequality. This aesthetic description is in its proper place in a revolutionary newspaper because this dismantling of the worker's body of experience is the condition for a worker's political voice.[79]

In the moment of aesthetic judgement, both questions of *knowledge* and *desire* are neutralised and a space is opened for the contemplation of *form* and *appearance* which, in turn, reveals the power that these aesthetic dimensions have in constituting the political subject. 'Neutralisation' involves suspending the viewer's own socially constructed knowledge and desire, making space for a somewhat naïve disposition which nonetheless has a disarming force, disarticulating the viewer from the social conditions that are usually taken to define them. Aesthetic judgement is, in this sense, undergirded by an all-important *as if* – *as if* ownership, class and power meant nothing – which opens a space of freedom in which the conditions of possibility for building a new sensible world become apparent. In this sense, the viewer comes to see the current 'distribution of the sensible' as something contingent and therefore eminently replaceable by some other aesthetic-political order.

It is my contention that an aesthetic reading of sovereignty retains this capacity to render contingent prevailing legal and political forms, opening up possibilities for imagining an alternative ordering of the sensible. As we turn to face the new climatic regime, the basic co-ordinates that have shaped both orthodox and critical readings of sovereignty are being fundamentally called into question. The prevailing approaches, which have focused on the complex reordering of governmental and legal competencies at 'global' registers, and the coincidence between sovereign power and biopolitical management, neither account for how sovereignty is implicated in the production and dissimulation of the forms of environmental harm that characterise the Anthropocene, nor do they adequately address the resurgence of sovereignty in the contemporary political moment. Neither of these approaches, which remain wedded to the sociocentrism of modern political thought, is well equipped to lead us away from the destructive status quo. The approach I pursue in what follows seeks to achieve a kind of neutralisation in which we assume an attitude of 'disinterestedness' with respect to the prevailing distribution of the sensible in an effort to speculate about an alternative aesthetic regime, fit for the Anthropocene.

Programmatically, we can see this as involving two steps. The first assesses how the aesthetics of sovereignty in the course of modernity – in terms of both *the appearance of sovereignty* and the production of a *sovereign imaginary* or *mode of perception* – produces a sense of the political which is constituted through the expulsion of a set of material and biogeochemical relations that are today pressing to take centre stage. What are the technologies, images and forms of representation, central to the articulation of sovereignty, that create a political world in which the environmental, the non-human and the earthly are all deemed to be politically irrelevant? In addressing this we will be particularly concerned with understanding the role that *jurisdictional technologies* play in producing the particular ordering of the sensible associated with sovereignty. The second step involves reimagining the political sphere from a range of perspectives which have largely been considered 'non-political' within the dominant paradigm, but that can nonetheless be recuperated in the context of the climate crisis. This approach hopes to find new meaning within those elements that the onward press of modernity has discarded or devalued in an effort to destabilise the prevailing aesthetic distribution. My wager is that at the limits of the modern sovereign imaginary we can find a set of co-ordinates that help us navigate the precarious politics of the new climatic regime.

3

Territory

The age of iron. After which comes the age of bronze. How long, how long
before the softer ages return in their cycle, the age of clay, the age of earth?
— J. M. Coetzee, *Age of Iron*[1]

There is an uncanny, vertigo-like feeling that often sets in when reading
scientific literature on climate change. I grew up in Norfolk, a corner of
England known for the flatness of its land, the vastness of its sky and the crum-
bliness of its coastline, and there is nothing that evokes in me a sense of the
uncanny or 'un-homely'[2] more than the literature on sea level rises. Business-
as-usual emissions could produce a rise in sea levels by the century's close of at
least 2 metres. This could happen gradually or vertiginously. At the end of the
last glacial period sea levels rose by almost 4 metres in a century, and a similarly
rapid transformation of coastlines is becoming increasingly likely as recent
studies have shown how the melt rate of Antarctic ice has tripled in the last
decade. Between 2012 and 2017 the Antarctic lost 219 billion tons of ice; from
1992 to 1997 it lost only 49 billion tons.[3] These numbers in themselves are dis-
concerting enough but if we translate this into a more concrete – or should we
say, pelagic – image of the earth's future, the reality depicted by these predictions becomes deeply unnerving. Without a rapid and fundamental change to
our GHG emissions, we can confidently bid farewell to the following by 2100:

> Any beach you've ever visited; Facebook's headquarters, the Kennedy Space
> Centre, and the United States' largest naval base, in Norfolk, Virginia;
> the entire nations of the Maldives and the Marshall Islands; most of
> Bangladesh, including all of the mangrove forests that have been the king-
> dom of Bengal tigers for millennia . . . Saint Mark's Basilica in Venice
> . . . the White House at 1600 Pennsylvania Avenue, as well as [President]
> Trump's 'Winter White House' at Mar-a-Lago, Richard Nixon's in Key
> Biscayne, and the original, Harry Truman's in Key West.[4]

This oddly selective list – compiled by an American climate science journalist,
and clearly designed to resonate with a Western, if not American, readership

– might make some baulk. Should we not foreground the devastation that rising seas will bring to millions of people worldwide who have contributed least to emissions and have the fewest resources to cope with the coming changes? Does this list not draw some odd equivalences between the loss of natural habitats; entire nations, home to millions; and the second homes of some of the most powerful, climate-change-denying men in the world? There is something to these criticisms but this partial list of future losses nonetheless speaks to the uncanniness that haunts contemporary climate science. It captures something of the disbelief that accompanies a realisation of the scale of the challenges and the extent of the changes that are coming. It is a list that seeks to evoke a sense of *homelessness*, suggesting that the coming century will see familiar landmarks, landscapes and ecosystems disappear from view. Political or economically engendered homelessness is of course a crushing reality for millions of displaced people worldwide but there is something uniquely disturbing about the particular form of homelessness induced by climatic transformation. This is not a matter of displacement or migration simpliciter, not a matter even of escape or diaspora. All these terms suggest a certain contingency and impermanence to the condition of mobility: we have left or have been evicted from our home but, one day, we might return; in the end the land itself remains, even though the politics, the people or the economy may have made life on that land unbearable. The homelessness that will mark the coming century is less about movement *off the land* or a matter of a *lost home* that yearns to be *re-found*, than it is a matter of the *erasure of land* and the *destruction of home*, with no promise of return.

We all struggle to imagine this strange world of erasures and in our imaginings we are perhaps inevitably drawn to particular places and people that define our *nostos* or homestead, our place of belonging and sanctuary. What would it mean for these places *to be lost to the sea*? How would we navigate such a world of unknown landscapes and altered vistas? And what kind of politics and polities might such transformations create?

One way of approaching this question of home and homelessness is through an attention to *ethos*, understood as not just a matter of the *ethical values* privileged by a given community but also a matter of *dwelling*, *belonging* or *habitation*. A *political ethos* refers to a political community's understanding of its place in the world and the institutions and values that mediate a sense of common belonging. Approached historically, a political ethos is always in state of transformation as rival institutions vie to be the predominant mediator of collective life and the ultimate arbiter of the bonds that constitute political community. For instance, the *ethos* that prevails within monarchical rule, where the king's word has the force of law and the monarch's personage is the chief means of mediating the communal bond, is quite distinct from that which emerges in the context of popular sovereignty. The sense of *to what* and *to whom* one is attached and the relevant principles that underpin political community are clearly transformed in this context where nationhood and a set of supposedly democratic and impersonal institutions install a distinctly modern political ethos. And in the context of globalisation, new forms of attachment are arguably taking hold, whether to sub- or supranational political forms, or even – as Neil Walker has suggested – to a nascent 'global community' that rivals more parochial national or ethnic identities.[5]

One of the animating features of modern sovereignty is that it renders the question of political ethos supposedly unproblematic by installing the territorially defined nation state as *the* institution that mediates the bonds of community, asserting an elision between questions of place, home, authority and belonging. And as we will examine below, this depends on the mobilisation of not only material and juridical but also *aesthetic* technologies. One of the great achievements of the aesthetics associated with territory is that it successfully naturalises a decidedly contingent articulation of the relation between place and power.

Territory is one of the foundational presuppositions of modern sovereignty but scholars have tended to treat the concept itself as largely unproblematic, focusing attention on territorial conflicts or the rights and obligations that lawful territorial claims legitimise.[6] Stuart Elden's seminal work on the history of the term displaces this view and turns our attention instead to the conceptual scope and historical trajectory of territory, unpacking the uniqueness of territory as a mode of representing and ordering legal and political space.[7] Elden situates territory as a *sui generis* concept, distinct from, though related to, other key terms in our spatial lexicon: land, place, terrain and territoriality. As a genealogical approach to the concept shows,[8] far from referring to a 'transhistorical' mode through which place and power are brought into relation, the modern understanding of territory emerges within seemingly esoteric debates concerning the nature and limits of papal authority in late medieval Europe. The question of how to define the contours of an emergent secular (or 'temporal') power was later combined with geometric and philosophical innovations in early modernity that fed directly into the early treatises that elaborated a putatively 'modern' form of sovereignty. In this sense, territory is best understood as 'a bundle of political technologies'[9] that draw on a range of practices (mapping, surveying, measuring), knowledges (juridical, geometric, geographic) and forms of power (martial, jurisdictional, political), testifying to a rich and varied conceptual history. Territory is not simply a 'container' for political life, or an uncontested 'object' to which (more or less contested) rights and duties are attached, but is itself *constantly being produced* through a range of legal, geographic and political practices. In

82   EARTHBOUND

this way, Elden's account of territory ends where most approaches to the topic begin, with Elden underscoring – rather than effacing – the contingency of territory as a mode by which legal and political space has been apprehended.

One of the distinctive aspects of territory is its reliance on, and reproduction of, what Henri Lefebvre calls 'abstract space'.[10] Indebted to Renaissance geometry, territory developed hand in glove with a conception of space which is reducible to *extension*, where space is defined not by its materiality, dynamism or particularity but through a set of points and positions on a single plane. This *res extensa* is at the heart of the spatial imaginary of modernity and is an important aspect of modern governmental practices that are able to 'see like a state' through techniques of calculation, measurement and surveillance.[11] Territory depends on technologies that re-present a material and dynamic earth in static, polygonal forms, bracketing the raw materiality of the earth, and its various biogeochemical cycles and systems, in order to render visible an 'abstract space' over which exclusive legal and political power can be claimed. Whilst we all know that rivers, coastlines and mountain chains are undergoing slow transformations, we understand these changes to be operating at a temporal rhythm so different from our own political-spatial histories that they appear to be conceptually irrelevant. In the Holocene this 'slow-motion' view of nature was perhaps understandable, but not today.[12] Territory need not exhaust our spatial-political imaginaries; if, as Hans Lindahl has stressed, territory is '*but* one of the historical permutations' of a more general relation between place and power,[13] it remains an open question whether the challenges augured by the Anthropocene require us to develop an alternative spatial imaginary and mode of perception.

The static, polygonal forms that define territory can only remain efficacious if the materiality of the earth, which territory aims to represent and over which it makes a juridico-political claim, is itself largely immobile. Not only does the Anthropocene thesis attune us to the complex interactions between all elements of the earth system – lithosphere, cryosphere and hydrosphere alike – but it also promises a reckoning with increasingly mobile terrestrial forms as landscapes, coastlines and ice floes are all being transformed by a warming climate. In this context, what work does territory do, or fail to do, for us, as a distinct means of grasping, representing, ordering and imagining space? To what extent does territory render us sensitive or insensitive to the various mutations that the Anthropocene heralds? In this chapter I explore the tensions between the aesthetics of territory – particularly as articulated through the jurisdictional technology of mapping – and the possibilities of an altered political aesthetics that I develop through the concept of *terrain*. Terrain is a term used and developed within geophysical, meteorological and strategic studies but rarely (if ever) used in legal and political theory.

Terrain – or more especially what I call the 'terrain prospect', a unique mode of apperception appropriate to the concept – offers a markedly different aesthetic framing and attunement to space, power and questions of political belonging than that installed and policed under the auspices of territory. The terrain prospect aims to resituate legal and political agencies *within* a lively, dynamic and processual geophysical environment rather than *set against* an abstract and conceptually empty territory.

Before we take these concerns further, I want to examine how territory has become so deeply embedded within our spatial and political imaginaries. This requires a historical perspective that assesses the contingency of territory. In particular, I examine how practices of mapping – read here as a specifically jurisdictional technologies – structure our sense of space, authority and social relations. This takes us to the heart of the aesthetics of sovereignty, examining both the aesthetic objects (maps) which have been central to the history of sovereignty and also the aesthetic disposition or imaginary which such objects help to install and reproduce. Mapping is central to the 'distribution of the sensible' that is distinctive to modern sovereignty. And the enduring force of the cartographic imaginary, so successfully naturalised in modernity, is central to our inability to properly *see*, *sense* and *feel* the challenges associated with climate change and the Anthropocene.

Mapping as a Jurisdictional Technology

Painted on a calf skin measuring over 2 metres squared, the Hereford *map-pamundi* is the largest extant example of a form of mapping that prevailed throughout medieval Europe. *Mappaemundi* are literarily 'cloths of the world', and the Hereford map aims to depict the entirety of our earthly reality. But to modern eyes this 'world map' is utterly unrecognisable. The map is orientated with east at the top, rather than north, showing 'Europa', 'Asia' and 'Affrica', three continents united in single disk, divided by what appears to be an internal sea and surrounded on all sides by water. At the centre of the map is Jerusalem, above which is an image of the crucifixion, affirming its theological significance. Across the three continents, places and peoples, animals and monsters, events and apparitions are scattered with no discernible geographic congruity. When recognisable spatial forms are represented, it is social relations that predominate over topographic felicity. In a gesture that might please contemporary nationalists, the Hereford map shows Scotland floating freely in the north sea, entirely detached from England, whilst Wales appears partially annexed, seemingly preparing for a similar fate; unionists are given some succour with the island of Ireland starkly partitioned by a band of water. Primarily, the map depicts places and events drawn from biblical history: at the top of the map is the garden of Eden, with Adam and

Eve shown to have recently departed Paradise and thereby destined to walk the earth that is represented by the map's remainder. Asia, by far the largest of the three continents, is home to a series of scenes and locations central to the Old Testament narrative: from Babylon to Mount Sinai, Noah's Ark to Sodom and Gomorrah. In the apex of the map's frame, situated beyond the terrestrial, Jesus sits in judgment of those souls that have recently departed the world. To his right, the saved are led towards heaven accompanied by an angel who assures them that they 'shall have everlasting joy', and to his left, the condemned are ushered towards hell.

One of the things that is so disorientating about the Hereford *mappamundi* is that it subverts modern mapping's hierarchisation of space over time.[14] The notion that maps depict a *spatial* reality is a banality but the *mappamundi* shows that to be historically contingent. The Hereford map privileges the *temporal* over the spatial, visually representing the historical trajectory of the Christian world from creation, through exile, incarnation, resurrection and the promise of redemption. In this way, the map aims to situate its medieval observer within a world defined by the promise of salvation, safeguarded by the all-encompassing authority of the church. As Jerry Brotton suggests, *mappaemundi*, like the one in Hereford, are able to 'embody all of human history in one image, and simultaneously to provide a sequential account of divine judgment and personal salvation'.[15] As this makes clear, maps are only legible from within a given discourse of power and a set of situated social relations; there is no map that 'stands alone', and each map can only find semiotic stability within a network of texts, processes and beliefs that help give it sense.[16]

As an aspiration to universality, and as a visual representation of plenary authority, the Hereford map is in so many ways alien to modern imaginaries of place and power. Nonetheless, underpinning the *mappaemundi* is the desire to capture a complex and unruly world, and its diverse social and political relations, in a single aesthetic object. In this way, *mappaemundi* affirm a very modern sense of mapping as a *technology of representation* that has the capacity to situate subjects in space and time, visualising the ligaments of authority that bind actors in social space. In the centuries that followed the Hereford map's creation, mapping would undergo a revolution in technique, form and style that would displace *mappaemundi* and the theological image of the world which they represent, ultimately contributing to fundamental shifts in the nature of authority in Europe. This transformation helps to show that maps articulate *modes of attachment* to place, power, time and the social world. If medieval maps sought to bind subjects to the authority of the church and a temporal trajectory defined by the biblical narrative, modern cartography binds subjects to the seemingly eternal authority of the nation state. The fact that modern maps and atlases depict a world divided into states, territorially delimited and defined, would be as alien to the medieval scribes who created that rich and variegated image of the world in Hereford as the *mappamundi* is to us.

At this juncture, it is worth recalling the fourfold view of sovereignty that we set out in the previous chapter. The analysis that follows seeks to draw out the different moments at which territory and the techniques of mapping are articulated as a matter of sovereignty's *appearance* (in particular maps); its *aesthesis* (as a particular *imaginary* or *ideal* of cartography); and in the *practices* of sovereignty in juridical reasoning. Furthermore, mapping and territory are implicated in the production of a *non-political remainder* in the form of both non-territorial forms of authority, which modern mapping renders imperceptible, and the geophysical stratum or 'terrain' from which territory is abstracted. And it is precisely with the supposedly 'non-political' concept of 'terrain' that we might begin to develop an alternative aesthetic disposition fit for the Anthropocene. As we will see, the great trick of modern cartographic technique is that it hides its contingency, managing to present itself as a putatively 'neutral', 'rational' and 'scientifically accurate' depiction of the natural world whilst occluding its legal and political implications.

The relationship between changes in cartographic technique and transformations to the nature of governmental authority has been widely commented on.[17] Central to this story is the rediscovery, translation and dissemination of Ptolemy's *Cosmographia* in the early fifteenth century, which reinjected techniques first developed in ancient Greece (the geometric graticule, astronomy and mathematical projection) into late medieval mapping. These transformative technological developments saw an explosion in the production of maps. In the early fifteenth century there are estimated to have been a few thousand maps in circulation in Europe, between 1472 and 1500 this ballooned to 56,000, and by the close of the following century there were millions of printed maps available.[18] In a recent study, Jordan Branch assesses the complementarity between the cartographic and the political as constituting a set of feedback loops that were crucial to the formation of the modern nation state.[19] Technological change produced new artefacts, which developed new perspectives on legal and political authority, which in turn 'fed back' into demands for technological refinement and so on. In this way, Branch highlights a complex and emergent set of relations between *mapping practices*, like surveying and projection techniques; *maps* themselves as novel political and technical artefacts; and a social and political *imaginary* through which the world is perceived, ordered and understood.

It is worth underscoring quite how dramatic was the change from medieval to modern forms of spatial representation, knowledge and sensibility.

Firstly, Ptolemaic mapping effectively removes the temporal dimension from maps. Indeed, geomorphic or political change that renders a map anachronistic has always been a source of great discomfort for map-makers. The secret dream of the modern cartographer is of a static, and therefore *non-historical*, world that can be plotted and represented in immaculate detail. But as Cassini III – the doyen of eighteenth-century French mapping – knew all too well, the 'fixed and invariable measurements' of the cartographer were never going to capture the ever changing topographic reality which the nation claimed as its 'homeland'.[20] Secondly, Ptolemaic mapping introduced a conception of *homogenous space*. Crucial to this is the geometric graticule, which allows for every corner of the earth to be represented at a uniform scale in which every physical point can be mapped onto an abstract polygonal plane. This method of representing the earth deliberately erases local differences, reducing the particularities of any given *place* to smooth and abstract *spaces* which are, by definition, undifferentiated. Maps were no longer orientated towards religious or culturally significant places, allowing every polity, in principle at least, to assert itself as 'the center of the world'. At the same time, however, each polity accepted a common set of co-ordinates through which its claims to particularity could be made. As Branch puts it, 'even as different actors argue in favour of a particular centre (or a particular boundary placement), they have all implicitly agreed to the fundamental structure of graticule-based cartography and hence have adopted the same understanding of space'.[21]

Most significantly for our own concerns, the widespread adoption of Ptolemaic mapping in Europe transformed the way in which political authority came to be represented and expressed. Legal and political power in late medieval and early modern Europe was defined by complex, nested, and often overlapping jurisdictional orders that combined territorial and non-territorial forms of authority. In this context, it was questions of a claimant's *status* or *form of activity*, rather than their presence in a particular territory, that were the central concerns in determining the jurisdictional competency of courts and tribunals. The technologies of representation developed by modern mapping offered a view of both space and political authority that left these non-territorial forms of power wholly unrepresented. Early modern mapping created a novel visual grammar which represented political space as a matter of bounded, homogenous and contiguous zones of authority. Throughout the sixteenth and seventeenth centuries – that is, before the consolidation of the territorial sovereignty of nation states in Europe – early modern maps regularly depicted the European continent as if it were neatly divided into discrete geopolitical units, very often with colour-coding that dramatised the claim in a way that foreshadows maps and atlases of the twentieth century.[22] Willem Blaeu's 'Map of Europe' of 1642, for instance, depicts 'Italia' and 'Germania' as homogenous geopolitical entities, some 200 years prior to their actual political unification.[23] Such maps sought to reflect cultural and linguistic affiliations but these representational devices sat in an uncomfortable relation to the messy reality of legal and political life in Europe which only shed the complexities of feudal jurisdictional ordering towards the end of the eighteenth century. In this way territory's aesthetic regime can be seen to precede its actualisation in practice: the political aesthetic precedes political practice.

The emergent political aesthetics of early modernity are indebted to specific technological devices which allow for the earth to be grasped in a particular configuration where non-territorial forms of authority and belonging disappear 'offstage'. As Branch puts it,

> It is inherent in the nature of Ptolemaic cartography, upon which these mapmakers had staked their intellectual and commercial fortunes, that space be treated geometrically: the co-ordinates system of latitude and longitude, applied to all points on the earth's surface, favours this conception. The effect on ideas of territorial political authority – homogenising the medieval collection of places into a geometric expanse – was . . . an unintended by-product of the visual language of maps [in early modernity].[24]

The technology of the geometric graticule which defined Ptolemaic cartography gave rise to a particular way of *seeing* and *sensing* a world – one defined by the territorial delimitation of political power within a putatively 'empty' or 'abstract' space – that was only later taken up in institutional disputes and reform. What is at stake in the proliferation of maps in early modernity is the dissemination of entirely novel politico-aesthetic artefacts that created a new way of imagining the nature of political authority. In this way we can understand modern mapping as a 'world-forming' power, underscoring the ways in which modern sovereignty, through a set of contingent techniques and practices, comes to mediate a prevailing sense of our earthly reality.

Following our association of 'juris-diction' with law's expressive and representative register, we can understand early modern mapping as a jurisdictional technology that helps shape both modern sovereignty's mode of appearance and its institutional form.[25] Jurisdiction is an expressly *creative* enterprise that has the unique capacity of needing nothing other than its own grounds in order to articulate a claim to authority. As Bradin Cormack suggests, jurisdictional claims are able to hide their contingencies by presenting themselves as eminently 'natural' – as unproblematic or naïve representations of an extant reality.[26] Early modern mapping conforms precisely to this form: the map, with 'functionally no other ground'[27] than its own technological enframing of the world, is able to project a novel form of authority that becomes utterly *naturalised* in the course of modernity. We can appreciate some of the implications of this insight more keenly if we turn to the role that mapping has played in the colonial context because it is here that we see the enduring power that mapping has had in shaping the aesthetics of sovereignty.

Mapping is one of the techniques crucial to colonial appropriation. In 1606 James I granted a licence to the newly created 'London Company' that gave it authority to claim for the crown land

> lying and being all along the sea coasts between four and thirty degrees of northerly latitude from the equinoctial line and five and forty degrees of the same latitude and in the main land . . . and the islands thereunto adjacent or within one hundred miles of the coast thereof.[28]

Similarly, in 1786 the jurisdictional scope of prospective settlements in New South Wales were defined by seemingly precise co-ordinates of longitude and latitude that, as Shaunnagh Dorsett has put it, granted Britain territorial jurisdiction over 'half a continent', long before any effective control of the land was ever exercised. In this way, the Ptolemaic graticule allowed states to make an apparently lawful claim to possession within a purely virtual and abstract space before any material acts of settlement. As Edgerton suggests, this illustrates the 'absolute faith Europeans of all religious persuasions had in the authority of the cartographic grid . . . troops were sent to fight and die for boundaries that had no visible landmarks, only abstract mathematical existence'.[29] The nascent political aesthetics of the period, which emptied out the messy reality of extant jurisdictional complexity in Europe and instead represented political space through unitary and contiguous zones of authority, found a natural home in the supposedly 'empty' places of the new world. In this way, the legal fiction of *terra nullius*, which asserts the right of colonial appropriation on grounds of the non-settlement of the land (irrespective of indigenous inhabitation), finds an aesthetic corollary in early modern mapping which had already developed a visual grammar that rendered non-territorial forms of authority and belonging invisible.

Throughout modernity the aesthetics of territory, first expressed in early modern maps that experimented with recently rediscovered Ptolemaic projection techniques and subsequently deployed within the project of European colonisation, was gradually integrated into the institutional ordering of European states themselves at the level of institutional practice. This evidences a process that Branch calls 'colonial reflection' where modes of authority that were key to the development of colonial power came to be mirrored in the colonisers' own political and juridical ordering.[30] As Ptolemaic maps began to more accurately reflect political practice within Europe and beyond, the visibility of the contingencies and particularities of modern mapping were gradually occluded as territorial maps were viewed as being apparently 'transparent', 'neutral' or simply 'accurate' depictions of the world. Matthew Edney has described this process as culminating in the formation of the 'ideal of cartography': a deeply engrained set of presuppositions about the nature and purpose of maps that came to define the modern spatial imaginary.[31] Central to the *ideal of cartography* – in contradistinction to multifarious *practices of mapping* – is the belief that maps are inherently rational, scientific and efficacious documents, free from political ambition or intent, and undergoing a progressive refinement in terms of geophysical felicity and navigational functionality.[32] What Edney makes clear is that the partiality of modern mapping is effaced as the *ideal* of cartography becomes entrenched within the collective European consciousness through the widespread proliferation of territorial maps, their inclusion in school curricula, and the development of surveying and observational technologies – from remote sensing devices to photography – that reinforce some of the ideal's central tenets. Throughout his study Edney is keen to show how the presuppositions that underpin this cartographic ideal are 'wrong', flawed', 'mythic' or 'erroneous' and urges instead an attention to the historically and geographically situated *practices of mapping*. Whilst there are important merits to his argument, Edney too quickly dismisses the function that the cartographic 'ideal' or 'imaginary' has played in constructing the moderns' apprehension of space, power and social relations. It is no good simply describing the idealised notion of a neutral, natural, rational and progressive cartography as 'wrong' or 'flawed' when the ideal itself has played such an important role in structuring dominant accounts of place and power. This becomes clear if we return to the contemporary (post-)colonial context where modern mapping techniques are presupposed by courts, and others, to be nothing more than a convenient means of delimiting and measuring space but in practice serve the ends of political power.

The statutory framework installed after the recognition of 'native title' by the Australian High Court in *Mabo v Queensland (No 2)* requires those seeking to establish native title to evidence their ongoing relation to the land and the spatial extent of their claim through the submission of cartographic evidence.[33] On its face, a requirement to illustrate the exact co-ordinates of the land over which a claim is being made might appear 'natural'. Indeed, Brennan J of the Hight Court seems to endorse this view in the opening paragraph of the *Mabo* decision when – echoing the abstract jurisdictional claims over the 'new world' referred to above – he identifies the Murray Islands (subject of the appeal) as being defined by its longitude and latitude.[34] In this way, the articulation of state authority relies on a supposedly objective, rational and efficacious technique through which the spatial extent of a dispute can be delineated. And this takes us to the heart of some of the contradictions that beset the post-*Mabo* native title regime.

The system of native title requires claimants to translate indigenous forms of authority, belonging and attachment to the land into a system of cartographic representation that is inimical to indigenous law and practice. The territorial delimitations of the colonies that were to become the Commonwealth of Australia cut through indigenous land, with no acknowledgement of, let alone respect for, indigenous knowledge, law or culture. In this way, the contemporary imperative to evidence native title claims with cartographic representation forces claimants to rely on the very mapping technologies that rendered indigenous life invisible to the coloniser's eye in the first place. The details of aboriginal attachment to land or 'country' are highly complex and are readily distorted when translated into Western concepts of 'ownership' and 'territory'. Nonetheless, it is worth noting some of the fundamental divergences from modern conceptions of territory:

> The boundaries of ruwi [indigenous land] were marked by beds in the creek or river, the rain shadow, trees, and rocks, as well as fabricated markers. While Aboriginal laws are specific to place and have a sense of boundary, they are boundaries unlike those constructed by Australian law, which mapped state boundaries in straight lines across Aboriginal territories. Aboriginal song lines do not travel in straight lines to make absolute boundary areas between different peoples. Aboriginal songs have sung the law, and those laws and stories are held in the land to form the song lines that lie across the entirety of the Australian landscape. Some regions were shared areas, while others were restricted, requiring permission to travel across the land and thus avoid conflict. The land was known in song and sung to by the custodians.[35]

Not only is the attachment to place mediated through song and story rather than claims of mimetic visual representation[36] but the scope of such bonds also fails to conform to the ideal of contiguous zones of clearly demarked territorial authority. The limits of ruwi might follow the contours of the land, but other times might not. And the relation that a community has to the land might be exclusive or shared. The insistence that claimants evidence native title by reference to clearly delineated boundaries, amenable to modern cartographic standards, imposes a foreign spatial imaginary onto these complex spatial practices and forms of attachment.

Australian law remains unreceptive to non-territorial forms of authority and belonging that are central to indigenous law and culture, and reduces indigenous modes of understanding place and power 'to a form that [settler] law can read and assess in its own terms'.[37] In this way, the jurisdictional technology of mapping is a key means through which a putatively 'natural' or 'efficacious' mode of expressing and representing space allows for the quiet imposition of a very particular set of legal and political commitments that animate settler colonialism. The native title regime illustrates the way in which mapping techniques are implicated in policing the limits of political life. Ultimately, this is achieved through techniques that constitutively render spatial practices and modes of authority variously *visible* or *invisible*; and these ways of *seeing* and *unseeing* have become deeply engrained in both the modern apprehension of space and the forms through which authority is legitimated and expressed.

Richard Ford calls modern, territorial jurisdiction 'synthetic' in that it makes no claims to any 'organic' relation a community has with a given tract of land.[38] Synthetic jurisdictions are deliberate constructions of state power, consciously artificial modes of delimiting authority that facilitate state interests. As we have suggested here, the jurisdictional technology of mapping plays a crucial role in maintaining such 'synthetic' jurisdictions. Not only do the surveying and projection techniques of cartography help to accurately delimit a self-consciously artificial imposition on the land and its peoples but so too do maps work to *naturalise* the contingencies associated with these claims. Mapping installs an *ideal* or *imaginary* that understands cartography as a neutral, rational and efficacious representation of space, which itself facilitates political power. This naturalised but wholly contingent way of grasping place and power is a crucial means through which notions of belonging and home are mediated and reproduced. For indigenous Australians, this is a particularly painful and disorientating experience because the very means by which Aboriginal Australians articulate a sense of political attachment and belonging is delegitimised by the state's jurisdictional technologies; as Irene Watson puts it, 'Aboriginal peoples who were homeless before *Mabo* (No. 2) remain that way.'[39]

As I have tried to show here, one of sovereignty's great tricks is to rely on technologies that occlude its own contingency and groundlessness, presenting itself *as if* it were constituted by nothing but a rational or efficacious representation. In the context of the Anthropocene we can see that the highly contingent ways in which territorial sovereignty frames our sense of place and power bracket a swathe of forces and relations that are central to our ensuing climate crisis. If in the Anthropocene political life must contend with the interlinking forces of biosphere, human infrastructures, the carbon cycle, melt rates of ice, atmospheric CO_2 concentration and much more besides, the aesthetics of territory renders these forces constitutively *invisible*, insisting that our political 'homelands' are irreducible to the flattened, polygonal spaces imagined and represented by modern cartography. What we can draw from the colonial experience of mapping is both how destructive this spatial imaginary can be, in occluding non-territorial forms of authority and belonging, and how deep-seated this mode of apperception is within a prevailing sense of legitimate political life. Indeed, as the post-*Mabo* native title regime shows, the technology of mapping has come to function as an *a priori* that prefigures the contours of legal and political claims.

In the remainder of this chapter I outline an alternative way of seeing, sensing and ordering relations between place and power through the concept of terrain. This aims to resituate the political, as well as a sense of home and belonging, *within* those forces that are central to the Anthropocene and the climate crisis. If we continue to allow our sense of place and power to be prefigured by the aesthetics of territory and the cartographic ideal, we will remain constitutively anaesthetised to some of the most pressing challenges of the contemporary moment. The 'terrain prospect' challenges the modern framing of the political which associates home, belonging and attachment to place with the territorially delimited state, a supposed 'homeland' to which citizens are both legally and affectively bound. In order to introduce these connections between home, territory and state authority in the context of ecological and climatic mutation, I first turn to John Lanchester's novel, *The Wall* (2019).[40] Lanchester helps us foreground the complex relations between authority, territory and the geophysical environment, posing stark questions about the nature of home and homelessness and the forms of disorientation that define life in the new climatic regime.

No Direction Home

Running through Lanchester's novel are interrelated concerns about the nature of territory, state power and a yearning for 'home' in the context of a dramatically altered climatic reality. The novel is set in an unspecified but not too distant future-world, fundamentally transformed by climate change: coastlines have been redrawn and possibilities for human flourishing have all but been obliterated. A significantly shrunken Britain has erected the eponymous 'Wall' to defend itself against rising seas as well as un-homed 'Others' that live beyond Britain's borders. Lanchester's prose evokes a strangely hollowed out, two-dimensional world, with each character reduced to an archetypical form: 'Defenders' guard the wall on a two-year-long form of national service, they are led by a 'Captain', a 'Sargent' and a 'Corporal', and are ultimately overseen by members of the 'Elite'. The latter are afforded the luxury of 'Help', comprised of those Others who both manage to scale the uncompromising border wall and are deemed useful enough to disbar immediate execution or deportation and effectively work as state-controlled slaves.

Defenders are allotted a singular responsibility: if they should let an Other cross the Wall, they themselves will be 'put to sea', banished from Britain and shorn of any citizenship rights, thereby becoming Others themselves.

'The Change' – the unspecified, worldwide climatic disturbance that has raised sea levels and dramatically cooled northern Europe – has caused new societal rifts not only between the Elite and the rest but, more strikingly, between young and old, between those responsible for the Change and those who have been left to deal with its consequences. Such is the sense of destitution amongst the young that few couples decide to have children and the state is forced to offer various incentives for the so-called 'Breeders' who are willing to bring new life into the world. The novel is narrated by Kavanagh, a Defender who secretly yearns to be a member of the Elite. Permeating Kavanagh's story is a profound sense of homelessness that speaks to broader political anxieties surrounding climate change and the waning power of territorial sovereignty.

On a break from his duties on the Wall, Kavanagh returns to his parents' home in the midlands, where he reveals the extent to which familial bonds have been severed by the Change:

> None of us can talk to our parents. By 'us' I mean my generation, people born after the Change. You know that thing where you break up with someone and say, It's not you, it's me? This is the opposite. It's not us, it's them. Everyone knows what the problem is. The diagnosis isn't hard – the diagnosis isn't even controversial. It's guilt: mass guilt, generational guilt. The olds feel they irretrievably fucked up the world, then allowed us to be born into it . . . The life advice, the knowing-better, the back-in-our-day wisdom which, according to books and films, was a big part of the whole deal between parents and children, just doesn't work.[41]

With the family home irreparably sundered by a sense of generational injustice, Kavanagh vainly searches for new places and forms of belonging: on a brief camping holiday with some of his Defender-friends, with his partner Kifa in their 'Breeders' accommodation, or with the floating community that takes in the exiled Defenders following their banishment. In each case the possibility of home and the promise of familial or communal attachment is suddenly broken, most dramatically – and most violently – when Kavanagh and Kifa's adoptive community is plundered by Pirates, an episode that ends leaving all but the couple dead. Kavanagh and Kifa's final resting place only serves to underscore the ambivalence of homelife in a world transfigured by the Change. After an arduous journey at sea the pair eventually arrive at an abandoned oil rig which is occupied by a mute and traumatised hermit-like figure who allows them some sanctuary onboard. Discovering supplies of food, fuel and water, Kifa and Kavanagh rejoice in their new-found comfort. Having lived without the prospect of heat and artificial light for so long, the discovery of an oil lamp, matches and sufficient fuel sends Kavanagh reeling: 'it was oil. I wanted to shout oil, oil, oil! Light and heat.'[42] The novel concludes, then, with the pair making a temporary home in the decaying architecture of late twentieth-century extractive capitalism, entranced by the power of fossil fuels to meet the human desire for comfort; as Kavanagh tell us, 'the light was yellow-blue, gold, the most beautiful thing I had ever seen . . . flickering but reliable, the most cinematic and biggest sight'.[43] This is the home, Lanchester appears to be telling us, that we are creating for ourselves in the present: an utterly unsustainable and derelict one, where we are unable to shake the expectations and obsessions that have precipitated our unfolding climatic catastrophe.

Throughout these scenes of displacement and itinerancy, Lanchester continually underscores how the Change has heralded a new confrontation with the *materiality* of the physical environment. Remarking on his first shift on duty, Kavanagh says the Wall is 'always water, sky, wind, cold, and of course concrete, so it's sometimes concretewaterskywindcold, when they all hit you as one thing, as a single entity, combined like a punch, concretewaterskywindcold'.[44] When Kavanagh's unit are moved to Scotland, he notes a change in the atmosphere: 'the sea smelt different . . . Greener, basically, it smelt greener. Of living things.'[45] Recounting an episode in which thick fog descended onto the Wall, Kavanagh remarks of the benefits this affords Defenders: 'in the super-humid silence, you could hear a cough or a metal clank hundreds of metres away. You could talk to the Defender at the next post without raising your voice.'[46] And once at sea, Kavanagh emphasises the enormity of the challenge of not only finding land but simply securing a foothold if one is lucky enough to come across it. Having chanced upon a small island, he realises a sad reality: 'there was nowhere to land. The island – beachless, like every coastline in the world after the Change – rose vertically out of the sea.'[47] Lanchester highlights in these different moments not only the disorientation felt by a changed climatic reality – no beaches, no landing grounds; novel smells, sights and atmospheres – but also the way in which the Change has immersed his characters within a shifting environmental scene to which they are becoming increasingly sensitive. This emphasis on the environmental and atmospheric itself returns us to the theme of homelessness for it is precisely a lack of shelter, protection, warmth and security that has necessitated this new-found attachment to the elements; indeed, Lanchester shows us that the pervasive threat of homelessness is to be become *permanently exposed* to these elements, unable to immunise oneself against a hostile environment.

The Wall plays on the fears of homelessness that haunt our climate imaginaries. But so too does the novel seek to underscore the naïve brutality of the 'walled state' solution to the challenges of climatic transformation. In this way the novel grapples with what Mark Neocleous has called the 'distinctive ecology of belonging' that connects territory, state and a sense of homeliness.[48] If, in the modern political imaginary, the territorially delimited nation state claims to be the chief mediator of collective belonging, turning a relatively arbitrary tract of land into a 'homeland', Lanchester reveals that the natural trajectory of this outlook lies in the wall-building instincts that have recently come to the fore in contemporary political debate. But as the novel shows, such walled communities offer nothing but a simulacrum of security in the context of a changing climate. The Wall allows for the dramatic changes to coastlines and the harsh realities of the 'concretewaterskywindcold' at the state's peripheries to be temporarily occluded for those living within the state's interior, whilst also blinkering citizens to the reality of the world that persists beyond their borders. State border walls, in this sense, are shown to be world-denying technologies, fundamentally abjuring the very possibility of a *common world* beyond the parameters of the nation state. The apparent security of the Wall offers nothing but a stark precarity for those charged with defending it; after all, Kavanagh, Kifa et al. are all readily abandoned by the state, rendered both stateless and homeless, as soon as they fail to satisfy the state's demand for absolute protection.

Powerfully drawing out the inadequacies of prevailing forms of attachment to home, place and nation in the context of a climatically altered world, Lanchester makes clear connections between the ethno-nationalisms of the present, the desire for walled borders and forms of climate denial. He forces us to ponder what kind of political ethos and spatial imaginary will come to the fore in the context of radical climatic upheaval. Will the practice of territorial delimitation that has come to define statehood evolve into more violent forms of securitisation and enclosure in the name of a supposed 'homeland'? Or might the new climatic order allow for an altered sense of home and political belonging to emerge? Lanchester's novel implies that if the worst excesses of the former trajectory are to be avoided, we must find new ways of mediating our political ethos that both reattune political thinking to the physicality of our material environment and renew the critical questioning of the artificial borders that nation states inevitably – violently and jealously – seek to defend. Lanchester questions how a shift away from territory, and its largely unquestioned association with state power, might attune us to a different sense of home, both privately and politically, within the uncertain future towards which we are implacably moving.

My contention is that the concept of 'terrain' can help us understand the transformation to the coding of place and power to which Lanchester's novel points. There is an important ambivalence to note about what I am calling the 'terrain prospect'. On the one hand, it signals new ways of imagining forms of belonging and attachment to place, foregrounding the immersion of subjects in a complex geophysical environment ahead of the bonds that tie us to the 'synthetic' borders associated with modern territory. On the other hand, and as is clear from Lanchester's novel, when changing climatic conditions disrupt the certainties of territory and the materiality of terrain comes into view, space tends to become militarised, tied to a marshal and strategic gaze.

The Terrain Prospect

A rarely used term in legal and political theory, terrain is central to both the geophysical sciences and strategic studies. In the former, studies are primarily concerned with the classification and measurement of distinct elements of the landscape – cliffs, slopes, alluvial fans and so on – and seek to understand how these elements combine to forms patterns or 'systems' of terrain over larger areas.[49] Whilst the emphasis of this analysis is on the material forms that constitute the landscape, terrain analysis in geomorphology is also sensitive to the complex interactions between 'landforms, soil, vegetation, topoclimate and hydrological regime[s]',[50] underscoring how terrain is both shaped by and shapes meteorological conditions. In strategic studies, taxonomies of terrain exist to understand the interaction between military strategy and the geophysical environment. This can include studies of geopolitical 'pinch points' or 'gateways' that separate nation-state territories or zones of conflict, examining how the use of military force will be limited or facilitated by the particular features of a given landscape and climate. Terrain is also studied in more localised accounts of the specific materialities of potential theatres of war in order to inform both defensive and offensive strategic decisions.[51] All of this amounts to a 'careful consideration of the whole spectrum of environmental factors including their interrelationships and effects on various military activities'.[52] Where the geophysical rendering of terrain foregrounds non-human systems and processes, the strategic approach is more concerned with the interactions between the human and the non-human, analysing how the landforms that constitute a given 'terrain system' will shape the capacity for the deployment of troops and ordnance.

My exploration of terrain seeks to supplement and extend the work of Gaston Gordillo and Stuart Elden who have both examined the theoretical significance of terrain for political and spatial theory.[53] For Gordillo, terrain is the only term in our spatial lexicon which indicates that 'space is made up of folds, textures, depths, and volumes'[54] and thus offers a means by which we can test the limits of modernity's spatial imaginary. Terrain articulates the meeting point between the geophysical and the political in a way that is particularly apposite for the Anthropocene where the materiality of the earth, its systems and processes, and the interactions between human and non-human agencies that constitute the particularities of a given place, are all becoming increasingly significant to legal and political life. A focus on terrain foregrounds the human interactions with the so-called 'natural world', emphasising that the earth system is not itself a *given* but is constantly being fashioned by human agency. In Gordillo's helpful formulation, terrain describes not simply the terrestrial but brings to the fore the 'affective geometry'[55] of a place, describing how human actors, meteorological conditions and the materiality of the earth form complex feedback loops that affect and are affected by one another.

The ability to move with confidence across a given terrain depends on a very particular set of capacities and capabilities: the fitness, experience or agility that allows the hiker to move through rugged, mountain terrain, for instance; or the local know-how that allows the cabby to find the quickest route through the backstreets of a city. In this way, terrain is known and navigated by particular, situated subjects that are themselves constituted by their material environment. Territory, in contrast, is associated with the flattening of subjectivity by tying legal and political status to legal forms, such as citizenship. In this way, where territory is associated with the formal equivalence of (legal) subjects, terrain is associated with their somatic, affective and cognitive differentiation. Beyond this, terrain brings a *temporal* dimension into view. However static it may seem, terrain is forever in a state of *becoming*: landscapes and atmospheres that shift with changes in temperature, precipitation patterns, erosion and so on.[56] But the geophysical dimensions of terrain also foreground the multiple temporalities that constitute the earth system itself: the carbon cycle, melt rates of ice, and 'tipping points' that can engender precipitous change to the earth's material fabric. Where modern cartography jettisons temporality in favour of an abstract and supposedly immobile space, the terrain prospect seeks to reattune political thinking to the varied temporalities of our material environment.[57]

I am especially interested in the *political aesthetics* that terrain evokes, the way in which the 'terrain prospect' alters our capacity to be rendered sensitive or insensitive to the various phenomena that are shaping the political sphere in the Anthropocene. As Alexandra Arènes et al. have recently shown, orthodox methods by which the earth has been represented – whether through classical cartography or as a 'blue planet', viewed from outer space – render strangely invisible the unique forces and relations that make the earth a living planet.[58] The terrain prospect aims to resituate modes of perception within these very forces. If territory is associated with a putatively mimetic representation, terrain is best approached through *aesthesis* where a broader range of our sensory life might be evoked. In this way, terrain escapes the techniques of mapping, surveying and representation on which sovereign power, and modern accounts of space more generally, so often relies. Where territory insists on reading space as *extension*, reducible to points on a single plane, terrain revels in the *intensity* and *multiplicity* of places and the various human and non-human forces that constitute them. Here I explore terrain along two trajectories, firstly through an attention to atmosphere, and secondly in relation to geophysical placement and the forms of attachment and belonging that this might evoke.

Atmospheric Envelopment

If the terrain prospect views space in volumetric and material terms, it draws attention to *atmosphere*. By foregrounding a spatial form other than the polygonal we can resituate ourselves *within* rather than *on* space, urging an encounter with the atmospheric envelope – that gaseous pellicle that extends roughly 100km from the earth – within which all terrestrial life is immersed and on which all organic life depends.[59] If we usually take the atmosphere to be a largely unremarkable *given* – hardly considered a subject of philosophical, sociological or political reflection[60] – the Anthropocene brings this unquestioned 'background' centre stage. It is, of course, the human reformation of our largely stable atmospheric conditions which is at the root of our current crisis, with the very nature of the air that we breathe undergoing unprecedented alterations. Properly attending to our atmospheric envelopment constitutes a fundamental shift in our political aesthetics: an account of the political in which disputes between and across the flat spaces of territory must give way to a theory of air-partitioning and atmospheric control.

As Derek McCormack has argued, 'envelopment' is a powerful means of reckoning with atmosphere because it 'provides a way of linking a condition of being elemental with the process of fabrication'.[61] For Emanuele Coccia, this dual aspect of atmospheric envelopment is best approached through the dynamics of *breathing* emphasising the somatic capacities that need to be foregrounded in this context. Whilst we might consign breath to one of life's background trivialities, we can think of respiration as actively fabricating the earth's elemental conditions. As Coccia puts it, 'the air we breathe is not a purely geological or mineral reality – it is not just out there, it is not, as such, an effect of the earth – but rather the breath of other living beings.'[62] In this way, Coccia encourages us to situate human agency within an atmospheric milieu which depends – in a deep, ontological sense – 'on the lives of others'.[63] We are not *set against* a putatively inert materiality that is open for exploitation, appropriation and division. Instead, our agency, as the Anthropocene thesis makes profoundly clear, is actively fashioning the conditions of the atmosphere to which we are fundamentally bound. Not only does this shift our attention towards the somatic and immersive qualities of space but it also highlights the processes by which the atmosphere can be *conditioned* or *immunised against*. The line-drawing obsessions of the cartographer, then, can give way to a renewed sensitivity to the practices of 'air-conditioning' and the various processes that manipulate our atmospheric envelopment.

Our Anthropocenic present is marked by profound changes to our atmospheric conditions. In 2013, for instance, northern China experienced a massive pollution event as the prevailing wind that usually clears the worst of the smog emanating from its industrial belt shifted direction, leaving an enormous, noxious cloud hanging across Shanghai, Nanjing and Jiangxi. The Air Quality Index provides a metric for air pollution. Before 2013, the uppermost range on the scale was 301–500. Breathing air graded at this level provokes 'serious aggravation of heart or lung disease and premature mortality in persons with cardiopulmonary disease and the elderly', and beyond this poses 'serious risk of respiratory effects in the general population'.[64] In 2013, the pollution levels in northern China peaked at 993 on the Air Quality Index: almost *double* what was until then considered the maximum range. The smog was estimated to be responsible for 1.37 million premature deaths in that year alone.[65] The technological means of immunising against this toxic air – gas masks, air purifiers, emigration to more breathable climes or simply staying indoors – are of course not evenly distributed within the community. The question of who can condition the air and by what means, then, becomes a significant point of differentiation between citizens.

In this context the pressing political questions are not simply where are you situated vis-à-vis a territorial jurisdiction but how are you enveloped, against what are you immunised, how are you attuned to the atmospheric milieu and what capacities do you, or given political institutions, have to condition the atmosphere in a such way that makes life liveable, and to what ends? Amongst other things, this raises significant questions about the inequalities implied by atmospheric conditioning, both within and between nations. But none of this can be sensed if we remain bound to a modern political aesthetics which insists on neatly delineated borders that operate in a strangely lifeless, two-dimensional world. If the Anthropocene necessitates an account of the atmospheric and what Peter Sloterdijk calls the 'aphralogical',[66] the volumetric and the air-conditioned, then it necessitates a very different *sensibility* to place and power than that constructed by modern cartographic technique. The processual, active and emergent qualities of the atmospheric serve to remind us that being *within* terrain is always a matter of an attuned, somatic sensitivity to the ebb and flow of materially complex places within which the capacity of human action is intricately enfolded.

Geophysical Entanglements

In some of his most recent work Elden has turned to the language of terrain in an effort to explore the materiality of territory, suggesting that through discourses of terrain we can foreground the ways in which territorial practices rely on interventions within, and a manipulation of, the geophysical environment.[67] To understand this intersection between state territory and the material environment, we might look to the ways in which states are increasingly 'weaponising terrain' in order to police migration. At the US–Mexico border, for instance, the ongoing project of border securitisation pushes migrants into increasingly hostile and unpopulated terrain. Similarly, regimes of security, profiling and deportation in southern Europe have forced undocumented migrants to find dangerous routes through the mountains in an effort to reach the more prosperous north of the continent. Here European states are deliberately using the 'rugged terrain of the Alps in an attempt to protect [themselves] against unwanted people'.[68] In both cases, this strategic use of hostile terrain has caused migrant deaths to increase.

These examples speak less to the materiality of territory than they do to the *supplementation* of a territory-view of place and power by a terrain-view. As the orthodox techniques of border control become less effective, the geophysical environment becomes increasingly significant in the projection of state power. If, as I am suggesting here, the Anthropocene heralds the waning significance of territory and the increasing relevance of terrain for political life, understanding what this shift entails is crucial. In this respect, as we noted above, the terrain prospect is ambivalent. On the one hand, terrain can be understood as sensitising us to new forms of attachment to place, land, atmosphere and the biogeochemical processes that constitute the earth system, transcending the 'bright lines' of territorial demarcation. On the other hand, however, the terrain prospect is deeply entwined with the militarisation of space and is often associated with strategies of domination, exclusion and legal exceptionalism. Notably, climate change has become fully integrated into almost every aspect of US Department of Defense strategic planning, illustrating how states' military powers are clearly readying themselves for the strategic challenges that the new climatic regime will inevitably bring.[69]

A contemporary illustration of how 'the terrain prospect' is tied to the militarisation of space is found in the dual projects of separation and occupation in the Occupied Palestinian Territories. As Eyal Weizman has convincingly shown in his study of Israel's 'architecture of occupation', settlement building, military control and resource allocation do not correspond to a unitary territorial rule but instead rely on fragmented, *ad hoc*, mobile claims over particular places of strategic or religious significance:

> Battlefield terms such as strongpoint, advance, penetration, encirclement, envelopment, control and supply lines, migrated from the military to the civilian sphere . . . The mobile home and later the small red-roofed single family house replaced the tank as the basic battle unit; homes, like armoured divisions, were deployed in formation across a theatre of operations to occupy hills, to encircle an enemy, to cut its communication lines.[70]

The mobilisation of a military vocabulary in this context only underscores the unique way that space is being apprehended here. There is a sensitivity to topographical variation, the distribution of material resources, and a knowledge of the situated capacities of human actors (settlers) to navigate and assume control over particular tracts of land. The unified, smooth spaces of territory and the geometric graticule of modern cartography are largely irrelevant. This mode of approaching space is nowhere clearer than in the construction of Israel's infamous 'security fence' (known as 'The Wall') that simultaneously works to surveil, enclose and exclude Arab communities in the West Bank. The Wall is a discontinuous and fragmented demarcation of a supposedly 'temporary' border, akin to a 'shifting frontier'[71] rather than a territorial 'bright line'. As Weizman suggests, 'the face of the territory has grown to resemble maps more redolent of Scandinavian coastlines, where fjords, islands and lakes make an inconclusive separation between water and land'.[72] Weizman's analogy with the angular coastlines of northern Europe should be taken quite seriously. More than creating a spectacle of plenary territorial power where in fact none exists,[73] The Wall indicates a more fundamental shift away from *territory* towards *terrain*, towards an articulation of place and power that is defined by the ability of political actors to exploit and defend a geophysical environment.

Weizman characterises the complexities of shifting, overlapping and 'temporary' claims to jurisdictional control in Palestine as constituting an 'elastic geography' where the stable linearity of the cartographic imaginary gives way to a splintered political geography where borders are 'dynamic, constantly shifting, ebbing and flowing'[74] in an effort to enclose Palestinian settlements. If 'elasticity' refers to the capacity of an object to return to its prior form having been distended, the political geographies of the Anthropocene would appear to be less *elastic* than they are *plastic*. Where elastic geographies of power can, in principle at least, return to the *status quo ante*, the plastic geographies of the Anthropocene offer no such consolation. Approaching the relation of place and power through the schema of terrain helps attune us to this changing reality and if, as I contend, the terrain prospect is likely to become increasingly significant as the stability of territorial claims fractures and shifts, becoming strangely serous as we endure coming climatic trans-formations, the legal and political strategies that accompany these changes ought to engender considerable concern. Indeed, the militarisation of space, the jealous protection of productive land, and the emergence of newly 'walled states', all evocatively depicted in John Lanchester's *The Wall*, are worryingly close to the bone.

Where Weizman's analysis concentrates on the itinerant frontiers of an occupying force, the Anthropocene requires that we contend with *peripatetic landforms*, alongside shifting legal and political claims over place. The new climatic regime promises the erosion and increasing indeterminacy of ter-ritorial borders as coastlines and other 'natural' features become increasingly mobile, affecting the distribution of productive land, freshwater supplies, aquifers, strategically significant outposts and so on. In the European Alps, for instance, melting glaciers are rewriting the territorial borders of states. Italy's border with Austria was originally defined by the location of the main Alpine drainage divide and subsequently given geometrically determined co-ordinates. The border, demarcated by physical markers since 1923, runs across glaciers that are now retreating with extraordinary speed. The drainage divide has moved in step with the glacier but the geometrically determined territo-rial line has remained in place. In order to address this changing reality, in 2005 the two states agreed a treaty acknowledging the existence of a 'moving border' that followed the drainage divide rather than the geometrically deter-mined 'bright line'.[75] Reminiscent of pre- or non-modern delimitations of political space, the border now corresponds to an ever shifting geophysical reality rather than co-ordinates that can be plotted within 'abstract space'. In order to trace this mobile border – which in places departs by hundreds of metres from the 1923 boundary – a team of architects and climate scientists mapped the glacial retreat through the installation of *in situ* sensing devices, reproducing their findings for an exhibition and a subsequent book. The *aesthetics* of this project are key to understanding the shifting reality that the team traced. Through a range of colour photographs, drawings, and data retrieved from remote sensing devices, a powerful account of a dynamic and indeterminate earth comes into view in a way that is utterly imperceptible within the aesthetics of modern mapping. In this way the team consciously situated themselves, and seek to situate their viewers and readers, *within* a mobile geophysical environment rather than as a viewer from the 'nowhere' of the cartographic gaze.

The 'terrain prospect' also seeks to describe modes of *political belonging* that transcend a territorial view of place and power. In order to explore this more generative aspect of the terrain prospect, I want to briefly turn to the Arctic where the mobile and indeterminate character of *ice* helps illustrate limitations of the aesthetics of territory in the context of a changing climate. The fact that the Arctic is, for most of the year, largely ice-covered poses a number of difficulties for states who make territorial claims in the region. Echoing Schmitt's famous division between a lawful land, subject of a so-called 'radical title', and a lawless sea, where no borders or lines of demarcation can be drawn, territory depends on a strict opposition between land and sea. Ice complicates this simply dichotomy. The ongoing territorial dispute between Canada, the USA and European states over the Northwest Passage – a route that promises to become increasingly significant for both strategic and commercial purposes as Arctic ice-cover continues to melt – illustrates the difficulties that ice poses to conventional modes of understanding place and power. In the eyes of international law, is ice land or sea; internal waters, enfolded within a sovereign territory, or beyond the reach of territory all together?

Canada now claims the Northwest Passage, which until 2009 was permanently frozen and treated 'just like the land',[76] as internal sovereign waters and therefore subject to its exclusive jurisdiction. The USA and others contend that the Passage ought to be treated as a continental strait and therefore open to international navigation, subject to the principles of the United Nations Convention on the Law of the Sea (UNCLOS). However, ice as a quasi-permanent, indeterminate geophysical feature subject to unique diurnal and seasonal patterns of change appears to directly challenge the spatial coding that informs either approach. If we presuppose sharp divisions between land and sea, internal water and the ocean, we are unable to grapple with the unique terrain of the region. Mapping the seabed, the delimitation of continental shelves, the planting of flags and the presence of weather stations have all been relied on in order to bolster sovereign claims in the Arctic. But these only emphasise the limited purchase that territorial sovereignty has in this context where the very materiality of the earth over which sovereignty is being asserted is itself constantly shifting, capable of fundamentally changing form – from land-like pack ice to open ocean, for example – with marked rapidity.

The distinct geophysical conditions in the Arctic prompt a number of technical challenges for international law and international relations. However, alongside the complexities that dog efforts to assert territorial control in the region, modes of governance and belonging that transcend sovereignty have also emerged. It is the development of a unique Arctic political imaginary that is particularly salient to the present discussion. Institutionalised within the Inuit Circumpolar Council (ICC), the Arctic

Council and other transnational groups, this Arctic imaginary purposefully foregrounds the *materiality* of the Arctic and the complex forms of place and power that cross territorial lines. The ICC, for instance, has emphasised how the dynamic places of the Arctic, which undergo dramatic seasonal transformations, require unique forms of pluralistic, transnational governance. And the Arctic Council, which comprises the eight Arctic states and recognises six institutions representing Inuit communities,[77] offers an indication of how the unique terrain that defines the region is a key mode through which political belonging is mediated and expressed. As Gerhart et al. comment, 'the Arctic Council's efficacy is dependent on recognising the Arctic as geophysically and sociopolitically distinct and on recognising that these two aspects of Arctic exceptionalism are linked'.[78] In this way the Council seeks to institutionalise a form of attachment to place which is primarily a matter of shared geophysical conditions rather than ethnic, national or linguistic identification. Central to this approach is an insistence on the complexity of Arctic materialities that cannot be reduced to a simplistic land/sea binary; contiguous territories are replaced by pluralistic, layered forms of political identity:

> Degrees and spaces of jurisdiction are downplayed in favour of the actual interactions between the various parties who maintain specific interests in the region, a phenomenon that also can be seen in other regional cooperative arrangements . . . [such as those which] allow Saami to travel freely between Norway, Sweden and Finland and intermittent proposals to allow free travel of indigenous peoples across the Bering Strait.[79]

What these practices and proposals suggest is the capacity for peoples living and working in indeterminate and dynamic geophysical terrain to code their political attachments through spatial categories other than territory. Forms of co-operation, solidarity and identity are mediated through a shared understanding of the terrain and the material interactions (the 'affective geometry') of human and non-human actors within the region. A key element of this Arctic imaginary consists in foregrounding the multiplicity of agencies, material forms and the human and non-human subjects entangled within them, ahead of the smooth spaces associated with sovereign space. As Gerhart et al. comment, the flattened ontology implied by the Arctic imaginary – where both non-human and human actors are all given their due – insists that political life does not begin and end with territorial division and the qualities of statehood. This 'challenges not just the ideal of the sovereign state with boundaries that are fixed in time and space . . . but also the modern notion of a world that is divided into distinct societies'.[80] In this way, the Arctic imaginary perceives a radically different world to that which is installed and policed by the aesthetics of sovereignty, one that is attuned to the particularities of our earthbound conditions.

We must be careful not to overstate the case. The Arctic Council has a limited mandate, restricted to environmental protection and sustainable development in the region. This has largely taken the form of commissioning and disseminating scientific research on climate change and biodiversity that then feeds into policy formation within member states. Indigenous groups, though recognised as 'permanent participants', are not given the same rights as member states, emphasising the continuing dominance of state power in this context. And the Council cannot legally bind its members as it is only able to use 'soft law' initiatives like offering best practice guidelines and outlining broad policy agendas. Furthermore, the innovative, transnational elements within Arctic governance might very well give way to traditional state interests as climatic change further disrupts the geopolitical reality of the region, prompting greater security and strategic concerns.[81] Nonetheless, the evolving governance practices in the Arctic illustrate the limitations of territory as a means of theorising place and power in the context of complex and changeable geophysical environments, and also illustrate how forms of formal and informal association are able to emerge through the recognition of shared geophysical situatedness.

The generative possibilities of generalising this mode of apprehending place and power were brought home to me by Fintan O'Toole, one of the most insightful commentators on the cultural and constitutional crises that have beset the United Kingdom since the Brexit referendum of 2016. Reflecting on the particular challenges that Brexit poses to political identity in Northern Ireland – where the imposition of a hard border between the Irish Republic and the North would have a devastating effect on the fragile peace settlement there – O'Toole notes the importance of fostering non-territorial forms of political belonging. In the context of an increasingly fetishised notion of British territorial integrity confronting the reality of newly robust assertions of English, Scottish and Welsh identities, O'Toole encourages us to re-pose these questions of belonging as a matter of *sharing space within this collection of islands*.[82] This subtle shift away from viewing the complexities of British nationhood and the civic institutions that mediate (or fail to mediate) a sense of political community, towards the question of *geophysical placement* – a concern with how those living within the British Isles share the space of their archipelago-home, the multiply folded, material reality of this place and the affective geometries which define its residents' lives – offers a very different mode of approaching the politics of place in this context. This is partly because this approach emphasises the *networks of dependence* that situate subjects in place and draws attention to the obligations that such networks imply, rather than the more abstract forms of belonging mediated by a language of citizenship rights. Of course, this is not going to solve the multifarious puzzles that attach to Brexit with the vexed questions of national and regional identity; undoubtedly the niceties of territorial delimitation remaining important issues. But O'Toole's foregrounding of the material entanglements that define this collection of islands and the actual interactions between the various parties that have specific interests in the region offers a glimpse of how the terrain prospect can help imagine political allegiance and belonging differently, where the abstractions of territory, and concomitant forms of legal subjectivity, give way to an altered political aesthetic that is sensitive to the situated complexity of material, geophysical and localised forms of attachment to place.

Towards an Earthly Politics

The political spaces that have defined – or at least have sought to define – our political attachments and *ethoi* in the course of modernity are losing their capacity to meaningfully locate subjects in space and time. In this way the Anthropocene accelerates processes that have been under way since at least the middle of the last century as the nation state has become increasingly challenged by globalised governance regimes, and the ease of transnational communication and commerce began to break down the ligaments that tie subjects to the largely taken for granted, nation-state ordering of place and power. If we are to return our politics to the earth and refocus our attention on the conditions of habitability that sustain community, the ways in which we *see, sense, represent, mediate* and *feel* that earth – in short, the political aesthetics we adopt – must be fundamentally reconceived. The exploration of terrain in this chapter ultimately urges a reassessment of the 'geo' that frames our sense of the 'geopolitical'. If geopolitics is primarily understood as the relation between territorially defined nation states, set against the horizon of an 'international' or 'global' community of states, the Anthropocene requires a different approach in which the materiality of the earth, its volumetric dimensions, its multiple temporalities and the affective geometry of the agencies that define place all become integral to contemporary (geo)politics. In this way, the terrain prospect helps recode 'geopolitics' as an *earthly politics* in which the complexities of our earthbound condition are at its heart. As we have seen, this mode of apprehending place can be associated with the securitisation and militarisation of space. But so too does the terrain prospect encourage alternative modes by which we become sensitive to the particularities of our geophysical environment and the forces and relations that increasingly define the contours of political community in our climatically uncertain times.

Such an earthly politics makes the abstractions of territory appear at best outmoded, at worst naïve. Nonetheless, territorial disputes and the importance of territorially defined citizenship are not going anywhere soon. These modes of apprehending and ordering social relations are deeply embedded in our sense of the (geo)political. The Anthropocene thesis suggests that territorial claims will increasingly be confronted by a range of earthly forces that territory constitutively ignores. This will see the interruption and complexification of territoriality and the disputes it engenders; to which the shifting ice floes of the Arctic and the Alps testify. At the aesthetic register, the challenge is perhaps greater. There is no affective imaginary of *terrain* in the same way that modern sovereignty has created a political imaginary built around *territory*. As changes to mapping and the nature of political power in early modernity suggest, the aesthetic will play a crucial role in any such transformation. In this sense, there is much work to be done at the symbolic and aesthetic registers if we are to reattune our political sensibilities to these earthly forces that the Anthropocene has pushed into social life. It is hoped that these reflections on the terrain prospect at least offer some sense of towards what this reimagination of place and power might be directed.

It should be noted in conclusion that a politics that foregrounds the earth, place, belonging and local attachment has a deeply compromised heritage, associated with 'blood and soil' nationalisms and a range of politically suspect thinkers – Heidegger and Schmitt perhaps chief among them.[83] The forms of attachment and belonging articulated here, I hope it is clear, are inimical to any such nationalism or localism of old. Terrain can never refer to some autochthonous lump of land over which a community can assert a supposedly 'natural' claim to legitimate occupation. Tracts of terrain, like the lifeforms that are enfolded within them, are mobile, dynamic and processual, always in states of becoming and therefore always necessitating ongoing negotiations amongst those who live in relation to them.

The recent resurgence of nationalism around the globe offers a very different form of 'place-centred' thinking which is far more readily associated with the fetishisation of territorial borders and the abstractions of citizenship than it is with attending to the complexities of geophysical and ecological entanglement. If the contemporary nationalist seeks to reassert the importance of their rights to a 'homeland' in the context of a globalised economy and an increasingly mobile global population, the terrain prospect seeks to foreground those bonds of attachment that persist beneath or prior to the bundle of rights that we commonly associate with citizenship. This aims to emphasise how political subjects and communities are bound to a dynamic geophysical reality, which is subject to various forms of reformation and change. This in itself challenges our sense of 'home', which is traditionally tied to a sense of *permanence* but today perhaps needs to be reimagined. The terrain prospect offers a corrective to the increasingly abstract notions of belonging that define globalism, forcing citizens of the 'global village' – a place that no one has ever visited – to answer some potentially unsettling questions. If the bonds of nationhood and sovereignty no longer mediate your attachments to place and define the ligaments that tie you in community, then to what, precisely, are you attached? What terrain do you occupy, in what atmospheric milieu are you immersed, and against what do your political institutions purport to offer protection? The terrain prospect aims to provide some co-ordinates that might organise a response and highlight some of the dangers that lurk within these questions. If, as Sloterdijk contends, being an adult consists in 'refusing to seek stability in the unstable',[84] we might think of the terrain prospect as gesturing towards a political aesthetics that at least aspires to maturity.

4

People

Are we Greeks? Are we Jews? But who we?
        – Jacques Derrida, *Writing and Difference*[1]

In August 2014 I moved to Hong Kong and was confronted on arrival by steamy tropical heat and an ensuing political storm that culminated in a seventy-nine-day occupation of streets and highways in the commercial and administrative districts of the city. This pro-democracy campaign sought to establish 'genuine universal suffrage' for the election of the Hong Kong Chief Executive. The mass mobilisation of tens of thousands of highly organised, non-violent, mostly young people in a city often characterised as little more than a shrine to Mammon drew the attention of the global media. At the time it was the biggest political mobilisation since the end of colonial rule in 1997.[2] The 'Umbrella Movement' – named after the umbrellas that protesters used to fend off police baton charges, tear gas and pepper spray, transforming an everyday item into an unlikely symbol of resistance – turned on a set of questions and tensions concerning the status of 'the people'. The Umbrella Movement, perhaps above all else, put in question the sense and direction of *the people of Hong Kong*: 'Are we Chinese? Are we Hongkongers? But who we?'

The movement resisted Beijing-backed reforms which, though intent on introducing universal suffrage for the Chief Executive for the first time in the territory's history, insisted on vetting candidates for the role ahead of any vote in order to ensure that any 'unpatriotic' elements could not find their way onto the ballot paper. This circumscribed form of democracy made clear the limited powers that 'the people of Hong Kong' were to be afforded in the context of 'one country, two systems'. Indeed, the 'Hong Kong people' have an ambiguous status within the Chinese constitutional settlement. From the perspective of the Chinese state 'the people', understood as an expression of popular sovereignty, can only be understood by reference to the state itself. As the constitution makes clear, 'all power in the People's Republic of China belongs to the people' but this power is exclusively exercised through the

National People's Congress.[3] There is no reference to 'Hong Kong people' in the Basic Law – the territory's 'mini-constitution' – which refers only to the rights and freedoms of 'residents'. The Beijing-sponsored reforms make this position absolutely clear: democratic procedures are conscionable only if the *Chinese people*, as constituted within the National People's Congress, has ultimate control over their operation.

The Umbrella Movement first argued for and then acted out, through democratically ordered assemblies and occupations, a very different interpretation of the meaning and status of 'Hong Kong people'. The assemblies temporarily created – within nothing but flyovers, commercial highstreets and highways – thriving civic squares in the city, replete with public meetings, study zones, artworks and food stalls. By insisting that 'one person one vote' alone was an inadequate reform and demanding, instead, the ability to nominate whomsoever they wished to represent the people of Hong Kong, irrespective of their palatability to the authorities in Beijing, the campaign insisted that political power was not reducible to 'the people' qua constituted power but must be understood as being held by the people of Hong Kong as a whole, an 'imagined community' to which all Hongkongers belong. Political power, the movement sought to make clear, is held, in principle at least, by *everyone* within the territory, neither exclusively mediated by nor entirely exhausted in the apparatuses of the Chinese state. For those heady seventy-nine days during which the Umbrella Movement took control of the centre of the city, a sense of popular sovereignty appeared to have been loosed from its confinement in representative and juridical structures: *a people in excess of 'the people'* assembled in homemade public spaces and enacted the meaning of democratic community. This was a people that was unauthorised but emergent, uncompromisingly *present* within the city but as yet *absent* from the juridical order; it articulated the claims of 'a people that was not . . . yet'.[4]

As was clear from Beijing's intransigence on the matter, all this was utterly inimical to the regime, which in a quintessentially totalitarian mode, insisted that the power of 'the people' is wholly subsumed within the Chinese Communist Party (CCP) and Chinese state institutions. 'Genuine universal suffrage' would have introduced – within Hong Kong at least – a dialectic between 'the people' qua constituted power and 'the people' qua constituent power, which is an essential element of any democratic order. Genuine democratic reform, even in an arguably limited, liberal and representative mode, would release political power from its confinement within its existing constitutional structures and, by embracing what Claude Lefort calls the 'empty place'[5] of democratic power, ensure that political power could never be fully exhausted by those who exercise it. To let political power slip from its grasp in this way was perceived to be an existential threat to both the power of the Party and the integrity of the state.

These disputations over the nature and status of 'the people' in Hong Kong are part of a wider questioning of this hugely significant term for law and politics in the contemporary moment. Bruno Latour has commented on a renewed condition of 'demogenesis' in the current conjuncture in which social movements that once took place *within* more or less clearly defined 'nations' or 'peoples' are today raising the question of peoplehood itself:

> Ta-Nehisi Coates made the provocative remark that Trump is the first white president – of course all the presidents before (except one) were white, but they did not claim to be the head of a United States made by and for white supremacists. So here we seize on the spot the refabrication of a people out of what was a vastly more complex assembly of Americans. And of course against other people who suddenly have to realize that they too have to define themselves as a people. It is very clear also in the realization by Europeans, suddenly abandoned by England [sic] and the US, that they have to redesign themselves as a people – but which one? Not a modernist one, not a universal one, not a national one?[6]

If we do live in period of demogenesis where the taken for granted existence of 'peoples' is being subject to renewed scrutiny and critique, it is also clearly true that 'old' national peoplehood has not gone away. In her 2016 address to the British Conservative Party, then Prime Minister Theresa May made a distinction between 'the people from somewhere and the people from nowhere', suggesting that the so-called 'global citizen' did not understand the meaning of national citizenship.[7] Similarly, the Brexit campaign insisted that the British people should to 'take back control' from the lofty cosmopolitans of Brussels, making a broadly populist assertion of the righteous return of an autochthonous 'people' in contradistinction to a transnational and flighty 'elite'. Whether in the patrician totalitarianism of the Chinese Communist Party; the democratic ambitions of the Umbrella Movement; the reflux of national populism in Britain and the United States; or the continuing search for an elusively cosmopolitan 'people of Europe', it is clear that 'the people' continues to structure our sense of the political, functioning as an *a priori* that predetermines the nature and ambitions of modern politics: *politics is of, for and by the people*. Of course it is! What else would it be about?

It was with the great upheavals of the eighteenth century that the people came to function as this prime political mover. In the Western tradition at least, its origins lie in medieval thought where 'the people' was understood to act as something of a 'reserve power' in the context of kingship: in many contexts representatives of the people were consulted by the prince in the course of his governance or, in a nonetheless ambiguous sense, the people's 'consent' was often deemed necessary to justify monarchical rule.[8] Similarly, many medieval scholars endorsed the principle of 'escheat' or 'reversion' which held that power was to be held by the people if no rightful ruler was in office, suggesting that the people functioned as the ultimate backstop to temporal authority.[9] As signalled by the seminal declarations of the late eighteenth century, the people came to take a central role as a *political actor* – in the form of popular government – not simply a kind of 'backstop' that guarded against the threat of tyranny. At the heart of this transformation from 'reserve' to 'actual' power is an Enlightenment commitment to human freedom and the promise of progress. A politics built on 'the people', rather than a natural or divinely created order, holds out a belief in the capacity for human beings to collaborate and institutionalise in an effort to make their own history, to rise above those 'natural attachments' that bind the human in various forms of servitude and indignity and, on the basis of a supposedly universal rationality, create a social world that is the product of and answers to expressly *human* needs and aspirations alone.

But the Anthropocene puts in question the enduring force of this Enlightenment – and decidedly anthropocentric – rendering of legitimacy. In a context in which human action has shown itself capable of disturbing the earth system's basic functioning and when continued human habitation of the planet requires an understanding the constitutive relations between human societies and a range of putatively 'natural' forces, systems and pro-cesses, should 'the people' continue to play a defining role in structuring our sense of the political? If we live in a time of demogenesis in which rival senses of the people are circulating, how might we render the people in a way that is sensitive to the realities of climatic transformation and the complex entanglements across national borders, not to mention between human and non-human life, that define our current condition? At first blush there appear to be two divergent responses to these questions.

On the one hand, we might argue that 'the people' has never been more important. Underlying the ambition of popular sovereignty is the belief in the power of collective human action to shape its own destiny. In this sense, the Anthropocene might be understood to confirm the power that modern 'peoples' have conferred on themselves: collective human action *has* remade the world, in a deep, geological sense. The political challenge in this respect might be understood to be a matter of harnessing and redirecting this power in order to get out of the crisis that we have created. In this respect, mobilis-ing 'the people' to take radical action in curbing emissions and greening the economy is precisely the kind of ambition that is required in this context. It is clear that the decisions that extant legal and political institutions will make

– acting in the name and through the purported 'will of the people' – in the coming decade or so will profoundly shape the nature of planet for thousands of years to come. Is there any greater proof that it is *people* and the institutions that marshal anthropic power – rather than some 'natural order' – that will shape the planet's destiny in the new climatic regime? As Clive Hamilton argues, the Anthropocene shows the modern myths of anthropocentricism have become all too true; and confronting this truth is precisely what political responsibility in the face of the climate crisis entails.[10] In this respect, reinjecting 'the people' with a renewed sense of purpose, responsibility and power might be considered essential if we are to both recognise and deal with the challenges that the Anthropocene names.

On the other hand, we might argue that the anthropocentricism and human exceptionalism that underpins 'the people', and the political thinking that it inspires, is precisely the problem that got us into this mess. After all, the Anthropocene shows that collective human action does not lord over the natural order and shape it as it wills, but is deeply *enmeshed* or *entangled* with a range of non-human forces that constitutively *limit* the capacity that any 'people' has to act. In this way, asserting the autonomy and supremacy of 'the people' as either the ultimate ground or the horizon of possibility for political life is woefully inappropriate; we therefore might have to finally give up on the fantasy that, unlike all other lifeforms on earth, 'humanity alone is not a spatial and temporal web of interspecies dependencies'.[11] It is precisely the forces that traverse the human and the non-human, the biotic and abiotic, that have shown themselves to be shaping the possibilities of collective action in the new climatic regime. In this way, we might approach the Anthropocene as opening new and radical possibilities within our prevailing sense of what constitutes the political, which is no longer considered to be an exclusively *human* affair but one which must place *non-human* actors as an integral aspect of any account of a 'political community'. Could we, in this way, construe the current moment as analogous to the transformations of the eighteenth century in which the monarch's authority was superseded by 'the people'? Today it perhaps 'the people' who must give way to a new constellation of forces in which human agency is but one actor amongst a range non-human 'counterforces'[12] that are redefining the very meaning of associative life.

These two trajectories are not mutually exclusive but *aporetic*, pointing to a conceptual impasse or blockage thrown up by the changed ontological foundations that the Anthropocene thesis describes, whereby the human is simultaneously aggrandised and humbled. Clearly, the state – and the demands made of those who seek to govern in the name of 'the people' of a given nation – is not about to wither away; and popular sovereignty continues to animate political passions and demands. But surely we cannot leave 'the people' untouched in its modernist formation which presupposes a hard binary between nature/culture and is associated with mythologies of progress and human freedom that the Anthropocene, and its various entailments, directly challenges. In this sense, I argue that the new climatic regime urges us to grasp 'the people' in an entirely new light, to begin to think its meaning and potentiality along radically different lines, lines that are nonetheless indebted to the traditions of democratic thought and practice. In this respect, Lefort's invocation of the 'empty place' of political power will be something of a guiding thread through this discussion as it reminds us that there is, by definition, an open potentiality at the heart of the democratic form, a sense that the occupation of the subject position of 'the people' always entails a risk or a wager that opens the possibility of something other than the *status quo*. In this sense, I continue to hold out some promise for 'the people' as a lodestar for a new political thinking in the Anthropocene.

Drawing on Donna Haraway, I suggest one avenue for reimagining the people through the heuristic of 'sympoiesis'. This allows us to explore the contours of a collective political subject that has sense only by virtue of its 'making-with' fellow earthbound critters as well as the geological forms and systems that allow for the flourishing of life. My concerns here are directed towards the *aesthetic* transformation that this kind of thinking entails, attending to the ways in which we might be rendered newly sensitive to a range of forces to which prevailing theories of popular sovereignty constitutively inure us. As is clear from the transfer of sovereignty from a monarchical to a popular form in the eighteenth and nineteenth centuries, institutional change requires a profound shift in the collective imaginary brought on by both political action and a range of aesthetic practices which can overturn the existing 'distribution of the sensible'. What I seek to examine in the latter stages of this chapter, then, is the meaning of a similar shift to the imaginary prompted by our Anthropocenic present. This involves challenging a pattern of thought which has been at the heart of Western culture, in which the properly 'human' is defined in opposition to an 'animal' other. As Haraway and others have argued, the emergence of new political possibilities at the dusk of modernity will be possible only if we challenge this largely taken for granted division of lifeforms into a 'human/animal' binary. Influential accounts of the biopolitical rendering of sovereignty in late modernity continue to work within this limited frame in which a 'politics of life' is largely understood to consist in powers that work to control *the human* alone. But the Anthropocene calls on us to radically expand our range of reference and attend to those non-human actors – both biotic and abiotic – that constitute the conditions of possibility for the continued habitation of the earth. In this way, the challenge of demogenesis that I examine in this chapter consists in articulating the sense of a 'people' that no longer relies on a mode of thinking in which the human is radically divorced from the non-human (animal or abiotic) but bears an inhuman trace within its very mode of appearance.

Before picking up this thread, I begin by returning to the modernist rendering of 'the people' and examine the aesthetic dimensions of popular sovereignty. This allows us to explore how popular sovereignty comes to be installed deep within our social and political imaginaries, making any effort to think the political otherwise – as indeed, I suggest, the Anthropocene requires us to do – incredibly challenging. The prototypical event which captures the transfer from monarchical to popular sovereignty is *the declaration* in which 'the people' appear for the first time as the legitimate authority that grounds the legal and political order. Here we look at this founding moment as a specifically 'juris-dictional' act, a moment when the law is spoken and, through the 'magic' of a performative speech act, a new civic order and subject of power is created. If in previous discussions of mapping and cartography we foregrounded the visual regime that modern mapping installs, in this context I am concerned less with the *visual* than I am with the *fictions* that help give popular sovereignty its sought-after effects. In this sense, it is the *as if*, the fictional or the consciously false, that lies at the heart of modern articulations of popular sovereignty. But as we examine below, the fictions and mythologies that animate political power are not merely symbolic or imaginary 'add-ons' to a material substrate but are operative at somatic and affective registers that foreground the embodied reality of political actors. In this way, I explore how the fictional and aesthetic dimensions of power are played out within what Eric Santner calls the 'flesh' of political subjects. This effort to connect the fictional and the fabulous with the corporeal and the affective offers some guidance for the kind of shift in our political aesthetics that, I suggest, the Anthropocene demands.

The Aesthetics of Popular Sovereignty

In his celebrated study of 'the king's two bodies', Ernst Kantorowicz traces the genealogy of a legal fiction that was central to the articulation of medieval and early Renaissance kingship. The doctrine of the two bodies holds that the monarch bears within himself a kind of doppelganger. Like every human being, the monarch's body is a *body natural*, subject to the infirmities of health and accident, infancy, old age and death. But unlike his subjects, the king is held to have a second, supernatural body, a *body politic* which, in Edmund Plowden's words, 'could not be seen or handled . . . [a body] utterly void of Infancy, and old Age, and other natural Defects and Imbecilities'.[13] Crucially the doctrine of the 'two bodies' allows for the reproduction of social relations and hierarchies of power by ensuring the continuity of kingship across time. Though the king's *body natural* withers and dies, the *body politic* lives forever; and succession is guaranteed through this device. These 'two bodies' – though giving rise to separable functions, as the theory of monarchical succession underscores – were nonetheless fused within the body of the monarch, considered to be separable only when the body natural died. As Plowden describes it, '[the king] has not a Body natural distinct and divided by itself from the Office and Dignity royal, *but a Body natural and a Body politic together indivisible*'.[14] In this sense, the supernatural or immaterial element of kingship – that transcendent quality that implies the monarch's participation in an eternal world underwritten by divine command – is inscribed within the fleshy reality of the king. The monarch, therefore, is thought quite literally to *embody* a transcendent quality in precisely the same way that the Christian church holds that Christ is the embodiment of God.

As Kantorowicz makes clear, the commingling of the material and immaterial; immanent and transcendent; somatic and symbolic is key to understanding the mediating role that the monarch played within social life. The king's body is the vehicle through which an imagined polity (in which individual parts are united into an abstract whole) can be made real: the transcendent body of the king, in which a mere man is made *more than human*, allows for an abstract bond to the realm to be materialised. Kantorowicz famously dramatises this argument at the opening of his study by reading Shakespeare's *Richard II* as a 'tragedy of the two bodies'. As Kantorowicz argues, the power of Shakespeare's drama consists in revealing how the symbolic, mythological and fictional accoutrements that accompany kingship are themselves written into the body of the king. This is what makes Richard's fall in Act IV, where he 'un-kings'[15] himself at the feet of Henry Bolingbroke, so affecting. In his newly humbled state, no longer adorned with the garbs of monarchy, Richard struggles to make sense of his own visage: 'Was this face the face / That every day under his household roof / Did keep ten thousand men?'[16] The king's supernatural *body politic*, once fused with the *body natural* in a way that beguiles his followers,[17] is, after Richard's inverse rite of de-crowning, rendered abject and barely recognisable. Rather than merely describing a disruption to the symbolic carapace of kingship, Richard's tragedy, in which he is forced to give up his kingly authority, is marked by a transformation within Richard's own body, giving rise to both a semiotic and a somatic degradation in which a man who was once in touch with the divine enters into a new relation to the sub- or barely human.

Eric Santner picks up these themes by seeking to understand what happens to this excessive, supernatural dimension inscribed within the king's body in the wake of the great transformations to public life brought about at the end of the eighteenth century.[18] The commingling of the semiotic and the somatic that was peculiar to medieval kingship – a marriage that was made possible through 'various rituals, legal and theological doctrines, and literary and social fantasies surrounding the monarch's singular physiology'[19] – participates, in Santner's terminology, in an economy of the 'flesh'. Santner describes 'flesh' as that excessive, symbolic and transcendent quality that was evoked within the body of the king. 'Flesh', he says, 'is the bit of the real that underwrites the circulation of signs and values',[20] it is a sublime excess, made real within a somatic presence. Santner refers to this as a 'surplus of imma-nence' in which the body can become either sublime or potentially abject, as indeed Richard does in his 'un-kinged' state at the close of Shakespeare's play. Santner argues that as sovereignty is transferred from a monarchi-cal to a popular form, those who are excluded from the dignities that are supposedly dispersed amongst the population as a whole – prototypically, the stateless but more generally the marginalised, dispossessed or excluded who have no power to shape or speak in the name of the body politic – are increasingly rendered as *abject bodies* that are understood to be less than fully human. Santner calls this 'a kind of negative or abyssal sublime' which is the shadow of that new-found power that has been conferred on the population at large.[21]

Santner's account of the 'flesh' is closely related to our doubled account of *aesthetics* that informs our approach to sovereignty. As we have described it, the aesthetics of sovereignty – that is, the aesthetic techniques through which sovereignty appears – also engages the question of *aesthesis*, the affective and somatic quality that *moves* subjects in often unexpected ways, structuring power at affective and somatic registers. In this way, Santner's 'flesh' points to sovereignty's aesthetic functioning, tying the affective, material and corporeal power of sovereignty to the fictional, symbolic and iconographic regimes which are central to its mode of appearance. With the end of monarchical kingship and the emergence of modern political forms throughout the late eighteenth and nineteenth centuries, what happens to the vicissitudes of 'flesh' that were once so central to binding subjects to kingly authority? Put differently, what happens to sovereignty's aesthetic dimensions when sovereignty becomes popular?

An orthodox response might be to say that this mysterious fleshy-affective-aesthetic dimension is precisely what the 'rationalisation' of the political sphere in the wake of the bourgeois revolutions worked to achieve. In lieu of the sacramental, mythic and spectacular presentations of pre-modern sov-ereignty comes recognisably modern, and purposively disenchanted, modes by which political authority is legitimated and performed. If, as Kantorowicz describes it, the supernatural *body politic* – taking form within the 'sublime flesh' of the king – was crucial to binding subjects to public authority, these mystical devices are displaced in modernity by more prosaic matters like the administration of citizenship and the technicalities of representative democracy. This trajectory might be seen to culminate in the Habermasian public sphere, constituted by 'rational discourse', in which sovereignty, shorn of spectacular and transcendent qualities, is reduced to little more than a set of 'procedures' which allow for a 'popular voice' to emerge.[22] However, as I have already argued, the aesthetic aspects of sovereignty – in terms of both its modes of appearance and the collective imaginary that it installs – remains crucial to understanding sovereignty's enduring force in the contemporary moment. And this is particularly true of discourses of popular sovereignty. As Edmund Morgan suggests, the notion that sovereignty is vested in the people as a whole

> is a much more complicated, one might say more fictional, fiction than the divine right of kings. A king, however dubious his authority might seem, did not have to be imagined. He was a visible presence, wearing his crown and carrying his sceptre. The people, on the other hand, are never visible as such. Before we ascribe sovereignty to the people, we have to imagine that there is such a thing, something we personify as though it were a single body, capable of thinking, of acting, of making decisions and carrying them out.[23]

It is precisely this fictional element that allows the people to appear *as if* rational, unified and agentic that I want to examine here. In Santner's own analysis, the affective-aesthetic supplement to the king's body is traced through to its re-emergence in biopolitical techniques of governance and control where a set of co-ordinated powers – governmental and otherwise – are directed towards 'the caretaking of the sublime (but also potentially abject) flesh of the new bearer of the principle of sovereignty, the People'.[24] In the efforts to measure, glorify, sculpt and test the health, well-being and fitness of bodies and populations, Santner argues that we can see an enduring power of the aesthetic, 'fleshy' dimension, which undergirded kingship's power but is now dispersed amongst the general populace. My aim is to supplement Santner's analysis by suggesting that we can understand the shifting dynamics of the 'flesh', in which bodies are rendered variously abject or sublime, through an attention to the moment of popular sovereignty's appearance in the declarative act that founds a political order. I approach this as a specifically 'juris-dictional' moment when a community comes to presence and speaks in the name of the law.

Juris-diction: Declaring the Law

Etymologically, jurisdiction connects law (*ius*) and speech (*dicere*). This can be understood to refer to moments of law's commencement in an act of constitution-making, in a moment of judgment or in the decision which determines the forum in which a case is to be heard. In all cases, what is at stake in this 'juris-diction' is the conjoining and articulation of *the general* and *the particular*: generally applicable rules are brought to bear on the particular case that falls before the court; or the particular assembly that drafts the constitution or declaration of independence speaks on behalf of the general will of the people. In Costas Douzinas's account of the 'metaphysics of jurisdiction' it is this hinge between the universal and the particular – and so too the performative and the constative modes of speech – which gives jurisdiction its sought-after effects.[25] The declarative act that founds a political community is Douzinas's key point of reference as it dramatises the dynamics that he identifies underpinning all jurisdictional pronouncements. In the celebrated form of the declaration that founds a new political order, the authors are taken to be 'we the people'. As Douzinas argues, what is at stake here is the elision between two distinct speaking positions: the *subject of enunciation* and the *subject of statement*. This distinction is best known in literary studies through which we can distinguish between the author who pens the words of a novel (the subject of enunciation) and the narrator who tells the story (the subject of statement). In the context of a founding declarative act, the subject of enunciation refers to the constitutional assembly, the authors or drafters of the declaration itself and the subject of statement is 'attributed to a totally different subject: God, humanity, or the people'.[26] The moment of declaration, the unrepeatable and singular *event* in which the people speak and in so doing create a new constitutional settlement, depends on an elision between these two registers: 'the particular and the universal are rolled together, as are the different subjects of enunciation and statement'.[27]

    In order for this elision to be successful, the imaginative and the fictional necessarily enter the scene: what has to be figured and imagined is a single speaking body, a unified and popular will expressed through the voice of the body politic which can play the role once fulfilled by the monarch in mediating the general and the particular, binding subjects to public authority. But as we noted above, the imaginative work required in this respect is all the more intense than that required in the monarchical mode where the king as *juris-dictator* can at least appear in his sublime presence. With the shift to *popular* sovereignty, as Derrida comments in reference to the American Declaration of Independence, the juris-dictator can only appear *as if*, in a fictional and imaginative mode where 'the people' are rendered as a device or contrivance which can channel popular power.[28] As Douzinas comments,

> the configuration of individual and universal creates a body politic which mirrors the individuality of the *juris-dictator* (he who speaks the law), a unified body, which while plural and therefore silent, wills the law singularly and speaks through its foil and representative, the sovereign, legislator or judge.[29]

In the moment of foundation, then, the fiction of the people's singular and unified voice allows for everyone to participate in the sublime act of lawmaking: for a moment we all become kingly, granted an excessive power beyond our limited and merely human station: *vox populi, vox Dei*. The excessive, aesthetic, 'fleshy' power that was part and parcel of the dignities that attached to the monarch finds a new mode of expression with the onset of popular sovereignty, with the fictional appearance of the people allowing individuals to participate in the plenary authority of the newly created order. We can think of the declarative act that founds a new order as the obverse of the state of exception where the law is temporally suspended in an effort to protect and sustain that order. The state of exception produces a legal void where the symbolic order that confers the human with a qualified, political existence is suspended and political power is able to work on a *bare life*, stripped of the dignities and protections that are the supposed guarantee of the political order.[30] The declarative act that founds the political order is the obverse of this anomic space: it allows the human to touch the sublime, participating in a register that was once reserved for the divinely ordained monarch alone.

Clearly, the people is not exhausted in the moment of foundation but continues to play a role within the modern democratic order, at the very minimum through some form of democratic participation. How should we understand the enduring significance of the people, qua constituent power, once its role in constituting a new order has been discharged? This returns us to what Lefort calls the 'empty place' of political power, created by the transition from monarchical to popular rule:

> The legitimacy of power is based on the people; but the image of popular sovereignty is linked to an empty place, impossible to occupy, such that those who exercise public authority can never claim to appropriate it. Democracy combines these two apparently contradictory principles: on the one hand, power emanates from the people; on the other, it is the power of nobody.[31]

As Lefort describes it, given that political authority emanates from the people, it can never be exhausted through its institutionalisation, making the actual seat of power always empty: those that occupy the offices of government can never fully actualise this power, which is always held in reserve by the people, imagined as a whole. In this way, there is an 'unresolved dialectic of determinacy and indeterminacy, of closure and openness'[32] at the heart of modern constitutionalism. This dialectic turns on the fact that the political sphere is founded in the name of a people understood as a unity, not a particular subset of people or a party, but *everyone* within a given community. This assertion of a plenary popular power can only ever be 'virtual' or 'symbolic' and therefore must be instituted within a constitutional order that seeks to actualise its promise. It is precisely a tension between a symbolic equality of power amongst all and the actualisation of that power in a hierarchy of ruler-and-ruled that ensures the enduring relevance of constituent power after the moment of foundation. The people is internally divided between its symbolic and institutionalised aspects, and this fissure, as Jacques Rancière reminds us, is not 'a scandal to be deplored . . . [but] is the primary condition of the exercise of [democratic] politics'.[33]

The 'emptiness' at the heart of political power, which modern discourses of popular sovereignty elaborate, has two implications. Firstly, constituted power produces an 'empty place' in the sense that the people can only ever rule *indirectly*. If the relatively small cabal who wield governmental power claim not to *represent* the people or *speak on their behalf* but to actually *be* the people, then the dialectical play at the heart of popular sovereignty is lost. The closure of that open space, where the nature of the people is apparently settled once and for all through its subsumption into 'the leader' or 'the party', is, as Loughlin suggests, the 'hallmark of totalitarianism'.[34]

The second implication of Lefort's 'emptiness' turns on the imagined unity of the people that – so theories of popular sovereignty contend – is the agent of political change, capable of dis-establishing and re-establishing a political institution. The difficulty with this conception of the people's *constituent* or *constituting* power lies in ascribing it any settled content. What is the nature of the bond that binds a people in a form of community *prior to* the foundation of the state? As Bernard Yack has argued, nationhood as a form of attachment and belonging built around a shared symbolic economy and sense of history is the most obvious and potent candidate capable of filling the 'empty space' that the pre-political 'people' evokes.[35] It is *national bonds* of belonging that allow us to conceive of a people that both *precedes* and *exceeds* the particular rendering of 'the people' given within the constituted order. For Yack, this means that nationalism will always accompany popular sovereignty if we subscribe to this theory of state legitimacy. Whether we endorse Yack's conclusions or not, it is clear that the substantive content of the people (qua constituent power) cannot be determined without referring to some form of community, mode of belonging or a communal bond that transcends 'the people' as it is rendered within existing state structures. And this is the question that *demogenesis* poses: are there forms of collective attachment and identity that both have a latent power within the collective imaginary and exceed the state's rendering of the people in a given constitutional form? Latour's contention that we live in a time of demogenesis holds open the possibility that, despite its institutionalisation within forms of constituted power, some other avatar or iteration of 'the people' may appear and speak in its name, that some other rendering of 'the people', defined neither in terms of constituted power nor in terms of national belonging, might be possible.

Following the argument developed thus far, this possibility depends on the mobilisation of an affective economy that animates the 'flesh' of political subjects. If we are to take on the task of demogenesis in the Anthropocene, we would have to describe 'a people' that is defined not by a kind of human exceptionalism, in which an entire nation is put in touch with the divine, but by an *earthly entanglement* with a range of non-human forces that is nonetheless capable of agitating the corporal and affective dimensions of human life. Can the pre-political form of belonging that gives content to the people qua constituent power be reimagined as a kind of *ecological imbrication*, a form of belonging that transcends the nation but nonetheless remains bound to the co-ordinates of popular sovereignty? This seems like an incredibly tall order, given not only the enduring force of nationhood in the contemporary moment but also the presuppositions of modern thought which hold that human freedom is defined through its capacity to rise above our *natural attachments*; indeed, theories of popular sovereignty are indebted to a logic in which *the human* is defined as constitutively separated from an *animal* or *natural* other. As we suggested via Santner, the aesthetics of the flesh that popular sovereignty inaugurates renders the human as somehow *more or less* than itself. Either the human reaches towards the divine – picking up the transcendent remnants of sublime kingship – or else it is diminished and denuded in the direction of the creaturely and animalistic. In this way, popular sovereignty appears to establish a set of co-ordinates in which the human, in order to become properly political, must detach itself from its animal nature, abstract itself from a physiological and natural milieu; and if it fails, is destined to become not *merely human* but *less than human*.

Can these co-ordinates continue to hold if we embrace the implications of the Anthropocene? If the mystical, aesthetic and affective dimensions that bind actors to forms of authority were once connected to the king's sublime body, and in modernity come to be associated with the dreams of a unified and purely anthropic community, in light of the Anthropocene can we not render these aesthetics otherwise? In what follows I want to speculate whether we can begin to think of the aesthetic, fictional and 'fleshy' surplus to political power as an *earthly excess*, evoking those forces that constitute the earth system's functioning. This would tie the 'surplus of immanence' that accompanies political claims, not to a revolutionary, sublime, unified and fictive 'people' but to the network of human and non-human, biotic and abiotic, forces that sustain a people's presence. In other words, I want to examine whether we can follow Santner's account of the vicissitudes of 'flesh' beyond its emergence in discourses of popular sovereignty and biopolitics and speculate instead on how this aesthetic supplement to power might emerge within the altered world that the Anthropocene describes. Part of the challenge that this presents lies in reimagining relations between human and non-human animal life, a bifurcation that has been central to the ideologies of modernity.

Responsibility and the Persistence of Anthropocentrism

Clive Hamilton, one of the most prominent commentators on the ethical and political implications of the Anthropocene, adamantly resists the kind of shift in political aesthetics that I am exploring here. Arguing against various thinkers who have sought to articulate the apparently complex entanglements between human and non-human animals in an effort to resituate human agency within a broader scenography, Hamilton calls for the reclamation of an anthropocentricism that is willing to reckon with humanity's unprecedented role as a geological agent.[36] This involves a confrontation with the entirely unique position that *Homo sapiens* have with respect to the earth system: we are, Hamilton argues, the only species that can actively, deliberately and consciously shape our planetary conditions. In this sense, 'the gulf between humans and the rest of creation is *blindingly apparent*'.[37] The peculiarity here is that Hamilton sees the Anthropocene as an unprecedented rupture in the history of modernity that calls for entirely new forms of ethico-political thought; as he suggests, 'the natural world inherited by modernity is gone, and all of the ideas built on it now float on its memory'.[38] Whilst insisting that the Anthropocene constitutes a decisive break with modernity, however, Hamilton readily relies on, and sees a continuing role for, the human/animal binary, one of the moderns' most potent conceptual distinctions, and seeks to build a supposedly 'new' ethical and political disposition on this basis. Hamilton shows, then, the difficulty of moving beyond the conceptual co-ordinates that have shaped modern political thought, and a brief account of his thinking illustrates the need to decisively break from these modes of thinking.

In Hamilton's effort to develop a 'new anthropocentricism' for the Anthropocene we can see what Giorgio Agamben calls the 'anthropological

machine' clunking into action.[39] The Anthropocene shows that all the modernist efforts to define the properly human through its 'will' or 'rationality'
were all wrong; what *really* defines the human is that it has become a *geological
force*, as revealed through contemporary Earth System Science. Whilst the
content is updated through a new decision on what constitutes the 'properly
human', the distinctively modernist *form*, in which the human must be understood in opposition to an animal-other, remains in place. Hamilton hopes to
stabilise the human/animal distinction by reference to humanity's unique
capacity for *responsibility*. As Derrida has shown, seminal thinkers within the
Western tradition – originating with Descartes and recapitulated by Kant,
Hegel and Heidegger – rely on the distinction between *reaction* and *response*
to justify the division between animal and man.[40] Animals, so the contention
goes, are only capable of *reacting* to their environment and external stimuli.
It is the capacity to *respond*, both in the sense of linguistic communication
and in the postulation of a hiatus between stimulus and action – that is, a
capacity for *decision-making* – that marks out the division between man and
animal. No animal is responsible because they only *react*, they are irredeemably tied to (their) nature. By rising above the environmental immersion
apparently common to all non-human animal life,[41] the human is capable of
decision, intention and therefore *responsibility* and it is this that sets human
life apart. For Hamilton, *being responsible* in the context of the new climatic
regime involves recognising the immense power of human action to shape the
planet: 'we may have acquired it foolishly, but we *now have a responsibility for
the Earth as a whole* and pretending otherwise is itself irresponsible'.[42] There
is, for Hamilton, a 'gulf of responsibility' between human and non-human
animals: when it comes to responsibility, 'we have it and they don't'.[43]

But the purity and uniqueness of a human 'responsibility' is constantly
confronted by the various parallels which Hamilton himself draws between
the supposedly *responsible human* and the purely *reactive non-human*.
Echoing Heidegger, Hamilton insists on the world-forming capacity of
humanity, stressing that humans have become the ultimate 'world-builders',
able, indeed, to shape the earth's basic functioning. But this unique capacity
that grounds our responsibility is no sooner asserted than it is given up: the
'worlds' of our creation, Hamilton says, 'grow up behind our backs', without
a 'deliberate plan'.[44] That human world-building happens *behind our backs*
implies that it does not pass through human consciousness and is not subject
to deliberate, *responsible* decision-making; it happens entirely naturally, then,
through a kind of *animal-like reactivity* over which we have no control.
Equally, Hamilton's aggrandising claim that human responsibility genuinely
understood is a responsibility for *the Earth as a whole* is hedged by the suggestion that humanity can never *master* the Earth, going even so far as to suggest

that 'the destiny of humans now lies as much in the hands of "Gaia" as in our own'.[45] Hamilton's equivocation between *responsibility* and *mastery* fails to reconcile his dual claims that the human is both uniquely responsible for the entirety of the earth system (*utterly unlike all other animals*) *and* bound to live in purely reactive relation to powers that are beyond our control (*just like all other animals*). The 'blindingly apparent' and 'unbridgeable' gap between human and non-human with which Hamilton begins his analysis very quickly closes. Indeed, Hamilton's insistence that the Anthropocene shows human life to be increasingly *subject to* the earth's natural forces in the form of extreme weather events, alterations to ecosystems, food cycles and so on ties the human more and more closely to its environmental milieu, making us ever more animal-like as we grapple to survive in our dynamic planetary conditions.

Hamilton's faith in the capacity for human responsibility is all the more ironic when we reflect on the fact that more than half of all historic GHG emissions have happened in the last thirty years; that is, since the formation of the IPCC and breakthroughs in climate science that conclusively demonstrated the impact of emissions on global temperatures. In this sense, the current environmental conditions which perch us on the edge of climate catastrophe have not been fashioned *behind our backs* but *in our faces*, with every possibility that *responsible* decisions to reduce emissions could have been made. Hamilton would surely retort that it is precisely this kind of *irresponsibility* that has to be confronted. But perhaps the problem lies not only with certain 'irresponsible actors' but also in a pervasive reliance on a supposedly autonomous and pure zone of 'responsibility' that denies our putatively 'animal' nature. In no way do I mean to deny historical contingency or the human capacity to bring about change – of course, things could always be otherwise than they are – but a 'responsibility' that defines itself in opposition to an animal-like 'reactivity' constitutively denies the complexity of the human, particularly its affective and preconscious dimensions, as well as the 'geosocial' conditions that shape our capacities. As Derrida suggests, the response/react dichotomy can be readily abandoned:

> It suffices as a minimal requisite to take into account the divisibility, multiplicity, or difference of forces of a living being, whatever it be, in order to admit that there is no finite living being (a-human or human) which is not structured by the force-differential between which a tension, if not a contradiction, is bound to localise – or localise itself – different agencies, of which some resist others, oppress or suppress others.[46]

This 'tension' of agencies – psychic, social, environmental and so on – that localise themselves within any actor (human or otherwise) implies that the capacity to act can only ever be formed in some indeterminate space *between* the poles of 'responsibility/irresponsibility' and 'reaction/passivity'. And Hamilton's insistence on a pure space of responsibility would deny this messy *in-between* to which the precipitation of the climate crisis directly speaks.

Hamilton's effort to assert the unique supremacy of the human is motivated by an entirely justified concern that human communities have not yet confronted the enormous impact that they have had, and will continue to have, in shaping planetary life. The decisions that states and intergovernmental bodies make in the coming decade or so, about the decarbonisation of economies and the implementation of adaptative technologies and infrastructures, will have profound effects on the viability of human and non-human life on the planet in the coming century and beyond. To dismiss the unique power of human agency in the context of the Anthropocene would be a gross mistake. But in doing so, we need not rely on an account of the human which constitutively disconnects it from an animal-other; under a little scrutiny, such claims are seen to rest on unsure foundations. Indeed, approaching these issues in terms of *responsibility*, as Hamilton does, already loads the dice in favour of a particular conception of the human, elevating human agency above a series of purely 'reactive' and 'natural' forces and cycles.

The legal-political-ethical lexicon that we use to unpack the challenges that the Anthropocene presents is significant. In this respect, the language and conceptual schema of *obligation* – with its implication of binding, attachment, ligament and alliance – open a set of issues that are largely foreclosed if we remain tied to the anthropocentricism of *rights* and *responsibilities*. As we outlined via Simone Weil in the opening chapter, obligation evokes those existential questions of our 'being-bound' and the forms of 'attention' – attunement or sensitivity – that our geosocial formations call on us to cultivate, emphasising matters of *relationality* and *need* that are routinely backgrounded within our prevailing 'rights-talk'. It is questions of how human collectives are *assembled, attached, linked* or *bound* to a range of non-human forces that we examine in the next section as we seek to elaborate the meaning of an *earthbound and sympoietic people*. I first turn to Judith Butler, whose innovative account of popular sovereignty seeks to foreground the material and ecological conditions of possibility for a people's appearance, and then by drawing on Donna Haraway I attend to the particularities of non-human agencies and their entanglement with the human. The approach taken here, which reads Butler and Haraway together, aims to articulate the aesthetic transformation that is needed in order to regrasp the people as *earthbound*.

A Sympoietic, Earthbound People

Judith Butler's work on popular sovereignty and the politics of assembly[47] makes an important connection between the assertion of 'we the people', made by an alliance of bodies that gather in public space, and the broad network of dependencies and relations that sustain the life of that community. The assemblies that Butler's study describes are broad coalitions that draw on disparate sections of society, often with no sense of obvious commonality prior to their gathering. Two of her most persistent references are the assemblies in Tahrir Square in 2011 and the Occupy Wall Street Movement of the same year. Central to Butler's analysis is the meaning and significance of the *bodies* that come together to form an alliance in such moments, focusing on the strategy of inserting bodies in public space. This strategy, Butler contends, foregrounds the bodily needs of subjects (for care, space, food and shelter) and poses questions of equality, precarity, publicity and relationality in the context of resistance to neoliberal governance. Furthering concerns introduced elsewhere, Butler examines a form of political equality that can be promoted through an understanding of the shared *precariousness* of embodied life.[48] In contrast to *precarity*, which Butler describes as being produced through forms of uneven economic distribution, Butler understands *precariousness* as a common condition to all human life: all life is finite, can be injured and exposed to harm, and in this sense is 'precarious'. The political assembly which foregrounds the basic needs of the body – space, shelter, sustenance and so on – can develop a renewed sensitivity to *both* the uneven distribution of precarity within a society, in which certain groups are marginalised, ignored or discarded, *and* a more generalised sense of the shared precariousness of the human condition. With this sense of equality, Butler suggests that we can understand assemblies of bodies in the street as *performing* the obligations of solidarity and reciprocity that make political life possible. In this sense, these assemblies make manifest the kinds of political obligations which equality demands; obligations which are sadly lacking within the contemporary moment in which basic needs for human flourishing are not met for many citizens.

The language of *obligation* is significant here as it not only foregrounds the inherently *relational* qualities that define political life, in way that the language of *rights* typically misses, but is directly tied to the question of *need*. In this way, Butler politicises the basic demands of the body – for food, water, shelter, protection from violence and so on – that are classically considered to be purely private concerns: that which should be taken care of in the *oikos* rather than in the *polis*. Writing in conversation with Hannah Arendt, who famously sought to reassert classical divisions between public and private spheres in order to reclaim the unique forms of action and association that define the political,[49] Butler argues that structurally induced economic precarity means that the very necessities of life have become central to contemporary political movements. The simple acts of sleeping, cooking, eating or studying in public break down the supposed dichotomy between public/private, and by extension complicate the domains of freedom and necessity, making the infrastructure that makes life liveable a primary political concern. As Butler suggests in reference to the occupations in Tahrir Square, but her comments could apply equally well to a range of similar occupations, including those in Hong Kong in 2014 with which we opened this chapter,

> The bodies [in the street or square] acted in concert, but they also slept in public, and in both these modalities they were both vulnerable and demanding, giving political and spatial organization to elementary bodily needs . . . Sleeping on the pavement was not only a way to lay claim to the public, to contest the legitimacy of the state, but also, quite clearly a way to put the body on the line in its insistence, obduracy, and precarity, overcoming the distinction between public and private for the time of the revolution.[50]

The movement's demands were made manifest *within bodies themselves*, irreducible to any discursive event, declaration or set of demands, but *acted out* or *performed* in a corporal and material presence that presented a complex topography of independence, need, freedom and necessity.

Key to Butler's argument is the inherently *relational* and *dependent* quality of the human body, which both serves as a critique of the isolated and 'responsiblised' neoliberal subject and also draws out those infrastructural and communal networks of support that allow for a body to appear at all. The body in this context is not some material *essence* or *substrate* that underpins political action but instead always points *elsewhere*, making manifest the network of support that allows a body to sustain itself: 'we cannot understand bodily vulnerability outside of this conception of its constitutive relations to other humans, living processes, and inorganic conditions and vehicles for living'.[51] Clearly, for Butler, the body is not reducible to the biopolitical and normalising gaze but is a site in which the dependencies that allow for life to flourish are localised. Indeed, the presence of a precarious body in public shows the forms of relationality that constitute the human to be essential to the articulation of political freedom. In this context, Butler highlights the environmental conditions which are essential to the sustenance of human life, suggesting that she 'seeks to offer an ecological supplement'[52] to Arendt's emphasis on the inter-personal (and thereby purely anthropic) conditions that secure cohabitation. This ecological supplement aims to evoke a 'broader

sense of life, one that includes organic life, living and sustaining environments and social networks that affirm and support interdependency'.[53] In this
way, Butler situates the human in constitutive relation to the 'inhuman': we
might even think of the human, she contends, as 'the name we give to this
very negotiation that emerges from being a living creature among creatures in
midst of forms of living that exceed us'.[54]

As Butler makes clear, accounts of popular sovereignty too often ignore
the *embodied, material, sensible* and *felt* realities that are essential to its mode
of appearance. Even if we concede that the prototypical moment of a people's
appearance is in the form of a performative speech act (a 'juris-dictional'
declaration), this moment of enactment itself requires bodies: bodies that
speak, that hear, that are moved or affected, and that are mediated by a
range of technologies, whether smart phones and social networks, television
screens or loudhailers. In this way Butler seeks to make the people a material,
corporeal and technological assemblage, rather than a disembodied *idea* or
a purely *discursive* or *textual* event. When the people appear – or when an
assembly speaks 'in the name of the people' – they necessarily carry with
them a network of other actors and forces that sustain the body itself. Indeed,
it is this broader network of forces to which assemblies are actively seeking
to draw attention under the conditions of neoliberal precarity where equal
access to the basic necessities of life is being routinely undermined.

In this way, 'the people' must always be understood as being a *more-than-
human constellation*; and this as recodes the 'flesh' of the people's two bodies.
The aesthetic supplement which accompanies a claim to peoplehood, making
a people *more than itself*, is no longer self-referential – as we saw in the context
of the founding 'juris-dictional' moment, where the people fashions itself
as a unified body – but implicates a range of non-human forces. As Butler
makes clear, these forces *transcend* a particular claim but are nonetheless *made
present* within the fleshy reality of those that gather and act in alliance. By
linking the claim of popular sovereignty to a network of more-than-human
actors, we see the human as an irredeemably *bound-being*: tied up to material,
social, environmental and infrastructural forces that constitutively limit and
enable the capacity to act. If the classic theories of popular sovereignty cultivate a myth of human exceptionalism whereby certain 'natural attachments'
are overcome, following Butler we can see that any such claims can only ever
be made in negotiation with a set of interdependencies on which human life
necessarily relies.

Nonetheless, the 'ecological supplement' that Butler points to in this
context is notably thin. Whilst she regularly gestures towards the environmental context within which political action is always already enfolded,
Butler invariably returns to an anthropic register in which social and ethical

questions predominate. As Cary Wolfe has argued, Butler's attention to the 'precariousness' and the variable 'grieveabilty' of life remains largely blind to non-human animal life, largely because Butler's theory of community depends on a theory of mutual recognition.[55] Further, Butler's account of differential precarity is largely concerned with *economic* questions of the distribution of harms and benefits, which ignores the forms of differential *ecological* precarity that are becoming increasingly pressing in the new climatic regime. As we repeatedly see with each new extreme weather event or environmental disaster, communities are inured and exposed to ecological threats in a multifarious ways. And though this differential precarity often mirrors uneven economic distribution, with the poor disproportionality affected by climatic change and extreme weather, this is not always or straightforwardly the case.[56] Whilst Butler regularly evokes the political significance of 'life' that transcends the purely human, there is minimal detail here beyond vague gestures to the 'organic', 'environmental' and 'inorganic', by which Butler invariably means humanmade infrastructure. In this sense, Butler situates the potentiality of human existence within a broad network of forces that are themselves largely undifferentiated and indistinct.

The implications of Butler's approach, however, are instructive. She shows that the pre-eminent political task that accompanies an assertion of peoplehood lies in tracing the connections that make life liveable, of making manifest the multifarious networks that at least sustain habitability if not allow for the flourishing of life. This opens a possibility for thinking a 'people' as a processual assemblage that reaches out across vast distances but is nonetheless felt in the highly localised, corporeal, *fleshy* reality of bodies that assemble and act in concert. In Butler's rendering, a claim to peoplehood, or assemblies that act in the name of the people, is always *local, grounded, felt* and *corporeal* but in a way that is never *parochial, national* or *neatly circumscribed.* Furthermore, Butler's conception of the human as a 'negotiation' amongst those living forms that exceed the human neither relies on a simple human/animal binary – specifically abjuring the postulation of an 'animal-other' through which a human exceptionalism can be asserted – nor does it suggest that the human's integration within other living networks implies a kind of *abjection* or *degradation* of the human. The human, in this sense, is brought purposively *down to earth*, and this opens a new aesthetic sensibility, in terms of both appearance and perception, through which the people might be felt and understood.

Donna Haraway can help us extend Butler's rendering of the people as a constellation of human and more-than-human forces and relations. Since the early 2000s Haraway has worked with the concept of 'companion species' in order to explore the challenges that arise if non-human life is included within the ambit of our ethical and political thinking.[57] In her most recent work, companion species thinking is directly related to the Anthropocene thesis and offers the basis for how we might live well and even flourish on a damaged planet.[58] Unlike Butler, Haraway – who originally trained as a biologist – is sensitive to the complex and highly specific relations that constitute any given lifeform. In lieu of giving an account of 'life' in a generic or abstract sense, Haraway draws attention to the material, particular and situated relations and assemblages that allow for lifeforms to subsist, with the concept of 'companion species' aiming to capture these constitutive relations. In Haraway's idiom, every species is a companion species in the sense that every living being is radically dependent on other 'companion' beings that, in co-constitutive relations, allow for the flourishing of life. This approach allows her not only to foreground the complexity of life at all scales of analysis but also to open up new forms of historical analysis that are sensitive to how imbrications between the human and non-human have been central to the development of civilisation. The story of modernity or the history of capitalism, for instance, can be recast as *multispecies*, rather than simply *social*, processes, with co-constitutive relations between the human and non-human at their heart. As Haraway puts it, 'living with animals, inhabiting their/ our stories, trying to tell the truth about relationship, co-habiting an active history: that is the work of companion species, for whom "the relation" is the smallest possible unit of analysis'.[59] This approach – where *relations between* rather than any individual unit in isolation (like an organism) is the object of analysis – involves eschewing classical divisions between nature/culture and thinking instead in terms of a continuum of relations across this presup-posed border that Haraway dubs 'natureculture'. As we find with Gaia, in natureculture there are no 'parts' that aggregate into a 'whole', rather there are only 'partial connections' that constitute what Haraway calls a series of 'incongruent translations necessary to getting on together'.[60]

Central to Haraway's approach to these themes is the notion of 'sympoie-sis', which aims to describe the situated practices that might attune us to the interlinked and fragile companion species relations that constitute a liveable planet. Haraway explains in the following terms:

> Sympoiesis is a simple word; it means 'making-with.' Nothing makes itself; nothing is really autopoietic or self-organising . . . earthlings are *never alone.* That is the radical implication of sympoiesis. *Sympoiesis* is a word proper to complex, dynamic, responsive, situated, historical systems. It is a word for worlding-with, in company. Sympoiesis enfolds autopoiesis and genera-tively unfurls and extends it.[61]

Autopoiesis has a rich history in both biological and social science, refer-ring to the capacity of a complex system, understood as a closed unity, to self-regulate and continually reproduce its own temporal and spatial boundaries. Autopoietic systems are 'self-making', and whilst cognitively open to an environment which exceeds the system are nonetheless 'normatively' or 'organisationally' closed. Sympoiesis describes a kind of 'distributed' control system, in which the ongoing functioning of a system of relations is irreducible to one factor in isolation. Sympoietic systems are *collectively* produced, emphasise the linked connections *between* a range of actors – rather than the operative closure of a set of relations in a *unity* – and are subject to ongoing, and often sudden, transformation and change.

The concept of sympoiesis was first coined by Beth Dempster in an effort to develop a heuristic that captured the nature of complex and adaptive ecosystems. Noting the dominant account of complex systems as *autopoietic*, Dempster argues that the concept is somewhat jarring in the context of ecosystems, which she claims are *sympoietic*. The two distinguishing features of sympoietic systems turn on the nature of their 'borders' and their 'organisational closure'. An autopoietic system – a tree, for instance – has clearly delineated and stable borders that are self-constituting: 'interactions *internal* to the system form the boundary, not external forces'.[62] In contrast, Dempster describes an ecosystem – like a forest – as being 'boundaryless' or at least without a clearly defined, self-constituting and stable boundary. As she suggests,

> Even at 'treeline' there exists small tree islands that may or may not be considered part of the forest. Even if considered as boundaries, these lines are either determined by the environment (hence not self-defined) or, the environmental factors determining the edge must be considered part of the system, in which case the boundary would not be at the treeline. Such forest systems, then, can be more appropriately characterised as boundaryless sympoietic systems.[63]

The edge of the forest is more like a 'frontier zone' than a boundary, where one system fades somewhat indeterminately into another and the exact delimitation between one system and another is impossible. The porous boundary of the sympoietic system ensures that it is never 'organisationally closed', like an organism, but is, in Dempster's terms, 'organisationally ajar', implying that sympoietic systems have the capacity to accommodate extraneous elements, as happens when foreign plant species or wildlife enters a forest. A sympoietic ecosystem need not translate extraneous elements into the system's predetermined co-ordinates (as in the autopoietic model); instead it 'relies on external sources yet limits these inputs in a self-determined manner'.[64] If autopoiesis works to reproduce the status quo within a given system, translating any input from an environmental outside into the predetermined coding of the organisationally closed system, sympoiesis describes a process that is constitutively open to change as new elements are incorporated or rejected in a process of becoming: sympoietic systems are 'continually, although not necessarily consistently, changing'.[65]

Haraway uses sympoiesis in both technical (biological) and metaphorical ways. For the former, she takes inspiration from Lynn Margulis's theory of symbiogenesis, which examines the way in which the evolution of cells, tissues and organs rely on complex dependencies and fusions between genomes in order to form largely stable assemblages referred as *holobionts* (literally 'entire beings'). A *holobiont*, though 'whole', is made up of a number of different species and cell types which combine to form an assemblage that can subsist through time. Though Margulis does not use the term – which did not circulate until after her initial research into these questions had been published – Haraway suggests that Margulis's theory is best understood as a form of 'sympoiesis' in which life is seen to flourish through unexpected couplings, alliances and fusions between seemingly distinct organisms. In a metaphorical sense, Haraway argues that sympoiesis might be a guiding concept for our thinking in the Anthropocene. Indeed, her rejection of the 'Anthropocene' and 'Capitalocene' nomenclature in favour of 'Chthulucene', which emphasises multispecies connections and non-human processes and systems,[66] indicates the kind of thinking that Haraway sees as being apposite for our current epoch: 'the earth of the ongoing Chthulucene is sympoietic, not autopoietic. Autopoietic systems are hugely interesting . . . but they are not good models for living and dying worlds and their critters.'[67] Haraway's injunction is to translate the art of sympoiesis – central to the evolution of microbial life – into our social, ethical and political lives, learning how to 'make-with' others in order to enable the continued flourishing of life on the planet.

Notwithstanding some important gestures towards the political – her study of 'companion species', for instance, is cast as a *manifesto* and deliberately situated in oblique conversation with Marx and Engels[68] – Haraway's work is directed towards a multispecies *ethics* much more than it is a multispecies *politics*. Her examples of 'sympoiesis' as a kind of interdisciplinary 'making-with' between science and art only underscores this point: collaborative artworks that crochet the shapes of the world's fast-disappearing coral reefs; narrative fiction which examines the lives of endangered lemurs in Madagascar; a computer game that intertwines indigenous and scientific knowledge in the high Arctic; and Navajo pastoralism and wool weaving that traces a history of colonial injustice and the possibility of ecological renewal.[69] This focus on what we might refer to as a kind of 'minor politics' of encounter, activism, intervention and artistic creativity is in keeping with Haraway's dismissal of orthodox political categories. It is this ongoing effort to trace the various ligaments that connect species and to understand how these bonds allow for the possibility of flourishing lifeforms and new modes of community that animates Haraway's thinking, rather than any reliance on an abstract, juridified and universalising discourse of 'right'. On this front, I think Haraway is correct but the political stakes of her thinking remain difficult to discern. Can the open-ended processes of 'making-with' really coalesce into meaningful political *action*, *decision* or *position*? More pointedly, how can the heuristic of sympoiesis inform a claim to 'peoplehood'?

As we examined in our discussion of the performative speech act in which 'the people' grants itself the legitimacy to rule, popular sovereignty imagines legitimate power to be entirely self-referential, with the people needing nothing other than itself to ground its authority. It is founded on an assertion of a *collective self*, what Derrida calls an *ipseity*, that lies at the heart of the history of sovereignty.[70] In this sense, the people is self-making, needing nothing other than itself to generate a system of order. What Butler's reading of constituent power points to is a way of reading the people as *sympoietic*, a 'making-with' rather than a 'self-making'. With a focus on the *bodies* that assemble in alliance in order to demand change, Butler draws attention to the various organic and inorganic networks and associations that allow for a body to appear at all. Each body necessarily implicates a range of material, infrastructural, environmental and communal networks of support. In this sense, a people might well achieve a 'unity' or 'stability' – just like Margulis's *holobionts* – but this stability is 'organisationally ajar', open to a range of non-human forces. Similarly, the boundaries of Butler's 'people' are indeterminate, something that is strikingly clear in the case of public assembly where participants, observers, critics and passers-by mingle in a kind of 'frontier zone' at the edges of a given assembly, where any clear division between those within and without 'the people' is held in abeyance. In Butler's reading, this is a crucial element of a new kind of 'open' popular sovereignty that resists any the *ipseity* or *selfhood* which undergirds orthodox accounts of popular power. Disavowing the *ipseity* of popular sovereignty would take up Haraway's plea to make 'relation the smallest unit of analysis' and move away from an account of political community in which *parts* aggregate to form a *whole* and instead bring to the fore the various means by which actors are *bound* in alliance.

We can discern this shift in perspective within contemporary climate activism. As Naomi Klein makes clear in her survey of what she calls 'Blockadia'[71] – a network of highly localised movements that resist fossil fuel extraction – diverse assemblies come together and form temporary alliances on the basis of a *shared need*. As the slogans suggests – 'water is life', 'you can't

eat money'[72] – it is the very necessities of life that are at stake in such movements and the fact that these necessities are being fundamentally ignored and
undermined by extractive industries. One of the most striking examples of
this emerging form of resistance has been the Standing Rock protests which
sought to resist the construction of the Dakota Access Pipeline (DAPL), a
1,172-mile pipeline designed to transport crude oil from North Dakota to
refineries in Illinois. The ultimately unsuccessful resistance to the building
of DAPL began in April 2016 and ended in February 2017 and sought
to defend perceived threats to water supply and water safety on unceded
Standing Rock Sioux Tribal land. Whilst the history of settler colonialism is
central to understanding the strength of feeling that the construction of the
pipeline prompted,[73] as Kyle McGee has argued, the movement was perhaps
most striking for its ability to draw support from diverse communities that
were all affected by the imposition of extractivist policies forming a novel
sense of the 'public':

> The Standing Rock public managed to translate a dispute framed originally
> as a Native American sovereignty question into a more complicated nesting
> of issues such as ecological and human health, religious freedom, freedom
> of speech, freedom from state repression, racial equality and ethnic dignity,
> and so on, through broad enrolment of allies interested in both the outcome
> and the means utilised to quash the pipelines opponents.[74]

The bonds that coalesce to form unlikely alliances – 'coalitions that brought
together vegan activists who think that eating meat is murder with cattle
farmers whose homes are decorated with deer heads'[75] – is testament to the
fact that the ligaments that tie a 'public' in alliance need not be reduced to
some shared 'essence' or substantive principle of belonging. Indeed, a claim
about 'sovereignty', 'property' and 'exclusivity' gave way to concerns that
drew a range of actors into an emergent assembly. This speaks precisely to
a *making-with*, in which it is the multifarious bonds that connect people
to place that allow for continued habitation, rather than any assertion of
identity or selfhood.

The Standing Rock protests help rethink the contours of the people in
two respects. Firstly, they make clear that highly situated, particular relations
between human and non-human agencies are central to the kinds of political
claims that emerge in the context of a changing climate and in resistance to
extractive capitalism. Discrete and unexpected alliances form around a shared
concern about *needs* that will necessarily entail *making-with* diverse human
and non-human actors. Secondly, the relevant 'forces' at play here are not a
matter of attending simply to 'animal life' but to the whole range of what
Elizabeth Grosz calls 'geopowers' that subtend the possibility of political

action.[76] Grosz insists that the Anthropocene requires political thinking which grapples with the geological, inhuman dimensions that undergird social life; Grosz's characterisation of geopower is worth quoting in full:

> Geopower has no outside, no 'place' or 'time' before or beyond it, it is the force, the forces, of the earth itself: forces which we as technical humans have tried to organise, render consistent and predictable, but which we can never fully accomplish insofar as the earth remains the literal ground and condition for every human and non-human action . . . If the inhuman is not understood as against the human, its opposite or overcoming, but rather as *both the preconditions and the excess within the human*, if we understand what is creative and inventive in the human as something impersonal, with forces that summon up rather than control, then it is a line that runs through human actions.[77]

What Grosz describes here is precisely an *earthly excess* that is nonetheless mediated through the capacity of human action, a kind of 'inhuman supplement' to the domain of human freedom, a *geopower* that is felt in the *flesh* of political subjects. Latour echoes this characterisation of the *excessive* powers of the earth system with which human collectives are always in negotiation when he describes Gaia, though without sovereignty and not to be mistaken for a supreme arbiter over human actions, nonetheless having the quality of *majesty*,[78] the very same quasi-divine quality that kingship evoked and wrote into the body of the monarch in order to bind subjects to the authority of the crown. It is this sense of the *majesty* of the earth system, the notion that the earth is constituted by forces that are always in excess of human agency but are nonetheless taken within the human in providing the preconditions for the capacity for action, that a sympoietic, earthbound people evokes.

The Political Aesthetics of Demogenesis

In reading Butler and Haraway together I have sought to outline an alternative political aesthetics for the people, hoping to make visible those forces and relations to which a purely anthropic, modernist discourse of popular sovereignty is constitutively blind. Following a line of thinking that stretches back to discourses of medieval kingship, I have suggested that any claim to political authority will have to work at an aesthetic register in which a seemingly transcendent quality is nonetheless brought within a fleshy and corporeal reality; indeed, it is this commingling of the fabulous and 'other worldly' with the somatic and the affective that captures one of the singular traits of *being-bound* to forms of authority. In the context of the Anthropocene, this aesthetic excess – what Santner calls a 'surplus of immanence' – might be reimagined in relation to the earthly forces that subtend social life but that can nonetheless be mobilised in moments of political action. This approach shifts the co-ordinates that are generally taken to define claims to people-hood by engaging a range of more-than-human actants within a people's claim to appear as an agent of political change. This approach aims to resituate the capacity for collective action within a set of 'earthly forces' that will engage both the organic and inorganic. Here, 'animal life' is no longer a negative referent for an isolated, rational and supposedly 'responsible' human agent, but is one force among many with which political life will have to contend in the ongoing process of sympoiesis. To approach the human through the heuristic of sympoiesis involves figuring anthropic agency otherwise than the modernist framework which situates 'Man' *in* 'Nature', embracing instead a more complex scenography of 'geopowers' that work both within and beyond the human. This foregrounds the forms of *dependence* and *need* that are the conditions of possibility for any claim to peoplehood.

In the context of resurgent nationalisms that can be felt in various locations around the world – not least in Hong Kong, where we began this chapter, with political movements actively relying on the bonds of a putative 'nationhood' to animate recent political campaigns – these speculations about the possibility of a 'sympoietic earthbound people' might feel hope-lessly disconnected from the affective economy and forms of attachment that seem to define so much of our contemporary political discourse. Whether this kind of thinking will ever rival the affective attachments that the nation state is able to evoke is an open question that is, today, almost impossible to answer optimistically. But it is worth recalling that at the time of high medieval kingship, the idea that 'the people' could hold sovereign power was likely to be viewed in a similarly sceptical manner. In the context of popular sovereignty, sympoiesis is an invitation to put in question the forms of associative life that have structured modern political thought and practice, opening the door to a radically altered account of what constitutes the political. In keeping with Lefort's insistence that the people always points to an 'empty place' of power, where its content can never be exhausted by those that speak in its name, the approach to popular sovereignty that we can develop through Butler and Haraway invites a sensitivity to the ongoing composition of a people, illuminating the geological, ecological, infrastructural forces, as well the multispecies networks of dependency, that allow for a people to emerge and make a claim to ground legitimate author-ity. These inhuman and impersonal powers that transcend a given polity should nonetheless be imagined as being immanent to a people's capacity to claim the mantle of political agency. Rather than abandon the notion of peoplehood entirely, the task of demogenesis in the Anthropocene therefore becomes how we might make claims to peoplehood that are sensitive to those *excessive, majestic, earthly* forces that run both through and beyond the human.

5

Scale

What is needed is a politics *of* place *beyond* place.
— Doreen Massey, *World City*[1]

Travelling by plane from the Gold Coast to Melbourne in December 2019, I could see a string of fires stretching out below me across that vast country. Great billows of smoke rose up from the flames and merged seamlessly into a thick blanket of clouds. In Sydney, some days previous, the air was acrid with smoke, an uncanny smell of the bonfire that pressed into the city ominously. The 2019–20 Australian bushfires killed as many as one billion animals and burnt over 18 million hectares of land, destroying many thousands of homes and farms, and killing thirty-four people. The flames destroyed dozens of habitats on which rare species depend and have further endangered a number of fragile ecosystems.[2] It was the sheer scale of the fires that so unsettled me as looked out of the plane window; at cruising altitude, no limit to the blaze was perceptible, extending as it did into a murky horizon of its own making many miles in the distance. Cormac McCarthy's stark vision of a burnt and blackened earth, brought on by some unnamed cataclysm, in *The Road* immediately came to mind. As I wondered what had become of the land below me, McCarthy's vision of the post-apocalypse had an eerie resonance: 'the ashes of the late world carried on the bleak and temporal winds to and fro in the void. Carried forth and scattered and carried forth again. Everything uncoupled from its shoring.'[3]

The sense of displacement and 'uncoupling' brought on by vast, all-encompassing destruction is one of the themes that runs through McCarthy's novel. But the drama is played out within the microcosm of a father-and-son tale of physical, moral and spiritual survival within the ruins. The movement that McCarthy depicts from the unimaginably vast to the intimate, familial and personal is at the heart of the challenges presented by the climate crisis and our entry into the new climatic regime. As I travelled thousands of feet above the burning Australian bush, I was no mere observer of some 'natural' phenomenon that might provoke a sense of wonder or awe. My journey, in some small part, was implicated in those flames that so disturbed me; I was bound up in a kind of loop that tied me to what was unfolding on the ground. It is the entanglement between our contemporary, technologically mediated lives and a natural world that we readily pose as its constitutive outside that is one of the central implications of the Anthropocene thesis. But so too is the telescoping of scales in which we appear to 'zoom' between dauntingly oversized scales like *planetary life* or *geological time* to the highly localised scales associated with extreme weather events, ecosystem vulnerability or something as mundane as sorting one's recycling or opting not to drive a car. There is a prevailing, if rather nebulous, sense that seemingly modest actions at a personal scale – shunning plastic bags, not eating meat, avoiding flights between the Gold Coast and Melbourne, and so on – can nonetheless have the effect of 'saving the planet'.[4]

This toggling between the apparently oversized and the highly localised is related to what Timothy Clark has called a kind of 'scalar blindness',[5] where dominant temporal and spatial scales tend to occlude the very issues that political thought and action ought to be addressing in the context of the climate crisis. This difficulty is encapsulated in Rob Nixon's account of the 'slow violence' of climatic change, where we fail to perceive dramatic alterations to the planet because they move at timescales that are readily ignored within contemporary social life which fetishises the spectacular and the eventful.[6] Timothy Morton's 'hyperobjects',[7] which describe processes like global warming that are so distributed in space and time relative to human life that they perennially evade our cognitive and political grasp, similarly speaks to the scalar challenges that the Anthropocene provokes. We might even think of climatic transformation as being *super-scalar* in the sense that there is never a single spatial or temporal scale at which the object of analysis can be rendered meaningful. If 'scale' derives from the Latin *scala* for 'ladder or flight of stairs', however high or low on the rungs of scale we are, we can never see all of the 'hyperobject' of climatic change that metes out its 'slow violence'; such phenomena either withdraw from or exceed the scalar units we commonly rely on to frame our social reality.

In this chapter I argue that the Anthropocene prompts us to think critically about the scales installed and reproduced through modern sovereignty. I approach scale with an emphasis on its aesthetic dimensions; that is, the extent to which dominant scalar units have the capacity to frame and give sense to social relations; scales allow us to imagine or depict a world. As Mariana Valverde puts it, 'there is no such thing as a scale-less seeing or depicting'.[8] The challenge in the context of the Anthropocene is to identify those scales which can help frame social relations in a way that is attuned to the ecological and geological forces that are at the heart of the unfolding climate crisis. Following Valverde, I understand scale to refer to more than a merely spatial designation. Scale gives rise to a particular mode of organising the sensible domain which involves attending to the *temporal, normative* and *affective* dimensions of a given scalar unit or series. It is this multifaceted account of scale which helps us assess those scales of authority which might open space for a new thinking of the political in the context of our changing climatic conditions.

A continued reliance on the nation-state scale, as the dominant mode through which we frame political life, fails to do the work that is required in this context. In lieu of this nation-state frame, it is commonplace to evoke 'the global' as the appropriate register at which the challenges associated with the quintessentially 'global' problem of 'global warming' can be addressed. The nature of a 'global outlook', represented in 'global institutions' that can order social life at a 'global scale', is at the heart of much of the contemporary discourse around the politics of climate change.[9] But as we examine here, 'the global' scale remains caught in a set of anthropocentric co-ordinates that are challenged by the Anthropocene concept and its various entailments, which invite us to take account of the inhuman milieu within which social life is situated. Rather than an account of *the global*, I explore the possibility of returning to an older and apparently smaller scalar unit in an effort to rethink the political in the context of our contemporary ecological mutation: *the city*. Drawing on contemporary writing in urban studies and spatial theory, I approach the city as a discrete legal and political form which might allow us to sense our changing planetary conditions and attune us to the forces and relations that define our entry into the Anthropocene. But this requires approaching the city as a material and infrastructural assemblage that engages a vast, planetary hinterland, rather than a bounded unit that posits 'nature' or 'the wild' as its constitutive outside. It is from this altered account of the city that, I argue, we might become sensitised to our earthbound condition and think through some of the implications that this entails for political and lawful relations. In this way I aim to outline how privileging the *city scale*, ahead of the *national* or the *global*, might form part of an altered political imaginary fit for our new climatic regime.

A Sense of Scale

Scale is central to spatial theory, and the meaning, significance and the supposed 'politics' of scale have been widely debated in human and political geography. Much of this work has sought to address the various social, economic and political transformations associated with globalisation; particularly the reorganisation of national, regional and urban sites of economic power which followed the economic crises of the 1970s and gave rise to new 'global'

scales of production and consumption. Neil Brenner provides a useful definition: scale refers to a 'hierarchically ordered system of provisionally bounded
"space envelopes" that are in turn situated within a broader, polymorphic
and multifaceted geographical field'.[10] It is worth unpacking this in order get
to grips with some of the theoretical co-ordinates that underpin the 'scale
question'.

Firstly, scale is understood here as *spatial* and though Brenner, relying on
Lefebvre's evocative term,[11] refers to the 'space envelopes' of a given scalar unit
in a way that suggests a volumetric rendering of space, spatial scale is often
conceived in purely areal terms. Secondly, scale has an essentially *relational*
quality in that each scalar unit has meaning only when combined in a series
or, at minimum, in relation to some binary opposite; as in 'Urban–National–
Regional–Global' or 'Global–Local'. The various metaphors for describing
scale, from an analogy with Russian Matryoshka dolls in which one scale is
'nested' within another, to the etymologically grounded metaphor of scale
as a 'ladder', or scale conceived as a set of concentric circles with smaller
scales at the centre being gradually enfolded by progressively larger scales, all
underscore the relational nature of scalar thinking. A particularly thought-
provoking way of capturing the relational quality of spatial scale is to draw an
analogy with musical scales. As Richard Howitt has argued, thinking of scalar
units by analogy with musical tones helps to emphasise that the significance
of each unit is radically altered by the scalar series within which it is situated.
In the same way that a given tone – the note 'C', for example – can feature
as a tonic, a third or a dominant fifth depending on the scale in which it is
situated, the spatial scale of 'the city' takes on a different significance when
included in the 'street–neighbourhood–city' series rather the 'city–national–
regional' series. As Howitt argues, 'the totality under examination in each case
is quite different, in a way that is similar to the way in which we might find a
C note in several scales playing quite different roles in the musical totality'.[12]
The focus on scalar *totalities* is crucial to Howitt's analysis of the relational
qualities of scale; scale always has a *gestalt* quality that allows for a 'world'
(qua social or geographic totality) to be grasped. Thirdly, scale is always a
provisional matter: though scales can become stabilised or become dominant
over time, they are processual and open to change; as Lefebvre puts it, scale is
always in a process of 'formation', 'stabilisation' or 'bursting apart'.[13] Lastly,
scale is always operative within a larger and more heterogenous field ('polymorphic and multifaceted', as Brenner has it) that exceeds the given scalar
ordering that one adopts. In this way, if scale is a technique of *enframing* and
ordering chaotic and refractory social or geophysical phenomena, there will
always be an *excess* to a given scalar order that threatens to interrupt or undo
the ordering that a scale or scalar series seeks to achieve.

Brenner's approach to scale challenges static and reified approaches to the concept by emphasising the processual, relational and interconnected nature of scalar series. In this way he describes scale as the product of – and therefore deeply entwinned with – other spatial concepts and practices like networking, territorialisation/de-territorialisation, and place-making. If the Matryoshka doll analogy aims to describe scales as bounded units that sit within a simply ordered hierarchy, Brenner emphasises the messiness of the connections between scales in a way that forms a 'mosaic' of interconnected socio-spatial relations; as he suggests,

> Insofar as terms such as 'local,' 'urban,' 'regional' and so forth are used to demarcate purportedly separate territorial 'islands' of sociospatial relations, they obfuscate the profound mutual imbrication of all scales and the densely interwoven, overlapping interscalar networks through which the latter is constituted.[14]

In fact, Brenner is less interested in scale *per se* than in the *processes* of scaling and rescaling within the context of contemporary political economy in which scales are routinely made/unmade by the processes of capital accumulation. Brenner accepts that scales and scalar series 'crystallize' or become 'fixed' both ideologically and within institutional practices; something that is key to his analysis of processes of urbanisation, which he describes as both a medium for and product of contemporary globalised capitalism. Relatively stabilised scalar orders (particular those undergirded by state power) provide the conditions of possibility for capital accumulation but, Brenner argues, capital also works to disrupt ossified scales of production and consumption in order to find new spaces within which it can circulate. Underpinning this approach is the contention that scale is not simply a matter of *ideation* or *ideology* – a mere way of 'seeing' or 'ordering' the world – but is what Brenner calls a 'real abstraction'[15] in the sense that a given scale, though a social construct, is *made real* through 'historically specific patterns, regularities, interdependencies, and systems of relations that crystallize through, and impact, sociospatial relations'.[16]

Brenner is clearly right to emphasise how scale is not merely ideological but is the result of instituted and patterned social practices. Scale, we might suggest in this respect, is analogous to what Foucault would call 'an apparatus': a complex assemblage of institutions, knowledges, beliefs and practices that mediates power relations.[17] But it is worth underscoring – contra Brenner – the differentiated ways in which scale functions at *economic*, *political*, *legal* and *cultural* registers, each of which will not necessarily coincide, and on the difference between the *practical* and *ideational* elements of scale, which the notion of 'real abstraction' perhaps too quickly elides. In particular, it does not follow that rescaling processes within institutionalised practices will necessarily be commensurate with rescaling at an ideational or aesthetic register. As we examined above, early modern maps depicted emically 'national' borders long before their juridical formalisation; the aesthetic ordering of social space, then, might well *precede*, and therefore shape, its later institutionalisation. The distinction between the *practical* and *aesthetic* aspects of scale is particularly relevant in the context of globalisation where the production of goods and the movement of capital are increasingly operative within 'global' and/or 'regional' rather than 'national' scales at the level of *socio-economic practice*, but as various recent political upheavals from the Brexit referendum to Trump's election indicate, the nation-state scale remains highly important at the level of the *perception*, *appearance* and the *enunciation* of political claims and forms of attachment. Contrary to the liberal mantra of 'think global, act local', we often *act globally*, in the sense that we rely on networks of production and consumption that are facilitated through globally dispersed supply chains and infrastructures, but *think locally*, in the sense that our dominant political frames of reference remain bound to the state scale.

Brenner's analysis suggests that static scalar models are guilty of a 'mis-reading' of a more nuanced social reality. But this too quickly ignores the structuring effect that scale has as an enduring and powerful mode of perceiving and thereby constructing a 'world'. This does not disregard the complex ways in which rescaling processes play out in instituted social practices but seeks to emphasise instead the enduring force that scalar 'fixes' can have in constructing our perception of social relations. Scale has an *aesthetic power* in that it allows us to *frame* a social reality, to categorise and organise a set of related units of space, and time, and to discard those phenomena that fall outside a scalar series as being irrelevant to a given mode of analysis or perception. What I want to draw from the literature on scale in spatial theory is the way in which prevailing scalar units combine to create a particular 'distribution of the sensible', as Rancière would describe it. Scale orders, and thereby constructs, 'a world' and allows for certain social relations and mate-rial realities to be seen and felt, whilst other scales are understood to form that 'polymorphic and multifaceted' background against which a given scalar unit or series is situated.

As we have already intimated with reference to its *gestalt* quality, scale is crucial to the work of world-building or what Donna Haraway calls 'world-ing', insisting that 'world' should be primarily understood as a verb rather than a noun.[18] As Derrida reminds us, a world is always constructed by 'a set of stabilizing apparatuses . . . [that] construct a unity of the world that is always deconstructible and never given in nature'.[19] Scale is instrumental to this work of 'worlding' where a provisional unity and stability to a set of perceptions is achieved. Derrida underscores the normative dimension to worlding techniques by recalling the etymological resonance between the French *monde* (world) and the Latin *mundus* denoting 'the proper'. *Immonde* (literally without a world) refers to something dirty, abject or impure and *émonder* means to clean, prune or purify. Derrida draws on this lexical heritage to underscore how world-making always involves a kind of 'clearing out' or 'purification' so that that which falls beyond a given world-construct is considered *immonde*, both unworldly and improper.

With this connection between *scale*, *worlding* and *normativity* in mind, let us recall the fourfold view of sovereignty with which we have been working in order to think about the work that scale does in crafting sovereignty's aesthetic dimensions. Much of the debate in the geographic literature on scale has turned on its ontological status: is scale a real feature of social and geophysical phenomena, or is it simply a mode of perception and a social construct? By mapping scale onto our fourfold rendering of sovereignty, we can circumvent this binary and instead approach scale as being a question of certain *practices* (evoking Brenner's processual definition of scale); a matter of *appearance* (posing the question of how different scales are represented); of *perception* (inquiring into how scales allow us to perceive social or material relations in an ordered constellation); and as producing a kind of *remainder* or *excess* that falls outside a given scalar unit or series. As we have suggested throughout, sovereignty has a world-forming power through the articulation of these four moments of *practice*, *appearance*, *perception* and *remainder*. Territorial sovereignty, for instance, appears through the technologies of mapping; installs a dominant 'cartographic imaginary' or mode of perception; depends for its continued power on certain juridical and material practices that reproduce and enforce this mode of articulating place and power; and produces a non-political *remainder* in which non-territorial forms are cleaned out (*émondé*) and considered to be largely irrelevant to a 'proper' account of the political. Scale works in precisely the same way with sovereignty privileging a given scalar series that centres on the nation state, through forms of appearance, perception, and material and juridical practice, at the same time as it jettisons or treats as irrelevant non-state centric scalar units and series.[20]

Mariana Valverde offers her own examination of the 'world-forming' power of scale by emphasising three elements that are either ignored or underplayed in the geographic literature on scale: *jurisdiction*, *time* and *affect*. Valverde's multifaceted approach to scale not only helps deepen our account of scale's aesthetic dimensions but also adds a degree of complexity that tends to be occluded in the geographic literature which, perhaps under-standably, tends to approach scale in purely *spatial* terms. It is striking that in so much of the geographic literature on scale there is scant reference to the law in general or jurisdiction in particular; jurisdiction is the legal technique *par excellence* which determines the limits to scales of authority. As we have already suggested, we can think of jurisdictional technologies as a 'hinge' between the practical and the aesthetic dimensions of sovereignty. At a juridical register, jurisdiction works to either enforce the predomi-nance of nation-state scales or create supra-state jurisdictional arrange-ments; and jurisdictional technologies like cartography help to represent dominant scales of authority in aesthetic and imaginative terms. The work of jurisdiction in delimiting zones of authority and organising governance programmes is essential to the production and maintenance of a given scalar unit.

Beyond a focus on questions of normativity, jurisdiction and govern-ance, Valverde also emphasises the temporal dimensions to scale. Drawing on Mikhail Bakhtin's notion of the 'chronotope' (literally, 'time-place'), Valverde argues that the purely spatial rendering of scale ignores 'how the temporal and the spatial dimensions of life and governance affect each other'.[21] As Bakhtin counsels, 'time, as it were, thickens, takes on flesh, becomes artistically visible; likewise, space becomes charged and responsive to the movements of time, plot, and history'.[22] For Valverde, Bakhtin's central insight is that any scalar unit – whether the 'household', the 'neigh-bourhood' or the 'globe' – will always carry with it a particular timescale, temporal rhythm or historical trajectory. The national scale, for instance, is often associated with a dominant historical narrative of the nation, orien-tated around a founding or revolutionary moment, for example, or else a past that supposedly stretches to the 'immemorial'. This temporal ordering of the national is also associated with particular rhythms of 'national life', whether election cycles or national or religious holidays and celebrations. These often contradictory temporal elements are essential to understanding the national scale in a way that a purely spatial rendering of the nation clearly ignores.

Scalar units are associated with a particular 'mood' or 'affect'. We might contrast a formal and procedural atmosphere associated with a 'national' scale with intimate or claustrophobic affects and feelings associated with the 'household', for instance. Drawing on the example of the regulation of zoning ordinances that aim to protect the 'character' of residential neigh-bourhoods from encroaching industrial units, Valverde argues that 'spatiali-zation, temporalization and affect'[23] all play a role in seeking to reproduce the neighbourhood scale. Howitt's analogy between spatial and musical scales noted above is apposite in this context because it underscores that each spatiotemporal scale is not only irredeemably *relational* but, just like a musical scale, evokes a distinct mood or feeling; major, minor or modal scales, as well as combinations and movements between such scales, are essential to the affective quality of melody and harmony. Similarly, distinct scalar units evoke and open possibilities for distinct affective dispositions, moods or atmospheres.

Valverde's multifaceted rendering of scale does not simply attend to a spatial delimitation but emphasises questions of *time, normativity* and *affect* in a way that deepens our appreciation of the world-forming quality that a given scalar ordering can achieve. If, as we indicated at the end of Chapter 1, the Anthropocene heralds 'the end of the world', in the sense that the prevailing ordering of background and foreground is fundamentally challenged by the onset of the new climatic regime, a crucial aspect of the disorientation that this engenders turns on the upending of the *spatial, temporal, normative* and *affective* ordering associated with modernity. As we think about the disruption to dominant scales instigated by the Anthropocene and begin to imagine alternate scales that help give order and meaning to the climate crises, it is all of these aspects of scale that are at stake. With this in mind, let us turn now to examine how the Anthropocene interrupts a scalar unit that is often posited as the natural successor to the state scale, particularly in the context of climate change: 'the global'.

Scaling the Anthropocene: From the Global to the Earthly

The Anthropocene disrupts the scalar ordering associated with globalisation. Dipesh Chakrabarty captures the problem: the global of 'globalisation' is not the same global as the global of 'global warming'.[24] Globalisation is an anthropic affair and the 'global' scale which it brings into view is a matter of legal and material infrastructures that allow for communication and trade in transnational networks. Whilst a sense of the 'global' clearly has a long history, stretching back to antiquity and given a new inflection in early modernity with the European 'discovery' of the New World, the contemporary 'global' of globalisation is chiefly concerned with the existence of markets for commodities and circuits of communication that place *human life* and human-centred institutions at its heart. The 'global' of global warming, in contrast, invites a reckoning with a non-anthropocentric framing of our planetary reality. Indeed, it is precisely an intrusion of the 'planetary' into the scalar ordering associated with the 'global' that the Anthropocene and the climate crisis appears to signal. In this sense, we might treat the 'global' of global warming as being largely synonymous with the 'planetary' scale.

Earth System Science is the discipline that perhaps best captures this altered perspective in which human life – in the form of habitation, consumption and production – is but one aspect (and until the very recent 200 years or so, a largely insignificant aspect) of a planetary system that is constituted by complex interactions between the earth's biosphere, hydrosphere, cryosphere, geosphere and atmosphere, describing interactions across and between abiotic and biotic elements within the planet's 'critical zone'. Indeed, this 'planetary' view not only provincialises human life and the institutions that enable 'globalism' but also provincialises, or at least contextualises, the earth itself within a broader inter-planetary environment. As Chakrabarty notes in reference to the Earth System Science framing of climate change, 'our current warming is an instance of what is called "planetary warming" that has happened both on this planet and on other planets, humans or no humans, and with different consequences'.[25] If the *global* is an anthropic affair, the planetary has only an incidental relation to human life. Thinking in terms of a planetary scale requires a kind of *abstraction* in which a systemic totality is imagined *as if* from the outside:

> The ideality of this 'globe' of Earth System Science is produced not only by a view of the planet from the outside but also by simultaneously reconstituting it in the imagination with the help of the sciences – including information obtained from satellites positioned in space as well as from ancient ice-core samples – while keeping all the time other planets in view. Earth System Science studies and produces a reconstituted planet, the Earth system, an entity no one ever encounters physically.[26]

In this way the planetary scale offers a non-anthropocentric vision of the Earth which foregrounds self-organising and integrated planetary processes and systems – including the carbon cycle, ocean currents and conveyors, rates of glacial retreat and so on. In many respects the earth system view helps situate human activity as being largely subordinate to the functioning of these autonomous systems. The notion of 'planetary boundaries' – which identifies the thresholds within nine planetary systems or processes that allow for continued human habitation of the earth – makes this clear.[27] This approach shows how dramatically different is the *scalar ordering* proper to the earth system model compared with that described through discourses of 'globalisation', which are generally content to trace the interactions between national, regional and sub-national institutions, infrastructures and their concomitant modes of perception.

As Latour has argued, the inadequacy of the 'global' scale was dramatically illustrated at the 2015 COP21 climate summit in Paris, when it became clear that the collective plans for modernisation and (putatively sustainable) economic growth endorsed by the nation-state signatories could not be accommodated within the planet's systemic functioning.[28] The planet, it seems, cannot accommodate the aspirations of a truly 'global' capitalism; non-negotiable planetary boundaries are being tested and in some cases breached as we try to cram 'global' aspirations for progress into the 'planet'. This is an example of what engineers and designers call a 'scale effect' in which a scaled-down model may be structurally sound but when scaled up to its intended final proportions suffers from instabilities and weaknesses.[29] The model for 'global' growth and prosperity, under the auspices of contemporary capitalism, has always depended on the logic of *scalability*; that is, where a simple expansion of productive capacity is considered to have no transformative effect on the nature of production itself.[30] Scale effects reveal the limitations of this quintessentially modernist attitude: if scaled up to reach every corner of the planet, contemporary forms of production and consumption would destroy the very conditions for continued human habitation of the earth itself.

But so many of us remain captivated by 'the global' with its promise of cosmopolitanism, growth, interconnectivity, borderlessness and 'progress' whilst the 'local' (the globe's antonym) remains, for many at least, a shorthand for the parochial, the closed-minded, insular, 'backward' even. As Latour makes clear, the 'global' scale is not simply a way of ordering space but also implies a *temporal* trajectory associated with modernity, a presupposition of a linear temporality and the aspirations associated with 'progress'. The global is precisely what the moderns are directed towards, it is the horizon that projects of modernisation have always held in view. Whether in global markets, global law, global constitutionalism or a more nebulous global ethos or outlook, the globe, as Latour puts it, features as an *attractor* within our political, legal and economic imaginaries. And though the global has been dominated by a liberal, free-market ideology in recent years, it is worth recalling that traditional leftist politics – as a creature of modernity and a self-consciously 'progressive' project – has similarly been directed towards a *global horizon* with a truly global political subject ('workers of the world', as the *Communist Manifesto* puts it) at its heart. In this way, 'the global' combines *normative, spatial, temporal* and *affective* elements that allow us to grasp social relations in a very particular configuration. This makes challenging the symbolic 'world' that the 'global' connotes extremely difficult. The 'global' engages an entire way of seeing and acting, it gives direction and meaning to one's political, legal or economic aspirations and values. But in the context of the Anthropocene, global, national and local scales appear to be utterly inadequate in the face of this 'planetary' challenge.

For Latour, as the global–local axis gives way, we need to come 'back down to earth' and feel the pull of an alternative attractor which he calls the 'terrestrial'. The 'terrestrial' denotes a related though distinct scale to 'the planetary'. As Chakrabarty describes it, the planetary scale, as conceived within Earth System Science, presents a *totality* which can only be imagined from the outside; the planetary conceives a complete *entity* but one which 'no one ever encounters physically'.[31] This mode of perceiving the planet finds an analogue in the well-known image of 'earthrise' taken from Apollo 8 in 1968 or the so-called 'blue marble' image of 1972. These powerful images of a unified but variegated, beautiful but tangibly fragile earth set against the inky black of deep space, not only were an extraordinary new vision of the planet but also signalled a dramatic alienation from our terrestrial reality. As Duncan Kelly puts it, 'what "earthrise" offered was the world as an image, a technically reproduced image at that, reducing humankind from being grounded beings with a place or a home in the world, to creatures holding merely temporary membership status of a planet'.[32] Whilst this form of displacement of the human can shift our imaginary away from an anthropocentric globalism, what is lost here is a sense of the intimate and immediate fact of our dwelling within a *terrestrial* home.

Latour's evocation of the 'terrestrial' is little more than a shorthand for Gaia, and thinking with Gaia involves a fundamental transformation of our sense of scale. As we discussed in the first chapter, one of the most striking things about Lovelock's Gaia hypothesis is that it cannot be analysed in terms of 'parts' and 'whole'. Each actant (biotic or abiotic) within Gaia is *always in relation* with other actants. As Latour puts it, glossing Lovelock,

> there cannot be, strictly speaking, any parts. No agent on Earth is simply superimposed on another like a brick juxtaposed to another brick. On a dead planet, the components would be placed *partes extra partes*; not on Earth. Each agency modifies its neighbours, however slightly, so as to make its own survival slightly less improbable.[33]

Lovelock's great innovation, which shows how organic matter shapes the chemical and geophysical conditions of the planet, with the 'goal' of maintaining the conditions of possibility for life, indicates that the modifications that each actant makes to 'its neighbours', as Latour puts it, move across commonly used scalar distinctions. As Latour suggests, these forms of interrelated agency constitute '*waves of action*, which respect no borders and, even more importantly, never respect any fixed scale'.[34] Gaia describes agencies that cut across extant scales of analysis – like organism, environment, biotic and abiotic – on which so many of the modern sciences rely. The great 'muddle' of Gaia[35] is a muddle of scales: the highly localised interactions of bacteria and the processes of photosynthesis, for instance, are integral to the planetary reality of an atmosphere that has been composed of 21 per cent oxygen for millennia. Lynn Margulis, the seminal theorist of symbiosis – which describes the ways in which different species interact and abide with and within each other to form complex assemblages or 'symbionts' – endorses the view that 'Gaia is just symbiosis as seen from space'.[36] The crucial point here is that the relations observable at the *microscopic* level, in which organisms depend on the ability to enfold themselves within other organisms in order to form life-sustaining processes, are precisely the relations that produce Gaia as a planetary phenomenon. In this sense, there is a relationality *all the way down* and *all the way back up again*, with any scalar division between part/whole, macro/micro and so on being artificial impositions on what is an always unfolding set of symbiotic relations. As with Morton's 'hyperobjects', Gaia – or the 'terrestrial' – is *super-scalar* in that it cannot be accommodated within the scalar units and series that we commonly rely on in order to frame our perception of social life.

But can we approach the political in these super-scalar terms? Despite the post-human turn within contemporary political and social theory, the political will always return us to the particularities of human collective life which will inevitably force us to grapple with the prevailing scales through which we perceive and order our social reality. Can a meaningful sense of the political really take hold at a 'planetary scale', a scale, Chakrabarty reminds us, that no one encounters physically? Can we really imagine political formations within the super-scalar 'muddle' of Gaia?

Latour's own account of how we might translate the 'terrestrial' into the political sphere makes this difficulty clear. Having established the 'terrestrial' as being composed of networks of relation that cut across many of our predominant and presupposed scales and scalar series, Latour concludes his effort to evoke a 'terrestrial politics' with a paean to 'Europe': it is, he says, 'in Europe that I want to come down to earth'.[37] Europe, for Latour, is partly a geographical designation, partly an 'idea' and partly the extant bureaucracy of 'Brussels', which 'by the intricacy of its regulations, which are attaining the complexity of an ecosystem',[38] might show us the way towards a post-national, post-global outlook. What is striking about Latour's attachment to Europe is the difficulty of translating the super-scalar, hyper-networked Gaia into a meaningful political form. Gaia is too dispersed, both too big (in that it engages planetary and even inter-planetary scales) but also too small (in that it draws attention to the most minute interactions within bacterial life), too slippery and too 'muddled' to provide a framework for meaningful political thinking and practice. In this sense, despite the reorientation from the 'global' to the 'terrestrial', Latour concludes his study by returning to existing political forms. Whilst acknowledging that the terrestrial 'lacks any political institution',[39] Latour appears ineluctably drawn to a scale of thinking and practice – regional, bureaucratic and inter-national – that is very much indebted to the 'old climatic regime'.

The challenge turns on how we can articulate a connection between the provocation of a planetary thinking and existing political and legal scales that might allow us to draw out dependencies and interactions between the geophysical and human social life. The challenge, as I understand it, is to describe those *earthly forms* that might capture the enfolding of human agency and planetary life that the Anthropocene describes. The 'earthly', I contend, is a more generative term than 'terrestrial' or 'planetary' in that it denotes a material, terrestrial reality but, as the *OED* reminds us, also refers to 'the material or lower elements of human nature'. The earthly in this sense directs us towards the elemental qualities of the human and the necessities on which human life depends in a way that the 'terrestrial' perhaps fails to evoke. The *earthly* is not directly concerned with the complex assemblages that constitute Gaia which, as Lovelock and Margulis are always keen to reminds us, will get on very well without us humans getting in their way; nor does the *earthly* correspond to those non-human, self-organising processes and systems to which the *planetary* scale draws attention. Instead, I take the *earthly* to describe the meeting point between the human and the planetary, denoting how particular social forms and scalar units are themselves integrated within the earth system and its various inhuman processes. In this way the *earthly* refers to a meeting point between seemingly heterogenous scales. It is, I argue, in the city that we might best understand this juncture between the social and the planetary.

Before we turn to this, however, I want to provide a brief historical sketch of the city in the context of Western political thought and practice. Central to this history is the growing significance of jurisdiction as a means through which the relative autonomy of a sphere of lawful authority can be asserted. The changing fortunes of urban jurisdictions, from a peak of significance in the high medieval period to a fundamental reorganisation in early modernity, illustrates sovereignty's overriding desire to suppress any rival scale at which the political might be conceived. The city, as a *sui generis* political form, is precisely what has to be jettisoned in early modernity in order for sovereignty to install and police a single scale at which the political can be enframed, sensed and imagined.

The Rise and Fall of the City Scale

Barring a handful of Roman and Moorish settlements in the south, the vast majority of today's European towns and cities can trace their heritage to the twelfth and thirteenth centuries, a period of extraordinary growth and transformation on the continent, of which these new urban centres were an integral part. This saw dramatic *climatic*, not just *institutional* transformation. The medieval warm period, a climatic anomaly within the Holocene epoch, saw temperatures rise in Europe from the tenth to the thirteenth centuries. This meant that average temperatures were comparable to those of the mid-twentieth century, a condition that lasted until cooler, wetter conditions returned in the fourteenth century, eventually culminating in the 'little ice age' of the following 300 years. The medieval warm period is associated with massive population growth, an uptick in agricultural surpluses and a military expansionism that established the European borders which hold an enduring relevance to this day.[40]

Though accurate records are unavailable, it is likely that the population of western Europe increased by at least a half, and possibly doubled, between 1050 and 1150, compared with stagnant and at times declining populations in the preceding centuries.[41] As agricultural surpluses grew, trade became increasingly significant and urban centres blossomed with as much as 20 per cent of the European population working outside of agriculture by 1300.[42] The money economy was central to this urban expansion, and towns became key sites in which innovations in finance, accounting and taxation were developed, crucial to the emergence of capitalism and new techniques of government and bureaucracy. As Fernand Braudel puts it,

> A new state of mind was established, broadly that of an early, still faltering, Western capitalism – a collection of rules, possibilities, calculations, the art of getting rich and living. And also gambling and risk: the key words of commercial language: *fortuna, ventura, ragione, prudenza, sicturta*, define the risks to be guarded against. It was certainly no longer a question of living day to day, like the nobles . . . the merchant was economical with his money, calculated his expenditure according to his returns, his investments according to their yield.[43]

Central to these social upheavals was the emergence of medieval towns and cities, which were entirely novel material, economic, infrastructural, legal and political formations. Whilst by no means the first urban settlements, they nonetheless represent a stark contrast to the towns and cities of the Roman empire, which were administrative and military outposts controlled by imperial agents, and the ancient city-states of Greece, which were self-contained republics constituting a *sui generis* political order. The medieval towns and cities were 'something in between'[44] these previous iterations. Medieval urbanisation created a unique legal, political and economic identity for towns and cities which was nonetheless integrated within a broader network of secular and ecclesiastical powers. Crucial to understanding this 'in between' status of medieval settlements are a set of innovations within juridical thought and practice that helped explain and justify the rise of secular legal regimes in general (mercantile, royal and manorial law, chief amongst them) and, more specifically, a discrete form of *urban law*. These transformations within the legal scenography of Europe were played out within an expressly *jurisdictional* register.

A novel understanding of jurisdiction emerged in the wake of the rediscovery of Roman law which helped jurists explain the changes which were taking place within medieval society. As Harold Berman indicates, the twelfth-century glossator Azo of Bologna is a key thinker in this context.[45] Azo's central insight was to understand jurisdiction (*iurisdictio*) as a form of political power (*imperium*) which though *lesser* in a hierarchy of competencies, nonetheless could claim to have an *independent* rather than a *delegated* claim to legitimacy. Azo's understanding of the Roman sources allowed him to conceive of a plurality of relatively minor but nonetheless autonomous jurisdictions, in lieu of a view that held that all legal orders derived their authority from some plenary source. Within the context of the church's universal claim to authority, this interpretation of jurisdiction was profoundly important as it established the view that 'jurisdiction did not descend downward from the emperor [or some other superordinate authority] but upward from the corporate community'[46] and embraced a meaningful form of legal pluralism within the context of the putative supremacy of ecclesiastical rule. This recognisably modern sense of jurisdiction as a relatively autonomous sphere of lawful authority helps understand the functional differentiation of secular legal orders, in which a mutual recognition of competencies – feudal, monarchical, urban and manorial laws, for instance – became widespread from the twelfth century.[47]

It is against this backdrop that we should understand the emergence of the new juridical regimes which took hold within the growing number of urban settlements in the twelfth and thirteenth centuries. Let me emphasise two aspects of the emergent *urban jurisdictions* of the high medieval period. Firstly, urban law was built around *communal*, not individual, rights and duties. The legal identity of a town or city was often founded on a sworn oath, taken by every citizen, which established the rights and obligations that the town afforded and demanded. This was reflected in obligations of mutual protection amongst citizens and a system of jury adjudication – displacing trials by ordeal or combat – which sought to find a formalised and rational mode of dispute resolution through the active participation of citizens. Urban government itself included important aspects of popular participation in the form of town councils or popular assemblies, as well as establishing a range of directly elected governmental and administrative offices. In the early twelfth century, for instance, London, which was referred to as a 'commune', emphasising its collectivist credentials, was chiefly governed through a folkmoot comprising the entire citizenry that met three times a year. The importance of the guilds within medieval towns – which controlled employment standards, apprenticeships, prices and production levels with a strict regime of licensing and quality control – only underscores that urban centres were *communal all the way down*, with no protections afforded to individuals qua individuals. As Berman suggests, 'the individual had no legal existence [in the town] except as a member of one or more subcommunities within the whole'.[48] The medieval town, in this sense, was a kind of *immanent corporation* – what Weber calls a 'fraternal association'[49] – in which the town's legal identity was indistinct from the citizenry. Otto von Gierke characterises this as a 'Germanic' conception of the corporation, in contrast to the 'Antique-Modern' definition which depends on the positing of an 'artificial personality' (a 'Town', with a capital *T*), to *represent* the town on the juridical plane.[50] The medieval towns and cities of the twelfth and thirteenth centuries conform to Gierke's 'Germanic' conception: they were an immanent and organic unity that had no 'personality' separable from the sub-communities which generated a distinctively urban form of life.

Secondly, towns and cities were *constitutional* in character: they were often founded on written charters which dictated the organisation of governmental competencies as well as citizen rights and duties. Berman describes these charters as 'the first modern written constitutions'[51] as they sought to establish the legal supremacy of the charter in the governance of a town's affairs, thereby establishing a set of legal constraints on economic and political life. The nascent constitutionalism of urban centres was the chief means through which the towns differentiated themselves from the feudal legal order which surrounded them. As Braudel describes it,

> Crossing its [the city's] ramparts was like crossing one of the still serious frontiers in the world today. You were free to thumb your nose at your neighbour from the other side of the barrier. He could not touch you. The peasant who uprooted himself from his land and arrived in the town was immediately another man . . . If the town had adopted him, he could snap his fingers when his lord called for him.[52]

The question of a newcomer being *adopted by the town* is key. Many towns guarded the status of 'citizen' jealously and established forms of semi- or quasi-citizenship for some residents that precluded full participation in the town's commercial and civic life.[53] And though relying on forms of popular participation, the towns were no democracies. As a 'community of communities' or *Ständestaat*[54] the town was usually dominated by an elite class of merchants and craftsmen, a power often wielded through the guilds which shaped so much of a town's affairs. Nonetheless, urban jurisdictions, built on distinctive liberties established in written legal codes, were discrete legal and political units, recognised as such by comparable secular jurisdictions within which they were nested. As Gianfranco Poggi suggests, the towns created 'a distinctive juridical space "immune" from the substantive and procedural rules characteristic of the feudal system'.[55] This degree of autonomy allowed for the lucky, the ambitious and the creative to generate new fortunes in urban centres which were unthinkable within the rural economy. This meant that towns provoked emotional and affective responses, with citizens fiercely loyal and protective of the town; Braudel calls them 'the West's first "fatherlands"', suggesting that a form of 'town-patriotism' emerged earlier, and was far stronger, than any kind of patriotism directed towards the territorially delimited nation state.[56]

Whilst constitutional innovations guaranteed a large degree of autonomy for urban life, particularly with respect to feudal and manorial law which, amongst other things, controlled the agrarian mode of production, it is worth noting the long-standing alliance between urban centres and monarchical power. Whilst some towns asserted their own claim to legitimate authority, irrespective of ecclesiastical or royal assent, most town or city charters were granted by the crown or a comparable quasi-sovereign authority. Both the monarch and the urban corporation benefited from this arrangement as it circumvented the complex network of personal relations that defined the feudal order. As centres of trade, towns were important sites for revenue generation and collection. Medieval urbanisation depended on a centralised, homogenous state, which had the power to protect a town from feudal or ecclesiastical infringements, but nonetheless granted it maximal legal and economic autonomy. Braudel goes so far as to suggest that large urban centres (London and Paris especially), in their demand for a stable common market, which could serve as an extended hinterland on which city expansion could rely, were instrumental in creating the conditions for the emergence of the nation state: large cities, Braudel argued, 'created national markets, without which the modern nation state would be a pure fiction'.[57] Braudel suggests that long before the political union of England and Wales, first with Scotland (in 1707) and then with Ireland (in 1801), the economic power of London worked to homogenise and unify a London-centric, trans-local market. London merchants sought the ever freer passage of goods throughout the

British Isles, installing wide-ranging networks that could extract ever greater surpluses; in this way London became 'an enormous demanding central nervous system which caused everything to move to its own rhythm, overturned everything and quelled everything'.[58] This point is worth underscoring as it reminds us that the process of urbanisation, starting in the twelfth and thirteenth centuries, was not simply a matter of *agglomeration* in which the urban form expanded and intensified but was part of a much wider series of societal transformations that had profound effects well beyond the city walls. Whilst the *legal* limits of the medieval town were often very clearly delineated – and forcefully policed by an emerging urban, proto-capitalist elite – the material impact of large settlements, in particular, ranged beyond the sphere of influence that the urban jurisdiction worked so hard to protect. As Braudel reminds us, with a piquancy that resonates with the inequities of our contemporary urban condition, 'the luxury of . . . [large urban centres] had always to be borne on the shoulders of others'.[59]

The great achievement of the towns and cities to sustain their economic power and legal distinctiveness reached an apogee at the end of the thirteenth century. The successes of urban centres ultimately contributed to their downfall. Urban elites increasingly viewed 'town interests', which in effect were indistinguishable from commercial interests, as being separable from 'town identity'. From the mid-fourteenth century, many towns 'transition from "community" to corporation', and in so doing 'the town . . . gets its capital *T*'.[60] This instigates a move away from the immanent, 'Germanic', conception of town unity to a more recognisably modern notion of the corporation endowed with legal personality and allowing for land ownership, the taking of rents, the lending and borrowing of money and so forth. This bifurcation of the town into a 'resident' class and an 'elite' that controls the functioning of the *Town*, qua corporate entity, led towns and cities to depend ever more strongly on monarchical power. Urban elites looked to the king for greater military and legal protection, and the king looked to the Towns for financial and administrative support.[61]

This relationship remained mutually beneficial only if there was a balance of powers between crown and town. Throughout early modernity, particularly in England and France where monarchical power became increasingly centralised and authoritarian, this equilibrium was lost in favour of the crown. As monarchical power grew, the town, as an autonomous source of communal political identity, legal authority and economic power, became an object of suspicion. As Gerald Frug has shown, the tensions between the plenary ambitions of monarchy and the vestiges of town autonomy were played out within a series of legal disputes over the status of town and city charters throughout the sixteenth and seventeenth centuries.[62] At the heart of these disputes was the capacity of the crown to revoke corporate charters in the event of any wrongdoing by a member of the corporation. At stake in these cases was the jurisdictional autonomy of the cities: did the liberties and privileges protected by a city charter ultimately owe their authority to the crown or did – as Azo's interpretation of the Roman sources articulated centuries earlier – the town have a *sui generis* claim to legitimacy? As Frug shows, in England these disputes were eventually resolved in favour, first of the crown, and then Parliament in wake of the Glorious Revolution in 1688. The result was a degree of continued autonomy for towns and cities but with the state ultimately reserving the right to revoke and control the charters. In this way, the city, rather than an anomalous legal and political space situated within, and held in productive tension with, a plurality of other secular legal orders, became a creature of the state, and its freedoms and privileges subject to the state's consent.

Saskia Sassen has argued that the medieval towns and cities were incubators for the political forms that are most clearly associated with modernity.[63] As we have seen, the medieval town was constituted by an alliance between a capitalist (or proto-capitalist) elite and a form of rational-formal law that was articulated in territorial terms: the very political form to which nation states in early modernity increasingly aspired. As the modern state grew in power and influence, cities became *rivals* rather than *allies* with respect to state authority, which was busy centralising and homogenising its power. As Sassen sees it, the political form of the medieval town – with its unique assemblage of quasi-constitutionalism, territorially defined jurisdiction and citizenship rights – 'jumped tracks' in early modernity and took hold at a nation-state scale, contributing to the displacement of the medieval rights and obligations that continued to define sovereignty well into the seventeenth century. What Sassen describes, then, is a *rescaling* of a particular constellation of *territory*, *authority* and *rights* from the urban to the national.

Tracing how this transformation was played out at the level of legal and political practice is highly complex. But as Frug points out, it is perhaps easier to understand the subsumption of the towns and cities within the sovereignty of the modern state in *ideological terms*.[64] What emerges in early modernity, alongside administrative changes that challenged towns and cities at the level *juridical practice*, was a new way of *perceiving and ordering* legal and political power, which focuses its gaze on the *individual* and *the state*, and nothing in-between. Hobbes captures this altered aesthetic, in characteristically colourful prose:

> Another infirmity of a Common-wealth, is the immoderate greatnesse of a
> Town, when it is able to furnish out of its own Circuit, the number, and the

expense of a great Army: As also the great number of Corporations; which are as it were many lesser Common-wealths in the bowels of a great, like wormes in the entrayles of a naturall man.[65]

Part of the work that Hobbes is undertaking in *Leviathan* is to clear out or purify (*émonder*) all those intervening scales of authority that muddle, what Hobbes saw to be, the primary political relationship between the individual and the sovereign institution. The rescaling of political power in early modernity meant that not only did towns and cities become *practically* limited – through a series of legal challenges to their claimed autonomy – but they also underwent an *aesthetic* transformation in that they no longer appeared relevant to *the political mode of perception*. Indeed, if we credit Hobbes with making a decisive contribution to the birth of a truly modern political imaginary, the city can be understood as precisely that which had to be *expelled* for a modern political aesthetics to emerge. Recalling both Derrida's account of 'worlding' and the fourfold approach to sovereignty that has informed our analysis throughout, we can think of the period of transition that Sassen, Braudel, Frug and others have charted in which the city scale becomes subsumed by the modern sovereign state in early modernity as producing the urban as a *non-political remainder*, a constitutive outside to the newly installed nation-state scale. The nation state became the scale *proper* to the political, a result of the administrative pruning (*émonder*) carried out in a seemingly mundane jurisdictional register.

As an irreducibly *communal* political form, intermediate between individuals and the modern sovereign state, the town all but disappeared in Europe by the eighteenth century. As the state form comes to dominate our sense of the political throughout early modernity, the unique status of the city as a bounded, jurisdictional unit within a plurality of other normative forms is quashed as sovereignty's monism comes to the fore. This is because states scaled up the very normative forms (constitutionalism, rights, territory, citizenship and so on) which towns and cities themselves had developed. Once these structures are adopted at the superordinate scale of the state, the city is thought to be entirely subordinate to state authority, ultimately owing existence to state grants and charters. Clearly, this does not mean that the *economic* significance of cities has waned. Indeed, as the nation state came to articulate the 'proper' domain of the political, capitalist production was given ever freer rein within urban centres, with cities becoming the key sites for industrialism in the nineteenth century and the urban fabric today central to contemporary forms of rentier capitalism. But the sense that the city constitutes a discrete articulation of the *polis*, carrying with it a unique set of normative and affective commitments, rarely features in the modern political imaginary. In the context of the contemporary climate crisis, however, this is changing. The unique political possibilities that inhere within the city form are increasingly being championed, and a number of writers are seeking to reclaim the status that cities once had as a *sui generis* political form.

City Redux

The recent resurgence of interest in the political possibilities of the urban form are driven by a recognition of both the disproportionate contribution that cities have made to our changing climate and the singular vulnerabilities that cities face in the context of a warming world. Cities are the chief source of GHG emissions and are key nodes in the contemporary fossil economy, responsible for 60–80 per cent of global energy consumption and approximately 75 per cent of global CO_2 emissions.[66] As Mike Davis argues, 'city life is rapidly destroying the ecological niche – Holocene climate stability – which made its evolution into complexity possible'.[67] At the same time, cities are amongst the most vulnerable places to climatic change. By 2025 it is estimated that 75 per cent of the global population will live within 120 miles of the sea,[68] and many of the world's most populous, 'global cities' are particularly at risk in the context of sea level rises – from Osaka to New York, London to Shanghai. In light of both the stark vulnerabilities that many urban centres face and the overriding sense that meaningful action on mitigation and adaption is not taking place either in national or international institutions, many urban theorists, and city institutions themselves, are seeking to reclaim their status as a unique political form vis-à-vis state authority.

Cities are playing an increasingly important role in the context of international affairs often taking the form of transnational, inter-city diplomacy and policy formation.[69] In the context of environmentalism such inter-city networks are at the forefront of contemporary debate with networks like C40 and ICLEI emerging as key sources of authority in the global climate change discourse.[70] These networks have led to the emergence of what Jolene Lin has called a transnational 'urban climate law'.[71] Through the development of voluntary standards, efforts to harmonise environmental policies across cities and the pooling and dissemination of knowledge, the internationally networked city has become a key site for the development of environmental policy. This move to reassert city power aims to counter the fact that cities remain partly 'invisible' in the climate change imaginary, which routinely focuses on either global or national scales, with many of the unique challenges that cities face being under-reported.[72] One particularly striking example of this is the 'heat island effect' that sees cities being on average 30 per cent warmer than surrounding countryside, exposing city-dwellers and the infrastructures that sustain urban life to enormous pressures in the context of increasingly extreme weather. In this sense, a political revival of the city aims to reimagine the heritage of this non-modern legal and political form for the twenty-first century in an effort to attend to the challenges that today's overwhelmingly urban global population face. If states are failing to address these challenges, perhaps city authorities will fare better.

This line of argument has been developed by Benjamin Barber, one of the most prominent advocates for a rearticulation of city power in the context of the climate crisis. As Barber argues, 'the constitutional subsidiarity of cities to national governments who have lost their capacity to protect and sustain cities remains a persistent hindrance to global urban action on climate change'.[73] What is needed, Barber contends, is a new form of 'urban sovereignty' in which cities are able to assume some of the governmental competencies usually reserved by states and co-ordinate their efforts within new inter-city networks, like the Global Parliament of Mayors, which Barber himself was instrumental in establishing. Indeed, the chief promise of cities lies in their natural interdependence, in contrast to states who remain caught in a logic of exclusivity, territoriality and independence. In order to claim a new form of 'urban sovereignty', cities need to articulate the right-capacity nexus that we generally assume to be the exclusive preserve of states. Where states are failing to act in the context of limiting GHG emissions, Barber argues that cities have a right to fill the vacuum of authority that states have produced. Drawing on the social contract tradition, Barber argues that cities can make a legitimate rights claim to protect their citizens from the threats of climate change when states are so drastically failing in this regard. As we have already intimated, the threat of rising sea levels and extreme weather events makes this an existential matter for many urban communities. And if states are failing these communities, Barber argues, they have a legitimate right to act in the interest of their own self-protection.

Despite his emphasis on *interdependence*, Barber's use of a 'rights' and 'sovereignty' frame to describe the prospect of augmented city power has the strange effect of reproducing the very co-ordinates that define the *independence* and *exclusivity* of states. If cities have unique 'rights' to self-preservation constituting a form of 'urban sovereignty', does this not naturally lead cities down a path towards confrontation, not only with each other as cities vie to control the supply chains and flows of capital and knowledge on which their existence depends but also with states themselves as they battle over the extent to which governmental competencies might be devolved to urban centres? As every social contract thinker has concluded, the individuated right to self-protection will ultimately lead to the evocation of some 'third' who can mediate and arbitrate between rights claims. And who will fulfil this function when it comes to arbitrating between city rights? By framing city power and the urban political form as a *rights* and *sovereignty* question we remain caught up in the very logics of exclusivity and supremacy that the turn to cities aimed to circumvent.

Furthermore, Barber's account of the city entirely embraces cities' extant institutional form. Ultimately, Barber is interested less in Lefebvre's 'right *to* the city' than he is in bolstering the 'rights *of* the city', arguing that existing urban institutions need to augment their collective power. Whilst I have some sympathy with this strategy and can see the benefits that might accrue to increased capacity for local authorities to shape the global climate policy agenda, what is under-theorised here is the nature of the urban form itself. If cities are becoming increasingly significant actors within global governance and there is an increasing push to recognise the unique political form that cities embody in the context of climate change, then how we define this form is crucially important. If there is some purchase to be found in privileging the city scale in the context of the Anthropocene, then, I argue, we need to think through the city as an *earthly form*, integrated in a broader set of planetary forces and relations. This is obviously a difficult task and requires a sensitivity to specific urban forms in specific locations, facing specific threats and vulnerabilities in the context of specific changes to climatic conditions. Nonetheless, we can, at a metatheoretical register, point to certain trajectories along which we might begin to rethink the nature of the city scale in the context of a changing climatic system. In conclusion, let me suggest three lines of inquiry to assist in this endeavour: a *spatio-temporal reorientation*, which situates the city in a 'planetary' rather than a 'global' context; an *aesthetic shift*, which reorganises our commonplace assumptions around the city's articulation of background/foreground; and a change in our *normative* rhetoric and modes of thinking in which we move away from a language of *city rights* and focus instead on the *dependences* and *obligations* which reproduce urbanity.

Earthly Cities

What might it mean to consider the urban form as having a planetary significance? Let us return to Neil Brenner who, following Henri Lefebvre's influential work in the 1970s, seeks to develop an account of 'planetary urbanisation'. To begin, it is worth emphasising the distinction – made by Lefebvre and mobilised by Brenner – between 'the urban' and 'the city'. 'The urban' is associated with a set of *processes*, driven by the logic of accumulation, that engage people and territories that lie far beyond the city's walls. The city, in contrast, is best understood as the material *outcome* or *manifestation* of these forces and processes. Brenner describes the urban in the following terms:

The 'urban' dimensions of urbanisation referred less to the spatial generali-sation of cityness *tout court* than to the consolidation of among other ele-ments, a specifically modern formation of industrial territorial organisation; the extension of large-scale, state-managed sociospatial interdependencies; and accelerated circulation (or labour, commodities, and politico-cultural forms), as well as variegated transformations, crises, conflicts, and insurgen-cies induced through those processes.[74]

Brenner situates his own approach to the 'urban question' against those that remain tied to a methodological 'cityism' where the sole object of study is a particular settlement type: '*the* city', usually described in terms of population density and diversity, or in relation to specific infrastructural characteristics, but always defined in contrast to the city's constitutive outside: *the rural, the natural, the wild* and so forth.

Brenner counsels against the universalising language of '*the* city' that purports to connote diverse forms of urban settlement that are the product of equally diverse forms of urbanisation. The recent explosion of interest in the city – of which Benjamin Barber's work is a part – regularly celebrates the unique qualities of '*the* city' as a space of ethnic and cultural heterogeneity, economic growth and creative potential, lumping together *all* urban settle-ments within a single morphology. Ashely Dawson attributes this recent wave of writing on the city to a new '*citerati* class' who offer a relentlessly optimistic vision of urbanism which is little more than paean to a way of life reserved for a handful of the wealthiest neighbourhoods in a handful of the wealthiest cities in the world.[75] For Brenner, a methodological 'cityism' attends to only one aspect of the urbanisation process, the moment of agglomeration or urban 'implosion', with the 'explosive' reach of urban life into various non-urban zones going largely unnoticed.[76] As Brenner argues,

> Today, it is impossible to grasp the essential elements of the urban question except in relation to diverse, extrametropolitan zones of the world that are now being enframed within and subordinated to the (il)logics of capital's industrial metabolism, and which directly support the 'growth of the city' upon which urbanists have for so long focused their analytical gaze.[77]

Any account of contemporary urbanisation requires spatial theorists to attend to the expansive hinterland which urban settlements instrumentalise and exploit. This extends the reach of urban theory into agricultural zones where industrial food production is mobilised to satiate urban appetites; onto the ocean floor where a network of communication cables facilitates urban mobile working practices; and even into outer space where GPS satellites allow today's urbanites to navigate the city jungle.[78] Brenner develops an urban theory which drops the 'city lens'[79] that has largely structured writing in urban studies, where the city is defined as having a constitutive outside. For Brenner, this involves developing an account of urbanism with *no outside* in the sense that processes of urbanisation have become truly *planetary*.

This approach is particularly apposite within the context of the Anthropocene. Cities are the sites in which human life relentlessly metabolises 'natural' forces and relations. But '*the* city' frame is invariably predicated on a constitutive opposition between the urban and the natural: in the city we are supposedly free from the bonds of nature, living in purely humanmade edifices in which the 'natural world' has been purposively walled out. Brenner draws back this ideological veil and reveals the messy entanglements within the city's putative outside, without which the urban form, as we know it, would crumble.

But is Brenner's 'planetary urbanisation' genuinely *planetary*? Recalling Chakrabarty's distinction between the 'globe' of globalisation and the 'globe' of global warming, Brenner's analysis remains bound to an anthropocentric framing of the 'globe', where human institutions and practices are the primary object of study. If we are to think the city in *earthly* terms, it is precisely the interrelations between the urban and the inhuman forces that define the earth system that are at stake. One way of grasping this altered mode of perception is through an attention to the city's role within the earth's *technosphere*; that is, the humanmade elements of the earth system, akin to the biosphere, cryosphere, atmosphere and lithosphere that constitute the fundamental elements of the earth system.[80] The technosphere refers to the 'summed material output of the contemporary human enterprise' and includes any technological material 'within which a human component can be distinguished, with part in active use and part being a material residue'.[81] Urban infrastructure (roads, buildings, docks, runways, landfills, metro systems and so on) – despite covering as little as 2 per cent of the earth's surface – constitutes over a third of the earth's technosphere.[82] The global explosion in urban population since the middle of the twentieth century directly corresponds to the wide-ranging transformations to the earth's biogeochemical systems that signal our arrival in the Anthropocene epoch. In this sense, our entry into a much vaunted 'urban age' represents one of the key markers that testifies to the recent rupture in planetary history: stratigraphers of the future will be able to point to deep scars in the earth's strata and a range of 'technofossils' left behind by *homo urbanus* as evidence of our transition into the Anthropocene epoch.

To conceive of the city in these terms allows us to connect the predominantly *urban* human condition of the present with the expansive reach of planetary time, displacing anthropocentric accounts of urbanisation in order to reimagine the urban as having a kind of *geological depth*. The vast networks of inhuman urban infrastructure – from pipes and cabling, to tunnels and roadways – have taken on a planetary and geological significance. Far from being places through which 'nature' is constitutively othered, this reminds us that cities are sites in which the human and the planetary are most tightly knit, forming socio-technical, socio-ecological and socio-geological entanglements.

Brenner's own project is concerned with tracing the economic forces that drive urban expansion and the modes of production and accumulation that sustain the urban form. My own interests lie elsewhere. In particular, I am keen to explore how privileging the city scale might reframe our sense of the political in the context of the new climatic regime; and in this respect Brenner's evocation of diffused, hyper-networked, multi-scalar processes of urbanisation falls foul to the same difficulties that beset Latour's evocation of Gaia. The object of study is too big, too slippery, too multifaceted to be able to allow for the political, which – as we have argued throughout – always needs to become *attached or bound to*, and *mediated by*, place and forms of belonging. In this way it seems imperative to return to 'the city' as a discrete legal and political form, whilst accepting the various caveats and qualifiers that Brenner's analysis insists on. This would involve a return to the specificities and intensities of urban agglomeration but would aim to situate the city within an expansive frame, in keeping with the Anthropocene and its various entailments. Most significant in this respect is the importance of avoiding universalising claims concerning '*the* city' and attending instead to the particularities of urban settlements and the possibilities of reimagining the political form that such attention might open up. What is needed, then – to echo our epigraph – is a theory of the city scale which attends to the particularities of place but nonetheless ranges beyond place. It is after all *cities*, not the vast hinterlands on which they depend, where the majority of the high-pollution, high-consumption, global north live, work, consume and pollute.

In returning our gaze to cities – rather than an exploded, planetary urbanism – we nonetheless need to strive for an *aesthetic reorganisation* where the human-to-human networks are backgrounded in favour of the inhuman assemblages which facilitate urban life. This kind of thinking has been developed within so-called 'assemblage urbanism' and the 'infrastructural' turn within urban studies. If the ambitions of the urbanists of the Chicago School was to understand the distinctive dimensions of early twentieth-century urbanism, in which 'neither the population aggregate nor the physical-cultural habitat but rather the *relations of man to man*'[83] are the focus of study, the 'infrastructural turn' of contemporary urban studies seeks to understand the complex post-human assemblages that constitute the city as a key actor within the earth's climatic system. Cities, on this view, are irreducible to any single – anthropic, economic or material – force and must instead be understood as forming complex *assemblages* between human and inhuman agencies. Whilst Brenner himself is suspicious of these theoretical positions because they tend to obscure what he sees to be the processes of accumulation and production which are the ultimate drivers of urbanisation,[84] there are useful insights in this literature if we are to return our attention to cities and give an account of how the city scale might attune us to the broader planetary reality within which urban life is embedded.

Sanitation, communication, transportation and financial infrastructures are often the taken for granted 'background' condition of a supposedly unique urban way of life. In their account of 'seeing like a city', Ash Amin and Nigel Thrift draw this background to the front and centre. To do this, they encourage us not only to *see* the city in a new way – momentarily bracketing the human encounters which tend to dominate our gaze, to focus instead on the inhuman apparatuses that allow for mobility within urban spaces – but to reattune *all* our senses to the meshwork of forces which constitute the city. As they suggest,

> Cities are chockful of noises which become their own associative landscapes . . . from the distant sound of aircraft overhead through the hum and honking of traffic to snatches of music and conversation, each with their own arcs . . . the main reason we can't get away from all this noise is – infrastructure.[85]

What Amin and Thrift counsel here is a retraining of our modes of perception in an effort to draw out the inhuman forces which subtend anthropic urban life. This involves an enlivening of the senses, what Weil would call cultivating new forms of *attention*, which allow us to sense our socio-technical conditions in a new way. There is a danger here that we fetishise the immediately perceived and sensed, that we give credence only to that which is presented to our sense perception within the city, amounting to a kind of naïve realism. And on this point, Brenner's more expansive conception of the urban form is a useful supplement: a renewed sensitivity to the more-than-human infrastructural networks which constitute the city need not lead to an obsession with the hyper-localised. Indeed, techniques through which we become immersed within a local urban infrastructural milieu can act as a useful adjunct to the kind of aesthetic practices that Brenner himself develops through the mapping of planetary infrastructures and flows.[86]

What this movement between the kind of *immersive aesthesis* that Amin and Thrift develop and the more abstract theorising and representation that

Brenner favours produces is precisely the kind of 'telescoping' of scales with which we opened this chapter and that marks the tensions and difficulties provoked by our entry into the new climatic regime. What I take from Brenner, and Amin and Thrift is a common effort to displace the affects and atmospheres of consumption and desire that are so often taken to structure city life, to puncture the atmospheric bubble of the city and look at the urban form 'slantwise', as a material assemblage that knits the human and the inhuman not only in *socio-technical* networks but within *geosocial* assemblages that have a truly planetary reach.

What kind of normative languages and modes of thinking are appropriate for this task? As a rallying cry for a renewed urban politics, the 'right to the city' is frequently evoked as a means through which those marginalised or displaced from urban centres might demand their right to shape urban development. Whilst not disregarding the productive potential of 'right to the city' claims which have been made in a number of important campaigns to resist urban exclusion, the privatisation of public space, to improve housing and infrastructural provision and so on,[87] the kind of shift in perspective that thinking of the city as an *earthly form* entails is perhaps less amenable to the language of rights than it is to a thinking of *needs, dependencies* and *obligations.*

In his expansive and theoretically rich study of spatial justice,[88] Philippopoulos-Mihalopoulos describes a teaching exercise in which students in his 'Law of the Environment' class are instructed to walk London's 'lawscape'.[89] Students are given a number of instructions to follow as they walk the city's street: keep in mind 'yourself, your movement, your surroundings' and reflect on how each alters within the different spaces you encounter, noting feelings of constraint or changes in demeanour and comportment. Students are instructed to keep track of their senses, noting what they smell and touch, what and how they see and the activities they might undertake as they walk. The purpose of the exercise is to attune students, at somatic and affective registers, to the multiple forms of normative ordering that the city produces and upon which urbanism depends. But so too does the exercise seek to reconfigure the very sense of the city as an assemblage of body/space/law in which human and non-human hybrids proliferate: the street – with its various signs, instruction and norms concerning where and when to walk, smoke or loiter, buy or donate, see and unsee – becomes a site where *law is everywhere*, constantly being reproduced through the very actions of the student-flâneurs themselves.[90]

We can think of Philippopoulos-Mihalopoulos's pedagogical exercise as urging a meditation, not on *rights of or to the city* but on the *urban obligations* that constitute the city as an associative form, an exercise in somatic attunement and 'attention' to legal–human–material relations that constitute the city's geo-eco-socio-material fabric. The 'urban obligations' to which Philippopoulos-Mihalopoulos attunes us are less concerned with a political demand to participate in the ongoing *oeuvre* of the city, than they invite a reflection on the network of bonds that constitute the urban reality in the first place. But in no way does this suggest that these urban obligations, or the city itself, can be *presupposed*; indeed, the import of the exercise consists in encouraging participants to take up the challenge of *assembly* and *composition*,[91] tracing the ligaments that produce the urban form. When we walk the city's lawscape we are immersed within a geological and planetary phenomenon. The concrete on which we walk; the social conventions that shape our behaviour and comportment; the property rights, licensing and tariff regimes that that facilitate the flow of goods, people and patterns of consumption, are perhaps the quickest route we have to connect our prevailing normative orderings with a sense of the *planetary scale* that the Anthropocene calls on us to face. Significantly, however, this approach does not *scale up* to the 'global' but instead brings these questions 'down to earth',[92] embedding them within highly localised somatic dispositions and sensitivities. This *aesthesis of urban obligations* urges us to become sensitive to the materials that shape our environment, the networks that facilitate our consumption and production habits, the material legacies that urban forms leave within the geological record, and the predominant role that contemporary urbanity plays within the earth's systemic functioning.

My intention here has been to sketch out some strategies of how we might begin to rethink the city scale in the context of the new climatic regime. This does not entail wishing away the state; clearly, state governance projects remain essential not only to the reproduction of the urban form but also to any effort to mitigate against and adapt to climate change. Instead, I have sought to identify an alternative point of departure for thinking about the nature of legal and political form in the context of the Anthropocene. The strategies that I have outlined here are intended to frame the city as an *earthly form*, a site in which human agency is enfolded within a broader set of planetary forces and relations. The details of such endeavour will only ever be worked out in the situated networks of particular urban settings. At a metatheoretical register, we can nonetheless characterise those themes and questions which might organise such an undertaking. The ultimate aim of such thinking is to develop a new mode through which we might *imagine the polis* that neither presupposes *state* or *global* scales, which constitutively ignore the inhuman, geological and ecological relations that are increasingly shaping social life, nor accepts the limited framework provided by existing city institutions. It is by accepting that a new sense of an urban politics, fit for the Anthropocene, *waits to be composed* that we might shift away from the scalar units associated with modernity, which continue to frame our political aesthetics and thereby limit the potential for legal and political renewal.

Afterword

I began working on this project in the aftermath of the Brexit vote, the election of Donald Trump, and in the context of rising nationalisms and localisms around the world, not least in my adoptive home of Hong Kong. I conclude the project in the midst of the 2020–21 coronavirus pandemic. In this sense, my research has been framed by two episodes that appear to signal an uncompromising reflux of modern sovereignty. The security of state borders; the reach of executive power; the privileges that attach to citizenship; and the enduring significance of nationhood and ethnic identity have all dominated our political discourse in recent years, something that has only accelerated in the context of today's 'viral times'. The response to the coronavirus pandemic amongst theorists of sovereignty was swift and largely predictable. Some heralded the return of the Leviathan, revealing the raw nature of political power and the pact that citizens make to limit their freedom in exchange for protection;[1] others focused on the deployment of exceptional powers, and raised the alarm over a creeping authoritarianism;[2] a number of commentators pointed to the biopolitical transformation of sovereignty within late modernity, claiming that recent events showed that state power has become ever more tightly coupled with medico-biological knowledge and practice;[3] and whilst some saw the pandemic as marking the high point of globalisation and urged the renationalisation of supply chains and greater state control of economic and social life, others continued to bang the drum for the post-war international order and the need for ever greater pooling of powers and resources within supra-national institutions.[4]

In these ways, the responses to the pandemic have remained fixed within the co-ordinates that have defined the debates around the nature of sovereignty for the last thirty years or more. Modern sovereignty is either thought to be waxing or waning within the context of 'globalisation' or is understood to be entwined with biopolitical techniques that measure, discipline and control populations and individuals. If, as has been suggested, the recent pandemic provides an opportunity to reflect more deeply about the crises to come, brought on by climate change, we have to move beyond these co-ordinates.

As I have argued in this book, some of the foundational presuppositions of modern sovereignty actively inure us to sensing, let alone addressing, the challenges associated with ecological mutation and our entry into the new climatic regime. Modern sovereignty engages a set of aesthetic practices in order to install a particular way of seeing, sensing, imagining and ordering the world that makes subjects constitutively insensitive to the ecological and geological relations that define the challenges of the Anthropocene. It is this doubled sense of the aesthetic – as a question of both *appearance* and *perception* – that has structured the preceding analysis. Sovereignty is an aesthetic or perspectival device which frames the world in a way that keeps the earthly relations and forces that ought to draw our attention resolutely 'offstage'.

If, as Latour has suggested, the pandemic is a 'dress rehearsal' for the upheavals to come,[5] we can read this in one of two ways. We might suggest that as the challenges associated with climate change mount, states will simply repeat what we have seen in response to the pandemic: borders will go up, liberties will be curtailed, power will be concentrated in the executive, biopolitical techniques will be deployed to control and immunise populations, citizenship will be a precious commodity, and nationalisms of various sorts will continue to hold sway. In this sense, John Lanchester's allegory of nation-state retrenchment in the face of climatic mutation in *The Wall* – discussed in Chapter 3 – would appear to be a sad forecast of things to come. The alternative is that we see the current crisis as a 'dress rehearsal' in the sense that things are going very badly and we require some fundamental reorganisation if we are to do anything more than embarrass ourselves on the opening night. If this is the case – as I believe it is – then we need to shift the co-ordinates that structure the debates around the nature of sovereignty in an effort to sensitise ourselves to, what I have called here, our *earthbound* condition. This must involve more than an understanding of the intersections between political power and the biological and more than a focus on the anthropic relations that define globalisation. Instead, this requires an account of the political that is attuned to the ecological, the geological and to the multiplicity of relations that sustain habitability on our planet.

It is this that I have attempted to do in admittedly suggestive ways in the more speculative aspects of the preceding chapters. At the limits of the modern framing of sovereignty, I have drawn on the work of a number of contemporary theorists in order to outline some alternative co-ordinates that might help us rethink the nature of the political in light of the Anthropocene thesis. At the limits of territory, I explored the possibilities of reimagining the relation between place and power through the heuristic of terrain; at the limits of popular sovereignty, I examined the possibility of including non-human actors within the ambit of political life through an account of 'sympoiesis'; and at the limits of the state scale, I set out what it might mean to privilege the city as a discrete legal and political form within the context of our new climatic conditions. These more speculative aspects of the preceding discussion intend to provide some new avenues for thought about the nature of legal and political form in the Anthropocene. Throughout, a key concern – inspired by the two chief influences of Weil and Latour – has been to reaffirm questions of *attachment, binding, placement* and *obligation* ahead of a pervasive discourse of *rights*. As Weil argues, to privilege obligation ahead of right is to foreground questions of *need* and *dependence*. It is through an attention to these themes that I have sought to articulate what it might mean to reimagine our legal and political commitments as emerging from our irredeemably earthbound condition.

All this might be taken as an injunction to transcend the structures of modern sovereignty entirely. And it is certainly true that one of the principal purposes of theory – as indicated by the etymology in *theōros* and *theōria*, to see, spectate and speculate – is to mobilise concepts and ways of thinking that allow us to imagine social, political and lawful relations beyond the confines of the present. As I have argued, the need for a 'new sensible world',[6] beyond the framing of social and ecological life that modern sovereignty installs and reproduces, is imperative in the context of the present ecological mutation and the onset of the Anthropocene. But it would be naïve to think that anyone has a clear sense of the form that political and legal power might take if completely shorn of the structures of modern sovereignty. Sovereignty, as the foremost means through which legal and political power has been theorised, organised and defined, has been with us for many centuries and it is not set to wither away any time soon. Indeed, it is my sense that too much 'critical' work on sovereignty labours under the misapprehension that if we were to simply rid ourselves of this concept and mode of political organisation, we would inevitably find ourselves somehow heading towards the sunlit uplands, finally freed from the kind of artificial constraint that sovereignty imposes on social life. Given the present state of things, I endorse the view that if modern sovereignty were somehow finally eclipsed, we would live in a 'much governed world'[7] but one largely controlled by the maddening logic of the market, on the one hand, and tightly determined by a set of ecological constraints that our planetary boundaries impose on us, on the other.

In lieu of a perspective in which we rather vaguely hope for some final transcendence of the sovereignty schema, I follow Donna Haraway's advice and aim to 'stay with the trouble' that our prevailing modes of thinking have themselves provoked.[8] In following the trajectories outlined in this book – with terrain, rather than territory; through a logic of sympoiesis that engages

the non-human; and in relation to a unique city, rather than the state, scale –
my hope is that we might undertake a 'reorganisation of the lighting system,
so to speak, that renders visible front lines . . . that were invisible before'.[9]
My effort has been to show sovereignty in a light not of its own choosing,
and to develop new strategies from which a critique of sovereignty might be
developed that is sensitive to the forces and relations that define our unhappy
arrival in the new climatic regime. If we are to do better than our current
'dress rehearsal' indicates, this remains an urgent task.

Notes

Introduction

1. Beckett, *Endgame*, p. 41.
2. Shugar et al., 'River Piracy'.
3. Ibid. p. 374.
4. Throughout the 1990s knowledge of the geological history of the earth dramatically increased as a series of projects analysed so-called 'deep cores' extracted from glacial ice, giving rise to unprecedented knowledge of earth's historic atmospheric composition, temperature and ocean levels. This has allowed for far greater understanding of the changes that have happened – and therefore can happen again – to the planet's climate system. Recent research suggests that tipping points within the earth system may already have been breached; see Lenton et al., 'Climate Tipping Points'.
5. Lenton et al., 'Tipping Elements'.
6. Stern, *Economics of Climate Change*, p. 193.
7. Anderson and Bows, 'Reframing the Climate Change Challenge'; referred to in Hamilton, *Requiem*, pp. 19–21.
8. IPCC, *Climate Change 2007: Impacts, Adaptation and Vulnerability*, 19.4.2.2, available at https://archive.ipcc.ch/publications_and_data/ar4/wg2/en/ch19s19 -4-2-2.html> (last accessed 8 December 2020).
9. Anderson and Bows, 'Beyond "Dangerous" Climate Change'.
10. IPCC, *Climate Change 2014: Synthesis Report*; IPCC, *Climate Change 2007: Synthesis Report*.
11. Barnosky et al., 'Approaching a State Shift', p. 54.
12. Barnosky et al., 'Has the Earth's Sixth Mass Extinction Event Arrived?'
13. Smil, *Earth's Biosphere*, p. 284, quoted in Bonneuil and Fressoz, *Shock of the Anthropocene*, p. 7.
14. Worm et al., 'Impacts of Biodiversity Loss'.
15. Barnosky et al., 'Approaching a State Shift', p. 54.
16. Welzer, *Climate Wars*.
17. Kelley et al., 'Climate Change in the Fertile Crescent'.

18. Simon Critchley; see Scratton, *Learning to Die in the Anthropocene*. The quotation is taken from the front pages where it is attributed to Critchley but otherwise unreferenced.
19. Steffen et al., 'Anthropocene', p. 842.
20. Hamilton, *Defiant Earth*, p. ix; see also Stager, *Deep Future*, pp. 34–42.
21. Sloterdijk, 'Anthropocene'.
22. For an assessment of these issues from two very different perspectives, see Slattery, 'First Nations and the Constitution'; Borrows, *Canada's Ingenious Constitution*.
23. Nadasdy, *Sovereignty's Entailments*.
24. It is worth noting here that the 'band' nomenclature owes its heritage to the federal Indian Act and is a term rejected by most Canadian Indians. As Nadasdy makes clear, the complex bonds of reciprocity and kinship that define the indigenous way of life in the Yukon are not accurately captured by the notion of distinct tribal groupings or band societies, which are themselves inventions of the state, created as instruments of rule; see ibid. pp. 20–45.
25. Ibid. p. 44.
26. Ibid. p. 302.
27. Ibid. p. 185.
28. Scott, *Seeing Like a State*, p. 2; my emphasis.
29. As Nadasdy makes clear, indigenous knowledges and forms of life have an enduring power within First Nations despite the adoption of 'modern' political forms. In a pattern common to post-colonial societies, the essential political and cultural struggle that now predominates within these communities does not concern a supposed *return* to older ways of living but how to successfully conduct a meaningful dialogue between indigenous practices and modern legal and political forms.
30. Rancière, *Politics of Aesthetics*.
31. Chakrabarty, 'Planetary Crises'.
32. Latour, 'On a Possible Triangulation'.
33. Latour, *Down to Earth*.
34. Latour, *Facing Gaia*.
35. Birrell and Matthews, 'Re-storying Laws for the Anthropocene'.
36. Rancière, *Politics of Aesthetics*.
37. Walker, 'Sovereignty Surplus'.
38. Haraway, *Staying with the Trouble*.
39. For a useful overview of this three-element account of sovereignty, see Jessop, *The State*, pp. 25–40.
40. Douzinas, *End of Human Rights*; Moyn, *Last Utopia*.
41. For an overview of these approaches, see Rogers, *Law, Fiction and Activism*, pp. 94–127.

42. See, for example, *Juliana v United States of America, et al.* (2020) (US Court of Appeals, Ninth Circuit).

Chapter 1

1. Hobsbawm, *Age of Extremes*, p. 287.
2. Latour, *We Have Never Been Modern.*
3. Indicative references that illustrate the range of disciplinary engagements with the Anthropocene include Turpin (ed.), *Architecture in the Anthropocene*; Davis and Turpin (eds), *Art in the Anthropocene*; Davies, *Birth of the Anthropocene*; Menely and Taylor (eds), *Anthropocene Reading*; Vidas et al., 'What is the Anthropocene?'
4. For overviews of this history, see Steffen et al., 'Anthropocene'; Angus, *Facing the Anthropocene*, pp. 27–37.
5. Hamilton, 'Getting the Anthropocene So Wrong', p. 103.
6. Hamilton, *Defiant Earth*, pp. 9–21.
7. Lawton, 'Editorial'.
8. Hamilton, *Defiant Earth*, p. 14.
9. Ruddiman, 'Anthropogenic Greenhouse Era'.
10. Lewis and Maslin, 'Defining the Anthropocene'.
11. It is estimated that between 45 million and 76 million people died over a 150-year period following the European colonisation of the Americas; this constitutes 90–95 per cent of the total indigenous population and about 10 per of the global human population. See Lewis and Maslin, *Human Planet*, pp. 147–87.
12. Zalasiewicz et al., 'When Did the Anthropocene Begin?' For a broader survey of these different approaches, see Davies, *Birth of the Anthropocene*; Bonneuil and Fressoz, *Shock of the Anthropocene*.
13. Hamilton and Grinevald, 'Was the Anthropocene Anticipated?', quoted in Angus, *Facing the Anthropocene*, p. 54.
14. Moore, *Capitalism in the Web of Life.*
15. Nancy, 'Existence of the World'.
16. Haraway, *Staying with the Trouble.*
17. Latour, *Facing Gaia.*
18. Angus, *Facing the Anthropocene*, p. 231; original emphasis.
19. Zalasiewicz et al., 'When Did the Anthropocene Begin?', p. 198.
20. See Malm and Hornborg, 'Geology of Mankind?'; Malm, *Fossil Capital*, p. 391.
21. Davies, *Birth of the Anthropocene*, p. 209.
22. Ibid. pp. 109–10; my emphasis.
23. Ibid. p. 76.
24. Heede, 'Tracing Anthropocentric', quoted in Malm, *Fossil Capital*, p. 328.
25. Hamilton, *Defiant Earth*, p. 30.
26. Hamilton, 'Getting the Anthropocene So Wrong', pp. 105–6.

27. Ibid. p. 105.
28. Malm and Hornborg, 'Geology of Mankind?', p. 66.
29. Moore, *Capitalism in the Web of Life*, p. 170.
30. Ibid. p. 191.
31. Ibid. p. 172.
32. Crutzen, 'Geology of Mankind'. For a good overview of some of the misconceptions over the science of Anthropocene, see Angus, *Facing the Anthropocene*, pp. 224–31.
33. Beck, *Metamorphosis of the World*, pp. 87–8.
34. See Chakrabarty, 'Politics of Climate Change'.
35. Malm, *Fossil Capital*, pp. 277–8.
36. Ibid. p. 278.
37. Ibid. pp. 367–88.
38. Ibid. p. 379.
39. Stoekl, 'Stocks and Shares', p. 62.
40. Clark and Yusoff, 'Geosocial Formations'.
41. Latour, *Down to Earth*, p. 84.
42. Latour, *Facing Gaia*.
43. See Lovelock, *Revenge of Gaia*.
44. Clarke, 'Rethinking Gaia', p. 13.
45. Latour, *Down to Earth*, p. 76; original emphasis.
46. Latour, *Facing Gaia*, p. 87.
47. Latour, 'Why Gaia is Not a God of Totality', p. 70; original emphasis.
48. Latour, *Facing Gaia*, p. 95; original emphasis.
49. Ibid. p. 97n71; original emphasis.
50. I borrow the notion of 'subscendence' from Morton, *Dark Ecology*, p. 114.
51. Latour, 'Waiting for Gaia', p. 10; original emphasis.
52. See Burdon (ed.), *Exploring Wild Law*; Burdon, *Earth Jurisprudence*; Rogers and Maloney (eds), *Law as if Earth Really Mattered*; for a more critical reading of Earth Jurisprudence, see Schillmoller and Pelizzon, 'Mapping the Terrain of Earth Jurisprudence'.
53. Berry, *Great Work*.
54. Burdon, *Earth Jurisprudence*, pp. 87–8.
55. See Bell, 'Thomas Berry and an Earth Jurisprudence'.
56. Ian Mason suggests that 'the principle of wholeness is the key principle running through the entire philosophy of Earth Jurisprudence'; see Mason, 'One in All', p. 36.
57. Cullinan, 'History of Wild Law', p. 13.
58. See Te Awa Tupua (Whanganui River Claims Settlement) Act 2017. It is worth noting that the legislation sought to not only safeguard the river from environmental harm and exploitation but also resolve a long-standing dispute between

Maori and state interests over the river and therefore needs to be read in this specific context.

59. For the seminal account of the error in this characterisation of scientific knowledge production, see Latour and Woolgar, *Laboratory Life*.
60. Howe, 'Making Wild Law Work', p. 27.
61. Latour, *Facing Gaia*, p. 97n71.
62. Manderson, 'Beyond the Provincial'.
63. Cullinan, 'History of Wild Law', p. 13.
64. Margulis, *Symbiotic Planet*.
65. Latour, *Facing Gaia*, p. 281; original emphasis.
66. A *vinculum* can be anything with which binding is done; see Birks, *Roman Law of Obligations*, p. 3, quoted in Veitch, 'Sense of Obligation'. In deploying the language of the *vincula juris* I am indebted to Kyle McGee who inspired this turn to a thinking of obligation, ligature, allegiance and alliance in the context of the ecological crisis; see McGee, *Heathen Earth*, pp. 117–44.
67. Serres, *Natural Contract*.
68. As Isabelle Stengers puts it, 'Gaia has no reason to be mixed up with anything that interests us, it's us that must pay attention to her'; see Stengers, 'Faire avec Gaïa', p. 15; my translation.
69. Weil, *Need for Roots*, p. 2.
70. Weil, 'Human Personality', p. 86.
71. Weil, *Need for Roots*; see also Weil, 'Draft for a Statement of Human Obligations'.
72. Weil, 'Draft for a Statement of Human Obligations', p. 225.
73. Weil, 'Human Personality', p. 83.
74. Ibid. p. 93.
75. The etymology of 'resolve' and 'dissolve' from the Latin *solvere*, to loosen, is worth noting here: in Roman Law a *solutio* was the mechanism by which the bonds of obligations could be undone. In this sense, we might think of rights-based 'solutions' to injustice as always entailing a loosening of prior and more fundamental obligations. On this point, see Veitch, 'Binding Precedent', p. 223.
76. MacIntyre, *After Virtue*, p, 69.
77. *Calvin's Case* (1608) 7 Co Rep 1a, 77 ER 377; my emphasis.
78. Christodoulidis, 'Dogma'.
79. Weil, 'Human Personality', p. 84.
80. Christodoulidis, 'Dogma', p. 11; original emphasis. Christodoulidis's point here is that this more radical sense of obligation *and* the languages of the middle region both form part of juridical language, broadly conceived.
81. Weil, 'Human Personality', p. 87.
82. Esposito, *Categories*, p. 152.
83. Davies, *Law Unlimited*, pp. 124–5; my emphasis.
84. Miles, 'Introduction', p. 8.

85. Christodoulidis, 'Dogma', pp. 9–10.
86. The direct connection that I am making here between obligation and the body does have a historical dimension. The primary form of obligation in Roman Law – debt – afforded a creditor the power to bind a debtor in chains until the debt had been repaid or some other 'solution' (*solutio*) to the bonds of obligation could be found. In this sense, the debt obligation had a material force that was felt on the body of the legal subject: 'debt was conceived very literally to inhere in or bind the body with a *vinculum juris*'. Wendall Holmes, *Common Law*, p. 10, quoted in Veitch, 'Binding Precedent', p. 222.
87. Latour, 'Attempt at a "Compositionist Manifesto"'.

Chapter 2

1. Arendt, 'Lying in Politics' in *Crises of the Republic*, pp. 3–13, 5, italics in the original.
2. Morton, *Dark Ecology*, p. 8; my emphasis.
3. See *R (Miller) v Secretary of State for Existing the European Union* [2017] UKSC 5.
4. *The Economist*, 'Interview with Steve Bannon'.
5. McGee, *Heathen Earth*.
6. See Bodin, *Six Books*.
7. Schmitt, *Political Theology*.
8. Consistent with Schmitt's well-known claim that all modern political concepts are secularised theological concepts; see ibid. On the association between sovereignty and 'awe', see Hobbes, *Leviathan*, p. 88.
9. See Agamben, *Kingdom and the Glory*, in which Agamben stresses the necessary connection between sovereign power and practices of 'acclamation', 'glory' and 'ceremony'.
10. Veitch et al., *Jurisprudence*, p. 15.
11. Martel, *Divine Violence*.
12. Walker, *After the Globe*, p. 61; my emphasis.
13. Bodin, *Six Livres*, p. 9, quoted in Minkkinen, *Sovereignty*, p. 65.
14. Walker (ed.), *Sovereignty in Transition*.
15. Tuck, *Sleeping Sovereign*.
16. Brown, *Walled States*.
17. Walker, 'Idea of Constitutional Pluralism'; Walker, 'Late Sovereignty'.
18. Loughlin, *Sword and Scales*, pp. 125–40.
19. Joyce, *Competing Sovereignties*, p. 1.
20. For an assessment of deconstructive approaches to sovereignty, see Gratton, *State of Sovereignty*, pp. 161–226.
21. See MacCormick, 'Beyond the Sovereign State'.
22. Foucault, *History of Sexuality Vol. 1*, p. 138.

23. Agamben, *Homo Sacer*; Agamben, *State of Exception*.

24. Motha, *Archiving Sovereignty*, p. 55.

25. Butler, *Precarious Life*; Santner, *On Creaturely Life*.

26. Mbembe, 'Necropolitics'.

27. On 'sociocentricism' in the context of the climate crisis, see Connolly, *Facing the Planetary*.

28. Walker, 'Postnational Constitutionalism'; Walker, *Intimations*.

29. Walker, 'Postnational Constitutionalism', p. 84.

30. Ibid. p. 82.

31. Sloterdijk, 'Anthropocene'.

32. Malabou, 'Will Sovereignty Ever be Deconstructed?'

33. Povinelli, *Geontologies*.

34. Ibid.

35. King James VI and I, *Political Writings*, quoted in Benite et al., 'Editors' Introduction', p. 16.

36. Agamben, 'Leviathan and Behemoth'; Richardson, 'Hobbes' Frontispiece'; Goodrich, *Legal Emblems*.

37. Goodrich, *Languages of Law*; Goodrich, *Legal Emblems*; Goodrich, *Oedipus Lex*.

38. Bagehot, *English Constitution*, p. 4.

39. Indicatively, see Neocleous, *Imagining the State*; Fitzpatrick, *Mythology of Modern Law*; Manderson, *Kangaroo Courts*; Manderson, *Danse Macabre*.

40. Frank, 'Living Image'.

41. Benton, *Search for Sovereignty*, p. 33.

42. Loughlin, *Idea of Public Law*, pp. 72–98; Loughlin, 'Erosion of Sovereignty'; Loughlin, 'Ten Tenets'.

43. Loughlin, *Political Jurisprudence*, p. 20.

44. Loughlin, *Idea of Public Law*, p. 78.

45. For a detailed assessment of this point in relation to British constitutional theory and Brexit, see Loughlin and Tierney, 'Shibboleth of Sovereignty'.

46. Loughlin, *Idea of Public Law*, p. 152.

47. Ibid. p. 145.

48. Motha, *Archiving Sovereignty*, p. 101.

49. Brown, *Walled States*, p. 109.

50. Baumgarten, *Aesthetica*; Baumgarten, *Reflections on Poetry*.

51. Eagleton, *Ideology of the Aesthetic*, p. 13.

52. Eagleton, 'Aesthetics and Politics', p. 62.

53. Clough and Halley (eds), *Affective Turn*; Gregg and Seigworth (eds), *Affect Theory Reader*; Anderson, *Encountering Affect*.

54. Gregg and Seigworth, 'Inventory of Shimmers', p. 1.

55. Berleant, *Re-thinking Aesthetics*, p. 78.

56. Rancière, 'Aesthetic Dimension', p. 1.

57. Rancière, *Politics of Aesthetics*, p. 8.
58. Ibid. p. 8.
59. Loughlin, 'Erosion of Sovereignty', p. 61.
60. Castoriadis, *Imaginary Institutions*, p. 145; original emphasis.
61. Thompson, 'Ideology and the Social Imaginary', p. 665.
62. Anderson, *Encountering Affect*, p. 31.
63. Böhme, 'Atmosphere as a Fundamental Concept'.
64. Anderson, *Encountering Affect*.
65. Walker, *After the Globe*, p. 228; my emphasis.
66. Povinelli, *Geontologies*.
67. Latour, *We Have Never Been Modern*.
68. *Mabo v Queensland (No 2)* (1992) 175 CLR 1.
69. See Dorsett and McVeigh, *Jurisdiction*; McVeigh (ed.), *Jurisprudence of Jurisdiction*; Barr, *Jurisprudence of Movement*; Rush, 'Altered Jurisdiction'.
70. Dorsett and McVeigh, 'Conduct of Laws'.
71. See Dorsett, '"Since Time Immemorial"'.
72. Dorsett and McVeigh, *Jurisdiction*, p. 37.
73. For instance, it was not until the Judicature Acts of 1870s – unifying Equity and the Common Law – that a single legal system operated with England and Wales.
74. Costa, *Iurisdictio*, pp. 142–3, quoted in Cormack, *Power to Do Justice*, p. 8.
75. Cormack, *Power to Do Justice*, p. 9.
76. Quoted in Rancière, 'Aesthetic Dimension', p. 7.
77. Bourdieu, *Distinction*. A similar argument is developed by Terry Eagleton (*Ideology of the Aesthetic*) in which aesthetic judgement is tied to the nineteenth-century struggle for political hegemony of the middle classes.
78. Rancière, 'Aesthetic Dimension', p. 7.
79. Ibid. p. 8; my emphasis.

Chapter 3

1. Coetzee, *Age of Iron*, p. 50.
2. For a seminal account of the uncanny (*das unheimliche*) and its relation to home and the 'un-homely', see Freud, *The Uncanny*, pp. 121–220.
3. Shepherd et al., 'Trends and Connections', quoted in Wallace-Wells, *Uninhabitable Earth*, pp. 63–4.
4. Wallace-Wells, *Uninhabitable Earth*, p. 60; see also Goodell, *Water Will Come*, pp. 13–14.
5. Walker, *Intimations*, pp. 1–28.
6. For instance, Moore, *Political Theory of Territory*; Sassen, *Territory, Authority, Rights*.
7. Elden, *Birth of Territory*; Elden, *Terror and Territory*; Elden, 'Thinking Territory Politically'; Elden, 'Land, Terrain, Territory'.

8. Elden, *Birth of Territory*.
9. Ibid. p. 322.
10. Lefebvre, *Production of Space*.
11. Scott, *Seeing Like a State*.
12. On this point, see Chakrabarty, 'Climate of History'.
13. Lindahl, 'Book Review', p. 146; original emphasis.
14. For a detailed discussion of some of the theological and philosophical presup-
    positions that structure *mappaemundi*, see Olsen, *Abysmal*, pp. 57–75; see also
    Harvey, *Mappa Mundi*.
15. Brotton, *12 Maps*, pp. 107–8.
16. Edney, *Cartography*, pp. 37–44.
17. Indicatively, see Jacob, *Sovereign Map*; Cosgrove, *Geography and Vision*; Black,
    Maps and Politics.
18. See Branch, *Cartographic State*, p. 54; see also Karrow, 'Centers of Map
    Publishing in Europe'.
19. Branch, *Cartographic State*.
20. See Brotton, *12 Maps*, p. 334.
21. Branch, *Cartographic State*, pp. 98–9.
22. On the use of colour in early modern maps, see Ackerman, 'Structuring of
    Territory'.
23. Branch, *Cartographic State*, pp. 81–3.
24. Ibid. p. 88.
25. The analysis here seeks to supplement and extend Dorsett and McVeigh's
    own explorations of mapping as a jurisdictional technology; see Dorsett and
    McVeigh, *Jurisdiction*, pp. 63–6.
26. Cormack, *Power to Do Justice*, pp. 3–10.
27. Ibid. p. 9.
28. The Virginia Charter (1606).
29. Edgerton, 'From Mental Matrix', p. 46.
30. Branch, *Cartographic State*, pp. 100–19.
31. Edney, *Cartography*.
32. Edney identifies ten specific aspects to the cartographic ideal; for a detailed
    assessment of each, see Edney, *Cartography*, pp. 50–102.
33. Section 62, *Native Title Act* (1993) (Cth).
34. *Mabo v Queensland (No 2)* (1992) 175 CLR 1.
35. Watson, 'Sovereign Spaces', pp. 37–8.
36. For greater detail on the nature of song and story in indigenous jurisprudence,
    see Black, *Land is the Source*.
37. Reilly, 'Cartography and Native Title', p. 14.
38. Ford, 'Law's Territory'.
39. Watson, 'Sovereign Spaces', p. 45.

40. Lanchester, *The Wall*.
41. Ibid. p. 55.
42. Ibid. p. 260.
43. Ibid. p. 275.
44. Ibid. p. 15.
45. Ibid. p. 161.
46. Ibid. p. 162.
47. Ibid. p. 199.
48. Neocleous, *Imagining the State*, p. 101.
49. Phipps, 'Terrain Systems Mapping'; see more generally Mitchell, *Terrain Evaluation*.
50. Minár and Evans, 'Elementary Forms'.
51. See Doyle and Bennett (eds), *Fields of Battle*.
52. Parry, 'Terrain Evaluation', p. 571.
53. Gordillo, 'Terrain as an Insurgent Weapon'; Elden, 'Legal Terrain'.
54. Gordillo, 'Opaque Zones of Empire', p. 2.
55. Gordillo, 'Terrain as an Insurgent Weapon', p. 57.
56. Ibid. p. 56.
57. Doreen Massey alerts us to these dynamics in her assessment of 'landscape' – a term similar to though distinct from 'terrain', which has artistic connotation which terrain lacks. Massey argues that an attention to the slow-motion transformation of landforms helps to displace the largely static conceptions that inform modern accounts of place; see Massey, 'Landscape as Provocation'.
58. Arènes et al., 'Giving Depth to the Surface'.
59. Beginning around three billion years ago, the Great Oxygenation Event provides the elemental composition of our largely taken for granted atmospheric conditions. Given that oxygen was a pollutant for most anaerobic lifeforms at the time of its emergence, the formation of our atmosphere killed off large swathes of earth's earliest life. This great dying event, the result of the then-emerging process of photosynthesis, evokes earth's 'deep time' and urges us to reflect on the ontological conditions which give rise to a habitable planet.
60. There are some important exceptions to this, notably Canetti, *Crowds and Power*; Irigaray, *Forgetting of Air*.
61. McCormack, *Atmospheric Things*, p. 29.
62. Coccia, *Life of Plants*, p. 47.
63. Ibid. p. 47.
64. Wallace-Wells, *Uninhabitable Earth*, p. 102.
65. Liu et al., 'Estimating Adult Mortality'.
66. Sloterdijk, *Foams*.
67. Elden, 'Legal Terrain'; Elden, 'Instability of Terrain'.
68. Ferrari et al. (eds), *Moving Border*, p. 19.

69. Department of Defense (USA), *Report on Effects of a Changing Climate*.
70. Weizman, *Hollow Land*, p. 84.
71. Ibid. p. 84.
72. Ibid. p. 177.
73. This is the argument developed in Brown, *Walled States*.
74. Weizman, *Hollow Land*, pp. 6–7.
75. Ferrari et al. (eds), *Moving Border*, pp. 20–1.
76. Gerhart et al., 'Contested Sovereignty', p. 995.
77. The Arctic Council comprises: Canada, USA, Russia, Finland, Norway, Iceland, Denmark (also on behalf of Greenland and the Faroe Islands) and Sweden; and six 'permanent participants'. For an introduction to the governance structure of the Arctic Council, see Nord, *Arctic Council*.
78. Gerhart et al., 'Contested Sovereignty', p. 998.
79. Ibid. p. 999.
80. Ibid. p. 999.
81. Bruun and Medby, 'Theorising the Thaw', p. 918.
82. O'Toole, 'Borders and Belonging'; see also O'Toole, *Heroic Failure*.
83. This point is well noted by Elden; see Elden, 'Legal Terrain', pp. 223–4.
84. Sloterdijk, *Foams*, pp. 30–1.

Chapter 4

1. Derrida, *Writing and Difference*, p. 192.
2. This has since been superseded by widespread civil unrest which engulfed the city in 2019–20. This began in June 2019, initially sparked by the proposed introduction of a controversial extradition law but the movement grew to encompass wide-ranging grievances about alleged abuse of police power, social and economic inequalities (particularly around housing policy), as well as renewed demands for democratic reform and the resignation of the Chief Executive, Carrie Lam. This saw an estimated 2 million residents take to the streets to resist the Beijing-backed extradition legislation, near-weekly confrontations with police, thousands of arrests and widespread disruption to the city's transportation infrastructure. The more militant strategies deployed in these recent actions explicitly depart from the non-violent orientation espoused by the 2014 Umbrella Movement.
3. Article 2, *The Constitution of the People's Republic of China*.
4. Frank, *Constituent Moments*, p. 5.
5. Lefort, *Democracy*, pp. 213–55; Lefort, *Political Forms*, pp. 237–319.
6. Latour et al., 'Down to Earth Social Movements', p. 360.
7. May, Conservative Party Conference Speech.
8. As Margaret Canovan argues, this can be traced to the legacy of *lex regis* inaugurated in Rome and discussed throughout the medieval period as the principle

that monarchical authority, despite its rejection of democratic legitimacy, none-theless depended in an indirect sense on the consent of the people. This theme was notably advanced by French Huguenot writers who articulated a sense of kingly authority which was conditional on a concern for the people's welfare. See Canovan, *The People*, pp. 10–16; Skinner, *Foundations*, pp. 239–301.

9. For an overview of the idea of popular sovereignty and discourses of 'the people' in medieval political thought, see Gierke, *Political Theories*, pp. 37–61.
10. Hamilton, *Defiant Earth*.
11. Haraway, *When Species Meet*, p. 11.
12. Latour, *Facing Gaia*, pp. 255–92.
13. Quoted in Kantorowicz, *King's Two Bodies*, p. 7.
14. Quoted in Kantorowicz, *King's Two Bodies*, p. 9; my emphasis.
15. Shakespeare, *Richard II*, IV, i, 220: 'God save King Henry, unkinged Richard says'.
16. Ibid. IV, i, 281–3.
17. Ibid. IV, i, 279–81: 'O flatt'ring glass, / Like to my followers in prosperity / Thou dost beguile me.'
18. Santner, *Royal Remains*.
19. Ibid. pp. ix–x.
20. Ibid. p. xv.
21. Ibid. p. 49.
22. Habermas, 'Popular Sovereignty as Procedure'.
23. Morgan, *Inventing the People*, p. 153.
24. Santner, *Royal Remains*, p. 34.
25. Douzinas, 'Metaphysics of Jurisdiction'. Following J. L. Austin's famous distinction, a constative utterance is descriptive and can be assessed in terms of its truthfulness; a performative, in contrast, *does* something through its utterance. Promises, declarations and refusals are all performatives that cannot be judged according to their truthfulness or falsity but, in Austin's terms, only according to their 'felicity', referring to the contextual conditions which determine their effectiveness; see Austin, *How to Do Things with Words*. Derrida examines the importance (and the instability) of the performative/constative distinction within the 'juris-dictional' moment of the declaration in 'Declarations of Independence'.
26. Douzinas, 'Metaphysics of Jurisdiction', p. 24.
27. Ibid. p. 24.
28. Derrida, 'Declarations of Independence', pp. 49–51.
29. Douzinas, 'Metaphysics of Jurisdiction', p. 26.
30. Agamben, *State of Exception*.
31. Lefort, *Political Forms*, p. 279.
32. Loughlin, 'Concept of Constituent Power', p. 228.

33. Rancière, *Disagreement*, p. 87.

34. Loughlin, 'Concept of Constituent Power', p. 228; see also Lefort, *Political Forms*, p. 280.

35. Yack, 'Popular Sovereignty'.

36. Hamilton, *Defiant Earth*.

37. Ibid. p. 40; my emphasis.

38. Ibid. p. 38.

39. Agamben, *The Open*. Agamben argues that the entire trajectory of Western politics is built on this fundamental division between the human and the non-human, justified in various ways and at different historical moments, which allows for the ongoing rearticulation of the political and the continuing production of *bare life*; that is, life which can be readily disposed of, without sanction.

40. See Derrida, *Animal That Therefore I Am*, pp. 29–35ff.; Derrida, 'And Say the Animal Responded'.

41. Derrida is particularly scathing of traditional accounts of the man/animal dichotomy on their treatment of difference, describing as *bêtise* (stupid, asinine or beastly) the regular homogenisation of all non-human animal life which embraces immense diversity under the singular concept of 'the animal'; see Derrida, *Animal That Therefore I Am*, pp. 1–51.

42. Hamilton, *Defiant Earth*, p. 43; my emphasis.

43. Ibid. p. 53.

44. Ibid. p. 63.

45. Ibid. p. 54.

46. Derrida, *Beast, Volume I*, p. 183.

47. Butler, *Notes*.

48. Butler, *Precarious Life*.

49. Arendt, *Human Condition*.

50. Butler, *Notes*, pp. 97–8.

51. Ibid. p. 130.

52. Ibid. p. 113.

53. Ibid. p. 214.

54. Ibid. p. 43.

55. Wolfe, *Before the Law*, pp. 17–21. On this theme, see also Stanescu, 'Species Trouble'.

56. On this point, see Beck, *Metamorphosis of the World*.

57. Haraway, *Companion Species Manifesto*; Haraway, *When Species Meet*.

58. Haraway, *Staying with the Trouble*.

59. Haraway, *Companion Species Manifesto*, p. 20.

60. Ibid. p. 25.

61. Haraway, *Staying with the Trouble*, p. 58.

62. Dempster, 'Sympoietic and Autopoietic Systems', p. 3; original emphasis.

63. Ibid. p. 8.
64. Ibid. p. 5.
65. Ibid. pp. 10–11.
66. Haraway, *Staying with the Trouble*, pp. 51–7.
67. Ibid. p. 33.
68. Haraway, 'When We Have Never Been Human'.
69. Haraway, *Staying with the Trouble*, pp. 72–98.
70. See Derrida, *Rogues*.
71. Klein, *This Changes Everything*, pp. 293–336.
72. Ibid. p. 303.
73. On this point, see Powys Whyte, 'Dakota Access Pipeline'.
74. McGee, *Heathen Earth*, p. 119.
75. Klein, *This Changes Everything*, p. 302.
76. Grosz et al., 'Interview'; Grosz, *Becoming Undone*.
77. Grosz et al., 'Interview', p. 135; my emphasis.
78. Latour, *Facing Gaia*, p. 283.

Chapter 5

1. Massey, *World City*, p. 15.
2. *The Lancet*, 'Australia on Fire'.
3. McCarthy, *The Road*, p. 9.
4. Clark, 'Scale', p. 150.
5. Clark, 'What on World?', p. 11.
6. Nixon, *Slow Violence*.
7. Morton, *Hyperobjects*.
8. Valverde, *Chronotopes of Law*, p. 58.
9. See, for example, Bosselmann, *Earth Governance*.
10. Brenner, 'The Limits to Scale?', p. 604. For a more detailed substantiation of Brenner's approach to scale, see Brenner, *New Urban Spaces*, pp. 46–114.
11. Lefebvre, *Production of Space*, p. 351.
12. Howitt, 'Scale as Relation', p. 55.
13. Quoted in Herod, *Scale*, p. xv.
14. Brenner, *New Urban Spaces*, p. 100.
15. Ibid. p. 100.
16. Ibid. p. 103.
17. See Agamben, *What is an Apparatus?*.
18. Haraway, *Staying with the Trouble*.
19. Derrida, *Beast, Volume 2*, pp. 8–9.
20. Marston, 'Social Construction of Scale', pp. 233–4. Marston makes this latter aspect of scale clear in her account of how the scale of the 'household' is routinely ignored in dominant accounts of political life which prioritises 'national',

‘regional’ or ‘global’ scales. As she argues, the household as a site of ‘micro-
level social processes . . . of social reproduction, biological reproduction and
consumption’, as well as economic production in the form of unpaid domestic
labour, is removed from the dominant scalar ordering that constructs a constitutively male ‘political world’.

21. Valverde, *Chronotopes of Law*, p. 9.
22. Quoted in Valverde, *Chronotopes of Law*, p. 10; italics removed.
23. Valverde, *Chronotopes of Law*, p. 82.
24. Chakrabarty, ‘Planetary Crises’, p. 260.
25. Ibid. p. 263.
26. Ibid. p. 265.
27. The processes are: climate change, ocean acidification, ozone depletion, bio-
    geochemical flows, freshwater systems, land use, chemical pollution, atmos-
    pheric aerosol overloading and biodiversity; see Rockström et al., ‘Planetary
    Boundaries’.
28. Latour, *Down to Earth*.
29. Clark, ‘Scale’, pp. 148–52.
30. Tsing, ‘On Nonscalability’.
31. Chakrabarty, ‘Planetary Crises’.
32. Kelly, *Politics and the Anthropocene*, p. 105.
33. Latour, *Facing Gaia*, p. 98.
34. Ibid. p. 101; original emphasis.
35. Ibid. p. 100.
36. Margulis, *Symbiotic Planet*, pp. 2, 113–28.
37. Latour, *Down to Earth*, p. 100.
38. Ibid. p. 100.
39. Ibid. p. 90.
40. Sassen, *Territory, Authority, Rights*, p. 55.
41. Berman, *Law and Revolution*, p. 102; see also Patel and Moore, *Seven Cheap
    Things*, p. 8.
42. Patel and Moore, *Seven Cheap Things*, p. 8.
43. Braudel, *Capitalism and Material Life*, p. 400.
44. Berman, *Law and Revolution*, p. 357.
45. Ibid. pp. 288–92.
46. Ibid. p. 292.
47. Sassen, *Territory, Authority, Rights*, pp. 57–67.
48. Berman, *Law and Revolution*, p. 394.
49. Weber, *The City*, p. 96.
50. Gierke, *Natural Law*, pp. 162–5.
51. Ibid. p. 396.
52. Braudel, *Capitalism and Material Life*, pp. 402–3.

53. Ibid. p. 403.

54. Poggi, *Development of the Modern State*, pp. 36–59.

55. Ibid. p. 40.

56. Braudel, *Capitalism and Material Life*, p. 399.

57. Ibid. p. 414.

58. Ibid. p. 414.

59. Ibid. p. 424.

60. Maitland, *Township and Borough*, p. 85.

61. Frug, 'City as a Legal Concept', p. 1091.

62. Ibid. pp. 1092–5.

63. Sassen, *Territory, Authority, Rights*.

64. Frug, 'City as a Legal Concept', pp. 1078–80.

65. Quoted in Frug, 'City as a Legal Concept', p. 1093.

66. Burdett and Rode, 'Living in an Urban Age', quoted in Amin and Thrift, *Seeing Like a City*, p. 13.

67. Davis, 'Who Will Build the Ark?', p. 41.

68. Dawson, *Extreme Cities*, pp. 5–6.

69. Nijman, 'Renaissance of the City'; Porras, 'City and International Law'.

70. Hirschl, *City, State*, pp. 151–71; Boutlegier, *Cities*; Lin, *Governing Climate Change*, pp. 105–26.

71. Lin, *Governing Climate Change*.

72. Dawson, *Extreme Cities*, pp. 130–1.

73. Barber, *Cool Cities*, p. 113.

74. Brenner, *New Urban Spaces*, pp. 354–5.

75. See Dawson, *Extreme Cities*, p. 136. A useful antidote to the *citerati* literature is Davis, *Planet of Slums*, which shows how most of our contemporary urbanisation is taking place within informal settlements within some of the poorest places on the planet.

76. See Brenner (ed.), *Implosions/Explosions*.

77. Brenner, *New Urban Spaces*, p. 388.

78. Ibid. pp. 358–61.

79. Hilary Angelo, 'From the City Lens'.

80. Haff, 'Technology as a Geological Phenomenon'; Zalasiewicz et al., 'Scale and Diversity'.

81. Zalasiewicz et al., 'Scale and Diversity', p. 11.

82. Ibid. p. 12.

83. Magnusson, *Politics of Urbanism*, p. 65; my emphasis.

84. Brenner et al., 'Assemblage Urbanism'.

85. Amin and Thrift, *Seeing Like a City*, pp. 52–3.

86. See Brenner, *New Urban Spaces*, pp. 334–94.

87. For a useful overview of this literature, see Butler, *Henri Lefebvre*, pp. 133–59.

88. Philippopoulos-Mihalopoulos, *Spatial Justice*.
89. For Philippopoulos-Mihalopoulos, the 'lawscape' refers to the 'tautology', or necessary co-implication, of law and space.
90. Philippopoulos-Mihalopoulos's approach to 'law' is expansive. The 'laws' that he encourages his students to see, think and feel as they walk the city do not necessarily refer to legislative provisions or formalised modes of enforcement but also engage social norms of comportment and etiquette.
91. Latour, 'Attempt at a "Compositionist Manifesto"'.
92. Latour, *Down to Earth*.

Afterword

1. Runciman, 'Coronavirus Has Not Suspended Politics'.
2. Agamben, 'Invention of an Epidemic'.
3. Lorenzini, 'Biopolitics in the Time of Coronavirus'.
4. See Gray, 'Why the Crisis is a Turning Point'; Miliband, 'Four Contests'.
5. Latour, 'Is this a Dress Rehearsal?'
6. Rancière, 'Aesthetic Dimension', p. 8.
7. Loughlin, 'Erosion of Sovereignty', p. 81.
8. Haraway, *Staying with the Trouble*.
9. Latour, *Facing Gaia*, p. 269.

Bibliography

Ackerman, James R., 'The Structuring of Territory in Early Printed Atlases', *Imago Mundi*, 47, 138–54 (1995).

Agamben, Giorgio, *Homo Sacer: Sovereign Power and Bare Life*, trans. Daniel Heller-Roazen (Stanford: Stanford University Press, 1998).

_____, 'The Invention of an Epidemic', *Quodlibet* (February 2020), <https://www.quodlibet.it/giorgio-agamben-l-invenzione-di-un-epidemia> (last accessed 18 December 2020).

_____, *The Kingdom and the Glory: For a Theological Genealogy of the Economy*, trans. Lorenzo Chiesa and Matteo Mandarini (Stanford: Stanford University Press, 2011).

_____, 'Leviathan and Behemoth', in *Stasis*, trans. Nicholas Heron (Stanford: Stanford University Press, 2015), pp. 19–54.

_____, *The Open: Man and Animal*, trans. Kevin Attell (Stanford: Stanford University Press, 2003).

_____, *State of Exception*, trans. Kevin Attell (Chicago: University of Chicago Press, 2005).

_____, *What is an Apparatus? And Other Essays* (Stanford: Stanford University Press, 2009).

Amin, Ash and Nigel Thrift, *Seeing Like a City* (Cambridge: Polity, 2017).

Anderson, Ben, *Encountering Affect: Capacities, Apparatuses, Conditions* (Abingdon: Routledge, 2014).

Anderson, Kevin and Alice Bows, 'Beyond "Dangerous" Climate Change: Emission Scenarios for a New World', *PTRSA*, 369, 20–44 (2011).

_____, 'Reframing the Climate Change Challenge in Light of Post-2000 Emission Trends', *Philosophical Transactions of the Royal Society A*, 366, 3863–82 (2008).

Angelo, Hilary, 'From the City Lens toward Urbanization as a Way of Seeing: Country/City Binaries on an Urbanizing Planet', *Urban Studies*, 54:1, 158–78 (2017).

Angus, Ian, *Facing the Anthropocene: Fossil Capitalism and the Crisis of the Earth System* (New York: New York University Press, 2016).

Arendt, Hannah, *The Human Condition* (Chicago: University of Chicago Press, 1998).

Arendt, Hannah, 'Lying in Politics', in *Crises of the Republic* (Harcourt Bruce & Company: New York, 1972), pp. 3–13, 5.

Arènes, Alexandra, Bruno Latour and Jérôme Gaillardet, 'Giving Depth to the Surface: An Exercise in the Gaia-graphy of Critical Zones', *The Anthropocene Review*, 5:2, 120–35 (2018).

Austin, J. L., *How to Do Things with Words*, 2nd edn, ed. J. O. Urmson and Marina Sbisà (Oxford: Oxford University Press, 1980).

Bagehot, Walter, *The English Constitution* (Cambridge: Cambridge University Press, 2001).

Barber, Benjamin R., *Cool Cities: Urban Sovereignty and the Fix for Global Warming* (New Haven, CT: Yale University Press, 2017).

Barnosky, Anthony D., Elizabeth A. Hadly, Jordi Bascompte et al., 'Approaching a State Shift in Earth's Biosphere', *Nature*, 485, 52–8 (2012).

Barnosky, Anthony D., Nicholas Matzke, Susumu Tomiya et al., 'Has the Earth's Sixth Mass Extinction Event Arrived?', *Nature*, 471, 51–7 (2011).

Barr, Olivia, *A Jurisprudence of Movement: Common Law, Walking and Unsettling Place* (Abingdon: Routledge, 2015).

Baskin, Jeremy, *Geoengineering, the Anthropocene and the End of Nature* (Basingstoke: Palgrave MacMillan, 2019).

Baumgarten, Alexander, *Aesthetica* [1750] (Hildesheim: Georg Olms, 1986).

_____, *Reflections on Poetry*, trans. K. Aschenbrenner and W. B. Holtner (Berkeley: University of California Press, 1954).

Beck, Ulrich, *The Metamorphosis of the World* (Cambridge: Polity, 2016).

Beckett, Samuel, *Endgame* [1958] (London: Faber and Faber, 2009).

Bell, Mike, 'Thomas Berry and an Earth Jurisprudence: An Exploratory Essay', *The Trumpeter*, 19:1, 69 (2003).

Benite, Zvi Ben-Dor, Stefanos Geroulanos and Nicole Jerr (eds), 'Editors' Introduction', in Zvi Ben-Dor Benite, Stefanos Geroulanos and Nicole Jerr (eds), *The Scaffolding of Sovereignty: Global and Aesthetic Perspectives on the History of a Concept* (New York, Columbia University Press, 2017), pp. 1–49.

Benite, Zvi Ben-Dor, Stefanos Geroulanos and Nicole Jerr (eds), *The Scaffolding of Sovereignty: Global and Aesthetic Perspectives on the History of a Concept* (New York, Columbia University Press, 2017).

Benton, Lauren, *A Search for Sovereignty: Law and Geography in European Empires, 1400–1900* (Cambridge: Cambridge University Press, 2010).

Berleant, Arnold, *Re-thinking Aesthetics: Rogue Essays on Aesthetics and the Arts* (Abingdon: Routledge, 2016).

Berman, Harold, *Law and Revolution: The Formation of the Western Legal Tradition* (Cambridge, MA: Harvard University Press, 1983).

Berry, Thomas, *The Great Work: Our Way into the Future* (New York: Bell Tower, 1999).

Birks, Peter, *The Roman Law of Obligations* (Oxford: Oxford University Press, 2014).

Birrell, Kathleen and Daniel Matthews, 'Re-storying Laws for the Anthropocene: Rights, Obligations and an Ethics of Encounter', *Law and Critique*, 31:3, 275–92 (2020).

Black, C. F., *The Land is the Source of the Law: A Dialogic Encounter with Indigenous Jurisprudence* (Abingdon: Routledge, 2011).

Black, Jeremy, *Maps and Politics* (London: Reaktion Books, 1997).

Bodin, Jean, *Les Six livres de la République* (Lyon: Jean de Tournes: 1579).

_____, *Six Books of the Commonwealth* (Oxford: Basil Blackwell, 1995).

Böhme, Gernot, 'Atmosphere as a Fundamental Concept in the New Aesthetics', *Thesis Eleven*, 36:1, 113–26 (1993).

Bonneuil, Christophe and Jean-Baptiste Fressoz, *The Shock of the Anthropocene*, trans. David Fernbach (London: Verso, 2017).

Borrows, John, *Canada's Ingenious Constitution* (Toronto: University of Toronto Press, 2010).

Bosselmann, Klaus, *Earth Governance: Trusteeship and the Global Commons* (Cheltenham: Edward Elgar, 2015).

Bourdieu, Pierre, *Distinction: A Social Critique of the Judgment of Taste* (Abingdon: Routledge, 2010).

Boutlegier, Sofie, *Cities, Networks and Global Environmental Governance* (Abingdon: Routledge, 2012).

Branch, Jordan, *The Cartographic State: Maps, Territory and the Origins of Sovereignty* (Cambridge: Cambridge University Press, 2014).

Braudel, Fernand, *Capitalism and Material Life 1400–1800*, trans. Miriam Kochan (New York: Harper and Row, 1967).

Brenner, Neil (ed.), *Implosions/Explosions: Towards a Study of Planetary Urbanisation* (Berlin: Jovis, 2014).

_____, 'The Limits to Scale? Methodological Reflections on Scalar Structuration', *Progress in Human Geography*, 25:4, 591–614 (2001).

_____, *New Urban Spaces: Urban Theory and the Scale Question* (Oxford: Oxford University Press, 2019).

_____, David J. Madden and David Wachsmuth, 'Assemblage Urbanism and the Challenges of Critical Urban Theory', *CITY*, 15:2, 225–40 (2011).

Brotton, Jerry, *The History of the World in 12 Maps* (London: Penguin, 2014).

Brown, Wendy, *Walled States, Waning Sovereignty* (New York: Zone Books, 2010).

Bruun, Johanne M. and Ingrid Medby, 'Theorising the Thaw: Geopolitics in a Changing Arctic', *Geography Compass*, 8:12, 916–29 (2014).

Burdett, Ricky and Philipp Rode, 'Living in an Urban Age', in Ricky Burdett and

Deyan Sudjic (eds), *Living in the Endless City* (London: Phaidon, 2011), pp. 8–43.

Burdon, Peter D., *Earth Jurisprudence: Private Property and the Environment* (Abingdon: Routledge, 2015).

_____ (ed.), *Exploring Wild Law: The Philosophy of Earth Jurisprudence* (Mile End: Wakefield Press, 2011).

Butler, Chris, *Henri Lefebvre: Spatial Politics, Everyday Life and the Right to the City* (Abingdon: Routledge, 2014).

Butler, Judith, *Notes Towards a Performative Theory of Assembly* (Cambridge, MA: Harvard University Press, 2015).

_____, *Precarious Life: The Powers of Mourning and Violence* (London: Verso, 2004).

Canetti, Elias, *Crowds and Power*, trans. Carol Stewart (New York: Farrar, Straus and Giroux, 1984).

Canovan, Margaret, *The People* (Cambridge: Polity, 2005).

Castoriadis, Cornelius, *The Imaginary Institutions of Society*, trans. Kathleen Blamey (Cambridge: Polity, 2005).

Chakrabarty, Dipesh, 'The Climate of History: Four Theses', *Critical Inquiry*, 35:2, 197–222 (2009).

_____, 'Planetary Crises and the Difficulty of Being Modern', *Millennium: Journal of International Studies*, 46:3, 259–82 (2018).

_____, 'The Politics of Climate Change is More than the Politics of Capitalism', *Theory, Culture & Society*, 34:2–3, 25–37 (2017).

Christodoulidis, Emilios, 'Dogma, or the Deep Rootedness of Obligation', in Daniel Matthews and Scott Veitch (eds), *Law, Obligation, Community* (Abingdon: Routledge, 2018), pp. 4–16.

Clark, Nigel and Kathryn Yusoff, 'Geosocial Formations and the Anthropocene', *Theory, Culture & Society*, 34:2–3, 3–23 (2017).

Clark, Timothy, 'Scale', in Tom Cohen (ed.), *Telemorphosis: Theory in the Era of Climate Change* (Ann Arbor: Open Humanities Press, 2012), pp. 148–66.

_____, 'What on World is the Earth?', *Oxford Literary Review*, 35:1, 5–24 (2013).

Clarke, Bruce, 'Rethinking Gaia: Stengers, Latour, Margulis', *Theory, Culture & Society*, 34:4, 3–26 (2017).

Clough, Patricia and Jean Halley (eds), *The Affective Turn: Theorising the Social* (Durham, NC: Duke University Press, 2007).

Coccia, Emanuele, *The Life of Plants* (Cambridge: Polity, 2019).

Coetzee, J. M., *Age of Iron* (New York: Random House, 1990).

Connolly, William, *Facing the Planetary: Entangled Humanism and the Politics of Swarming* (Durham, NC: Duke University Press, 2017).

Cormack, Bradin, *A Power to Do Justice: Jurisdiction, English Literature, and the Rise of the Common Law, 1509–1625* (Chicago: University of Chicago Press, 2008).

Cosgrove, Denis, *Geography and Vision: Seeing, Imagining and Representing the World* (London: I.B. Tauris, 2008).

Costa, Pietro, *Iurisdictio: Semantica del Potere Politico nel Pubblicistica Medievale (1100–1433)* (Milan: Giuffrè, 2002).

Crutzen, Paul, 'The Geology of Mankind', *Nature*, 415, 23 (2002).

Cullinan, Cormac, 'A History of Wild Law', in Peter Burdon (ed.), *Exploring Wild Law: The Philosophy of Earth Jurisprudence* (Mile End: Wakefield Press, 2011), pp. 12–23.

Davies, Jeremy, *The Birth of the Anthropocene* (Oakland: University of California Press, 2016).

Davies, Margaret, *Law Unlimited* (Abingdon: Routledge, 2017).

Davis, Heather and Etienne Turpin (eds), *Art in the Anthropocene: Encounters among Aesthetics, Politics, Environments and Epistemologies* (London: Open Humanities Press, 2015).

Davis, Mike, *Planet of Slums* (London: Verso, 2007).

_____, 'Who Will Build the Ark?', *New Left Review*, 61, 29–46 (2010).

Dawson, Ashely, *Extreme Cities: The Peril and Promise of Urban Life in the Age of Climate Change* (London: Verso, 2017).

Dempster, Beth, 'Sympoietic and Autopoietic Systems: A New Distinction for Self-Organising Systems' [Presented at the International Society for Systems Studies Annual Conference, Toronto, Canada, July 2000], in J. K. Allen and J. Wilby (eds), *Proceedings of the World Congress of the Systems Sciences and ISSS 2000*.

Department of Defense (USA), *Report on Effects of a Changing Climate to the Department of Defense* (Office of the Under Secretary of Defense for Acquisition and Sustainment, January 2019).

Derrida, Jacques, 'And Say the Animal Responded', in Cary Woolfe (ed.), *Zoontologies: The Question of the Animal* (Minneapolis: University of Minnesota Press, 2003), pp. 121–46.

_____, *The Animal That Therefore I Am*, trans. David Wills (New York: Fordham University Press, 2006).

_____, *The Beast & the Sovereign, Volume I* (Chicago: University of Chicago Press, 2011).

_____, *The Beast & the Sovereign, Volume II* (Chicago: University of Chicago Press, 2011).

_____, 'Declarations of Independence', in *Negotiations: Interviews and Interventions 1971–2001*, trans. Elisabeth Rudinesco (Stanford: Stanford University Press, 2002), pp. 46–54.

_____, *Rogues: Two Essays on Reason*, trans. Pascale-Anne Brault and Michael Naas (Stanford: Stanford University Press, 2005).

_____, *Writing and Difference*, trans. Alan Bass (London: Routledge, 2008).

Dorsett, Shaunnagh, '"Since Time Immemorial": A Story of Common Law

Jurisdiction, Native Title and the Case of Tanistry', *Melbourne University Law Review*, 26:1, 32–59 (2002).

Dorsett, Shaunnagh and Shaun McVeigh, 'Conduct of Laws: Native Title, Responsibility, and Some Limits of Jurisdictional Thinking', *Melbourne University Law Review*, 36:2, 470–93 (2012).

_____, *Jurisdiction* (Abingdon: Routledge, 2012).

Douzinas, Costas, *The End of Human Rights* (London: Hart, 2000).

_____, 'The Metaphysics of Jurisdiction', in Shaun McVeigh (ed.), *Jurisprudence of Jurisdiction* (Abingdon: Routledge, 2007), pp. 21–32.

Doyle, Peter and Matthew R. Bennett (eds), *Fields of Battle: Terrain in Military History*, The GeoJournal Library, vol. 64 (Dordrecht: Springer, 2002).

Eagleton, Terry, 'Aesthetics and Politics in Edmund Burke', *History Workshop Journal*, 28:1, 53–62 (1989).

_____, *The Ideology of the Aesthetic* (Oxford: Blackwell, 1990).

The Economist, 'An Interview with Steve Bannon' (20 September 2018), <https://www.economist.com/open-future/2018/09/20/an-interview-with-steve-bannon> (last accessed 18 December 2020)

Edgerton, Samuel Y., 'From Mental Matrix to *Mappamundi* to Christian Empire: The Heritage of Ptolemaic Cartography in the Renaissance', in David Woodward (ed.), *Art and Cartography: Six Historical Essays* (Chicago: University of Chicago Press, 1987), pp. 10–50.

Edney, Matthew H., *Cartography: The Ideal and its History* (Chicago: University of Chicago Press, 2019).

Elden, Stuart, *The Birth of Territory* (Chicago: University of Chicago Press, 2013).

_____, 'The Instability of Terrain', in Marco Ferrari, Elisa Pasqual and Andrea Bagnato (eds), *A Moving Border: Alpine Cartographies of Climate Change* (New York: Columbia Books on Architecture and the City, 2019), pp. 51–61.

_____, 'Land, Terrain, Territory', *Progress in Human Geography*, 34:6, 799–817 (2010).

_____, 'Legal Terrain – The Political Materiality of Territory', *London Review of International Law*, 5:2, 199–224 (2017).

_____, *Terror and Territory: The Spatial Extent of Sovereignty* (Minneapolis: University of Minnesota Press, 2009).

_____, 'Thinking Territory Politically', *Political Geography*, 29:4, 238–41 (2010).

Esposito, Roberto, *Categories of the Impolitical* (New York: Fordham University Press, 2015).

Ferrari, Marco, Elisa Pasqual and Andrea Bagnato (eds), *A Moving Border: Alpine Cartographies of Climate Change* (New York: Columbia Books on Architecture and the City, 2019).

Fitzpatrick, Peter, *The Mythology of Modern Law* (London: Routledge, 1992).

Ford, Richard T., 'Law's Territory (A History of Jurisdiction)', *Michigan Law Review*, 97:4, 843–930 (1999).

Foucault, Michel, *The History of Sexuality Vol. 1* (New York: Vintage Books, 1990).

Frank, Jason, *Constituent Moments: Enacting the People in Postrevolutionary America* (Durham, NC: Duke University Press, 2010).

_____, 'The Living Image of the People', *Theory and Event*, 18:1 (2015), <https://www.muse.jhu.edu/article/566086> (last accessed 18 December 2020).

Freud, Sigmund, *The Uncanny*, trans. David McLintock (London: Penguin, 2003).

Frug, Gerald E., 'The City as a Legal Concept', *Harvard Law Review*, 93:5, 1059–149 (1980).

Gerhart, Hannes, Philip E. Steinberg, Jeremy Tasch, Sandra J. Fabiano and Rob Shields, 'Contested Sovereignty in a Changing Arctic', *Annals of the Association of American Geographers*, 100:4, 992–1002 (2010).

Gierke, Otto von, *Natural Law and the Theory of Society 1500–1800*, trans. Ernest Barker (Clark, NJ: The Law Book Exchange, 2010).

_____, *Political Theories of the Middle Age*, trans. F. W. Maitland (Cambridge: Cambridge University Press, 1922).

Goodell, Jeff, *The Water Will Come: Rising Seas, Sinking Cities and the Remaking of the Civilized World* (New York: Little, Brown, 2017).

Goodrich, Peter, *Languages of Law* (Cambridge: Cambridge University Press, 2004).

_____, *Legal Emblems and the Art of Law* (Cambridge: Cambridge University Press, 2013).

_____, *Oedipus Lex* (Berkeley: University of California Press, 1995).

Gordillo, Gaston, 'Opaque Zones of Empire: Notes Toward a Theory of Terrain' (2013), <https://www.academia.edu/3795770/Opaque_Zones_of_Empire_Notes_Toward_a_Theory_of_Terrain> (last accessed 18 December 2020).

_____, 'Terrain as an Insurgent Weapon: An Affective Geometry of Warfare in the Mountains of Afghanistan', *Political Geography*, 64, 53–61 (2018).

Gratton, Peter, *The State of Sovereignty: Lessons from the Political Fictions of Modernity* (New York: State University of New York Press, 2012).

Gray, John, 'Why the Crisis is a Turning Point in History', *New Statesman* (April 2020), <https://www.newstatesman.com/international/2020/04/why-crisis-turning-point-history> (last accessed 18 December 2020).

Gregg, Melissa and Gregory J. Seigworth (eds), *The Affect Theory Reader* (Durham, NC: Duke University Press, 2010).

Grosz, Elizabeth, *Becoming Undone: Darwinian Reflections on Life, Politics and Art* (Durham, NC: Duke University Press, 2011).

_____, Kathryn Yusoff and Nigel Clark, 'An Interview with Elizabeth Grosz: Geopower, Inhumanism and the Biopolitical', *Theory, Culture & Society*, 34:2–3, 129–46 (2017).

Habermas, Jurgen, 'Popular Sovereignty as Procedure', in James Bohman and William Rehg (eds), *Deliberative Democracy: Essays on Reason and Politics* (Cambridge, MA: MIT Press, 1997), pp. 35–66.

Haff, Peter, 'Technology as a Geological Phenomenon: Implications for Human Well-being', in C. N. Waters, J. A. Zalasiewicz, M. Williams, M. A. Ellis and A. M. Snelling (eds), *A Stratigraphical Basis for the Anthropocene* (London: Geological Society Special Publications, 2014), pp. 301–9.

Hamilton, Clive, *Defiant Earth: The Fate of Humans in the Anthropocene* (Cambridge: Polity, 2017).

_____, *Earth Masters: The Dawn of the Age of Climate Engineering* (New Haven, CT: Yale University Press, 2014).

_____, 'Getting the Anthropocene So Wrong', *The Anthropocene Review*, 2:2, 102–7 (2015).

_____, *Requiem for a Species* (Crows Nest, NSW: Allen & Unwin, 2010).

Hamilton, Clive and Jacques Grinevald, 'Was the Anthropocene Anticipated?', *Anthropocene Review*, 2:1, 59–72 (2015).

Haraway, Donna, *The Companion Species Manifesto: Dogs, People, and Significant Otherness* (Chicago: University of Chicago Press, 2003).

_____, *Staying with the Trouble: Making Kin in the Chthulucene* (Durham, NC: Duke University Press, 2016).

_____, *When Species Meet* (Minneapolis: University of Minnesota Press, 2007).

_____, 'When We Have Never Been Human, What is to be Done?', *Theory, Culture & Society*, 23:7–8, 135–58 (2006).

Harvey, P. D. A., *Mappa Mundi: The Hereford World Map* (Toronto: University of Toronto Press, 1996).

Heede, Richard, 'Tracing Anthropocentric Carbon Dioxide and Methane Emissions to Fossil Fuel and Cement Producers, 1854–2010', *Climate Change*, 122, 234 (2014).

Herod, Andrew, *Scale* (Abingdon: Routledge, 2011).

Hirschl, Ran, *City, State* (Oxford: Oxford University Press, 2020).

Hobbes, Thomas, *Leviathan* (Cambridge: Cambridge University Press, 1991).

Hobsbawm, Eric, *The Age of Extremes* (London: Abacus, 1995).

Howe, Helena, 'Making Wild Law Work – The Role of "Connection with Nature" and Education in Developing an Ecocentric Property Law', *Journal of Environmental Law*, 29, 19–45 (2017).

Howitt, Richard, 'Scale as Relation: Musical Metaphors of Geographical Scale', *Area*, 30:1, 49–58 (1998).

IPCC, *Climate Change 2007: Impacts, Adaptation and Vulnerability*, Contribution of Working Group II to the Fourth Assessment Report of the IPCC (New York: Cambridge University Press, 2007).

IPCC, *Climate Change 2007: Synthesis Report. Contribution of Working Groups I, II and III to the Fourth Assessment Report of the Intergovernmental Panel on Climate Change* (Geneva: IPCC, 2007).

IPCC, *Climate Change 2014: Synthesis Report. Contribution of Working Groups I, II and III to the Fifth Assessment Report of the Intergovernmental Panel on Climate Change* (Geneva: IPCC, 2014).

Irigaray, Luce, *The Forgetting of Air in Martin Heidegger* (Austin: University of Texas Press, 1999).

Jacob, Christian, *The Sovereign Map: Theoretical Approaches in Cartography throughout History* (Chicago: University of Chicago Press, 2006).

Jessop, Bob, *The State: Past, Present, Future* (Cambridge: Polity, 2016).

Joyce, Richard, *Competing Sovereignties* (Abingdon: Routledge, 2013).

Kantorowicz, Ernst, *The King's Two Bodies: A Study in Medieval Political Theology* (Princeton: Princeton University Press, 1997).

Karrow, Robert, 'Centers of Map Publishing in Europe, 1472–1600', in David Woodward (ed.), *The History of Cartography, Volume 3: Cartography in the European Renaissance, Part I* (Chicago: University of Chicago Press, 2007), pp. 611–21.

Keith, David, *A Case for Climate Engineering* (Cambridge, MA: MIT Press, 2013).

Kelley Colin P., Shahrzad Mohtadi, Mark A. Cane, Richard Seager and Yochanan Kushnir, 'Climate Change in the Fertile Crescent and Implications of the Recent Syrian Drought', *Proceedings of the National Academy of Sciences*, 112:11, 3241–6 (2015).

Kelly, Duncan, *Politics and the Anthropocene* (Cambridge: Polity, 2019).

King James VI and I, *Political Writings*, ed. J. P. Summerville (Cambridge: Cambridge University Press, 1994).

Klein, Naomi, *This Changes Everything: Capitalism vs the Climate* (London: Penguin, 2014).

Latour, Bruno, 'An Attempt at a "Compositionist Manifesto"', *New Literary History*, 41:3, 471–90 (2010).

_____, *Down to Earth: Politics in the New Climatic Regime* (Cambridge: Polity, 2018).

_____, *Facing Gaia: Eight Lectures on the New Climatic Regime* (Cambridge: Polity, 2017).

_____, 'Is this a Dress Rehearsal?', *Critical Inquiry Blog* (26 March 2020), <https://critinq.wordpress.com/2020/03/26/is-this-a-dress-rehearsal/> (last accessed 18 December 2020).

_____, 'On a Possible Triangulation of Some Present Political Positions', *Critical Inquiry*, 44, 213–26 (2018).

_____, 'Waiting for Gaia: Composing the Common World through Arts and Politics' [Lecture at the French Institute, London, November 2011], <http://www.bruno-latour.fr/sites/default/files/124-GAIA-LONDON-SPEAP_0.pdf> (last accessed 18 December 2020).

_____, *We Have Never Been Modern*, trans. Catherine Porter (Cambridge, MA: Harvard University Press, 1993).

_____, 'Why Gaia is Not a God of Totality', *Theory, Culture & Society*, 34:2–3, 61–81 (2017).

_____, Denise Milstein, Isaac Marrero-Guiliamón and Israel Rodríguez-Giralt, 'Down to Earth Social Movements: An Interview with Bruno Latour', *Social Movement Studies*, 17:3, 353–61 (2018).

Latour, Bruno and Steve Woolgar, *Laboratory Life: The Construction of Scientific Facts* (Beverly Hills: Sage, 1979).

The Lancet, 'Australia on Fire' [Editorial], *The Lancet*, 395:10219, 165 (2020).

Lanchester, John, *The Wall* (London: Faber and Faber, 2019).

Lawton, John, 'Editorial: Earth System Science', *Science*, 292:5524, 1965 (2001).

Lefebvre, Henri, *The Production of Space* (Oxford: Basil Blackwell, 1991).

Lefort, Claude, *Democracy and Political Theory*, trans. David Macey (Cambridge: Polity, 1988).

_____, *The Political Forms of Modern Society* (Cambridge: Polity, 1986).

Lenton, Timothy M., Hermann Held, Elmar Kriegler et al., 'Tipping Elements in the Earth's Climate System', *Proceedings of the National Academy of Sciences of the United States of America*, 105:6, 1786–93 (2008).

Lenton, Timothy M., Johan Rockström, Owen Gaffney et al., 'Climate Tipping Points – Too Risky to Bet Against', *Nature*, 575, 592–5 (2019).

Lewis, Simon L. and Mark A. Maslin, 'Defining the Anthropocene', *Nature*, 519, 171–80 (2015).

_____, *The Human Planet: How We Created the Anthropocene* (London: Penguin, 2018).

Lin, Jolene, *Governing Climate Change: Global Cities and Transnational Law Making* (Cambridge: Cambridge University Press, 2018).

Lindahl, Hans, 'Book Review: *The Birth of Territory* by Stuart Elden', *Political Theory*, 44:I, 144–5 (2015).

Liu, Jun, Yiqun Han, Xiao Tang, Jiang Zhu and Tong Zhu, 'Estimating Adult Mortality Attributable to $PM_{2.5}$ Exposure in China with Assimilated $PM_{2.5}$ Concentrations Based on a Ground Monitoring Network', *Science of the Total Environment*, 568, 1253–62 (2016).

Lorenzini, Daniele, 'Biopolitics in the Time of Coronavirus', *Critical Inquiry Blog* (2 April 2020), <https://critinq.wordpress.com/2020/04/02/biopolitics-in-the-time-of-coronavirus/> (last accessed 18 December 2020).

Loughlin, Martin, 'The Concept of Constituent Power', *European Journal of Political Philosophy*, 13:2, 218–37 (2014).

_____, 'The Erosion of Sovereignty', *Netherlands Legal Philosophy Journal*, 2, 57–81 (2016).

_____, *The Idea of Public Law* (Oxford: Oxford University Press, 2004).

_____, *Political Jurisprudence* (Oxford: Oxford University Press, 2017).

_____, *Sword and Scales: An Examination of the Relationship between Law and Politic* (Oxford: Hart, 2000).

_____, 'Ten Tenets of Sovereignty', in Neil Walker (ed.), *Sovereignty in Transition: Essays in European Law* (Oxford: Hart, 2003), pp. 55–86.

Loughlin, Martin and Stephen Tierney, 'The Shibboleth of Sovereignty', *Modern Law Review*, 81:6, 989–1016 (2018).

Lovelock, James, *The Revenge of Gaia: Earth's Climate Crisis and the Fate of Humanity* (New York: Basic Books, 2006).

McCarthy, Cormac, *The Road* (New York: Picador, 2007).

McCormack, Derek P., *Atmospheric Things: On the Allure of Elemental Envelopment* (Durham, NC: Duke University Press, 2018).

MacCormick, Neil, 'Beyond the Sovereign State', *Modern Law Review*, 56:1, 1–18 (1993).

McGee, Kyle, *Heathen Earth: Trumpism and Political Ecology* (New York: Punctum Books, 2017).

MacIntyre, Alasdair, *After Virtue* (London: Duckworth, 1981).

McVeigh, Shaun (ed.), *Jurisprudence of Jurisdiction* (Abingdon: Routledge, 2007).

Magnusson, Warren, *Politics of Urbanism: Seeing Like a City* (Abingdon: Routledge, 2011).

Maitland, F. W., *Township and Borough* (Cambridge: Cambridge University Press, 1964).

Malabou, Catherine, 'Will Sovereignty Ever be Deconstructed?', in Brenna Bhandar and Jonathan Goldberg-Hiller (eds), *Plastic Materialities: Politics, Legality and Metamorphosis in the Work of Catherine Malabou* (Durham, NC: Duke University Press, 2015), pp. 35–46.

Malm, Andreas, *Fossil Capital: The Rise of Steam Power and the Birth of Global Warming* (London: Verso, 2016).

Malm, Andreas and Alf Hornborg, 'The Geology of Mankind? A Critique of the Anthropocene Narrative', *Anthropocene Review*, 1:1, 65–9 (2014).

Manderson, Desmond, 'Beyond the Provincial: Space, Aesthetics and Modernist Legal Theory', *Melbourne University Law Review*, 20, 1048–71 (1996).

_____, *Danse Macabre: Temporalities of Law in the Visual Arts* (Cambridge: Cambridge University Press, 2019).

_____, *Kangaroo Courts and the Rule of Law: The Legacy of Modernism* (Abingdon: Routledge, 2012).

Margulis, Lynn, *Symbiotic Planet: A New Look at Evolution* (New York: Basic Books, 2008).

Marston, Sallie, 'The Social Construction of Scale', *Progress in Human Geography*, 24:2, 219–42 (2000).

Martel, James, *Divine Violence: Walter Benjamin and the Eschatology of Sovereignty* (Abingdon: Routledge, 2012).

Mason, Ian, 'One in All: Principles and Characteristics of Earth Jurisprudence', in Peter Burdon (ed.), *Exploring Wild Law: The Philosophy of Earth Jurisprudence* (Mile End: Wakefield Press, 2011), pp. 35–44.

Massey, Doreen, 'Landscape as Provocation: Reflections on Moving Mountains', *Journal of Material Culture*, 11:1/2, 33–48 (2006).

_____, *World City* (Cambridge: Polity, 2007).

May, Theresa, Conservative Party Conference Speech (2016), <https://www.tel egraph.co.uk/news/2016/10/05/theresa-mays-conference-speech-in-full/> (last accessed 18 December 2020).

Mbembe, Achille, 'Necropolitics', *Public Culture*, 15:1, 11–40 (2003).

Menely, Tobias and Jesse Oak Taylor (eds), *Anthropocene Reading: Literary History in Geologic Times* (University Park: Pennsylvania State University Press, 2017).

Miles, Sian, 'Introduction', in Sian Miles (ed.), *Simone Weil: An Anthology* (London: Penguin, 2005), pp. 1–68.

Miliband, David, 'The Four Contests that Will Shape the Post-Covid-19 World', *New Statesman* (April 2020), <https://www.newstatesman.com/2020/04/david-miliband-four-contests-will-shape-post-covid-19-world> (last accessed 18 December 2020).

Minár, Josef and Ian S. Evans, 'Elementary Forms for Land Surface Segmentation: The Theoretical Basis of Terrain Analysis and Geomorphological Mapping', *Geomorphology*, 95:3–4, 237 (2007).

Minkkinen, Panu, *Sovereignty, Knowledge, Law* (Abingdon: Routledge, 2009).

Mitchell, Colin, *Terrain Evaluation*, 2nd edn (London: Routledge, 2014).

Moore, Jason W., *Capitalism in the Web of Life: Ecology and the Accumulation of Capital* (London: Verso, 2015).

Moore, Margaret, *A Political Theory of Territory* (Oxford: Oxford University Press, 2017).

Morgan, Edmund, *Inventing the People: The Rise of Popular Sovereignty in England and America* (New York: W. W. Norton, 1989).

Morton, Timothy, *Dark Ecology: For a Logic of Future Coexistence* (New York: Columbia University Press, 2016).

_____, *Hyperobjects: Philosophy and Ecology after the End of the World* (Minneapolis: University of Minnesota Press, 2013).

Motha, Stewart, *Archiving Sovereignty: Law, History, Violence* (Ann Arbor: University of Michigan Press, 2018).

Moyn, Samuel, *The Last Utopia* (Cambridge, MA: Harvard University Press, 2010).

Nadasdy, Paul, *Sovereignty's Entailments: First Nation State Formation in the Yukon* (Toronto: University of Toronto Press, 2017).

Nancy, Jean-Luc, 'The Existence of the World is Always Unexpected', trans. Jeffery

Malecki, in Heather Davis and Etienne Turpin (eds), *Art in the Anthropocene: Encounters among Aesthetics, Politics, Environments and Epistemologies* (London: Open Humanities Press, 2015), pp. 85–92.

Neocleous, Mark, *Imagining the State* (Maidenhead: Open University Press, 2003).

Nijman, Janne E., 'Renaissance of the City as Global Actor: The Role of Foreign Policy and International Law Practices in the Construction of Cities as Global Actors', in Gunther Hellmann, Andreas Fahrmeir and Miloš Vec (eds), *The Transformation of Foreign Policy: Drawing and Managing Boundaries from Antiquity to the Present* (Oxford: Oxford University Press, 2016), pp. 209–41.

Nixon, Rob, *Slow Violence and the Environmentalism of the Poor* (Cambridge, MA: Harvard University Press, 2011).

Nord, Douglas C., *The Arctic Council: Governance within the Far North* (Abingdon: Routledge, 2016).

Olsen, Gunnar, *Abysmal: A Critique of Cartographic Reason* (Chicago: University of Chicago Press, 2007).

O'Toole, Fintan, 'Borders and Belonging: British and Irish Identities in a Post-Brexit Era' [Lecture at Queens University, Belfast, January 2019], <https://www.youtube.com/watch?v=1SeadvWsn_k&t=3766s> (last accessed 18 December 2020).

_____, *Heroic Failure: Brexit and the Politics of Pain* (London: Head of Zeus, 2018).

Parry, J. T., 'Terrain Evaluation, Military Purposes', in Charles W. Finkl, Jnr (ed.), *The Encyclopaedia of Applied Geology* (New York: Van Nostrand Reinhold, 1984), pp. 570–80.

Patel, Raj and Jason Moore, *A History of the World in Seven Cheap Things: A Guide to Capitalism, Nature and the Future of the Planet* (Los Angeles: University of California Press, 2017).

Philippopoulos-Mihalopoulos, Andreas, *Spatial Justice: Body, Lawscape, Atmosphere* (Abingdon: Routledge, 2015).

Phipps, P. J., 'Terrain Systems Mapping', *Geological Society, Engineering Geology Special Publications*, 18, 59–61 (2001).

Poggi, Gianfranco, *The Development of the Modern State: A Sociological Introduction* (Stanford: Stanford University Press, 1978).

Porras, Ilena, 'The City and International Law: In Pursuit of Sustainable Development', *Fordham Urban Law Journal*, 36, 537–601 (2008).

Povinelli, Elizabeth A., *Geontologies: A Requiem for Late Liberalism* (Durham, NC: Duke University Press, 2016).

Powys Whyte, Kyle, 'The Dakota Access Pipeline: Environmental Injustice and U.S. Colonialism', *Red Ink*, 19:1, 154–69 (2017).

Rancière Jacques, 'The Aesthetic Dimension', *Critical Inquiry*, 36:1, 1–19 (2009).

_____, *Disagreement: Philosophy and Politics*, trans. J. Rose (Minneapolis: University of Minnesota Press, 1999).

_____, *The Politics of Aesthetics* (London: Continuum, 2006).

Reilly, Alexander, 'Cartography and Native Title', *Journal of Australian Studies*, 27, 1–14 (2003).

Richardson, Janice, 'Hobbes' Frontispiece: Authorship, Subordination and Contract', *Law and Critique*, 27:1, 63–81 (2016).

Rockström, Johan, Will Steffen, Kevin Noone et al., 'Planetary Boundaries: Exploring the Safe Operating Space for Humanity', *Ecology and Society*, 14:2, 32 (2009).

Rogers, Nicole, *Law, Fiction and Activism in a Time of Climate Change* (Abingdon: Routledge, 2020).

Rogers, Nicole and Michelle Maloney (eds), *Law as if Earth Really Mattered: The Wild Law Judgment Project* (Abingdon: Routledge, 2017).

Ruddiman, William, 'The Anthropogenic Greenhouse Era Began Thousands of Years Ago', *Climatic Change*, 61:3, 261–93 (2003).

Runciman, David, 'Coronavirus Has Not Suspended Politics – It Has Revealed the Nature of Power', *The Guardian*, 27 March 2020, <https://www.theguardian.com/commentisfree/2020/mar/27/coronavirus-politics-lockdown-hobbes> (last accessed 18 December 2020).

Rush, Peter, 'An Altered Jurisdiction: Corporeal Traces of Law', *Griffith Law Review*, 6, 144 (1997).

Santner, Eric L., *On Creaturely Life: Rilke, Benjamin, Sebald* (Chicago: University of Chicago Press, 2006).

_____, *The Royal Remains: The People's Two Bodies and the Endgames of Sovereignty* (Chicago: University of Chicago Press, 2011).

Sassen, Saskia, *Territory, Authority, Rights: From Medieval to Global Assemblages* (Princeton: Princeton University Press, 2008).

Schillmoller, Anne and Alessandro Pelizzon, 'Mapping the Terrain of Earth Jurisprudence: Landscape, Thresholds and Horizons', *Environmental Law and Earth Law Journal*, 3, 1–32 (2013).

Schmitt, Carl, *Political Theology: Four Chapters on the Concept of Sovereignty*, trans. George Schwab (Chicago: University of Chicago Press, 2005).

Scott, James C., *Seeing Like a State: How Certain Schemes to Improve the Human Condition Have Failed* (New Haven, CT: Yale University Press, 1998).

Scratton, Roy, *Learning to Die in the Anthropocene* (San Francisco: City Lights Books, 2015).

Seigworth, Gregory J. and Melissa Gregg, 'An Inventory of Shimmers', in Melissa Gregg and Gregory J. Seigworth (eds), *The Affect Theory Reader* (Durham, NC: Duke University Press, 2010), pp. 1–25.

Serres, Michel, *The Natural Contract*, trans. Elizabeth MacArthur and William Paulson (Ann Arbor: University of Michigan Press, 1995).

Shakespeare, William, *Richard II* (Oxford: Oxford University Press, 2011).

Shepherd, Andrew, Helen Amanda Fricker and Sinead Louise Farrell, 'Trends and Connections across the Antarctic Cryosphere', *Nature*, 558, 223–32 (2018).

Shugar, Daniel H., John J. Clague, James L. Best et al., 'River Piracy and Drainage Basin Reorganization Led by Climate-Driven Glacier Retreat', *Nature Geoscience*, 10, 370–5 (2017).

Skinner, Quentin, *The Foundations of Modern Political Thought, Volume Two: The Age of Reformation* (Cambridge: Cambridge University Press, 1978).

Slattery, Brian, 'First Nations and the Constitution: A Question of Trust', *The Canadian Bar Review*, 71:2, 261–93 (1992).

Sloterdijk, Peter, 'The Anthropocene: A Process-State at the Edge of Geohistory?', trans. Anna-Sophie Springer, in Heather Davis and Etienne Turpin (eds), *Art in the Anthropocene: Encounters among Aesthetics, Politics, Environments and Epistemologies* (London: Open Humanities Press, 2015), pp. 327–40.

_____, *Foams: Spheres, Volume III* (Los Angeles: Semiotext(e), 2016).

Smil, Vaclav, *The Earth's Biosphere: Evolution, Dynamics, and Change* (Cambridge, MA: MIT Press, 2002).

Stager, Curt, *Deep Future: The Next 10,000 Years of Life on Earth* (New York: Thomas Dunne Books, 2011).

Stanescu, James, 'Species Trouble: Judith Butler, Mourning and the Precarious Lives of Animals', *Hypatia*, 27:3, 567–82 (2012).

Steffen, Will, Jacques Grinevald, Paul Crutzen and John McNeill, 'The Anthropocene: Conceptual and Historical Perspectives', *Philosophical Transactions of the Royal Society*, 369, 842–67 (2011).

Stengers, Isabelle, 'Faire avec Gaïa: pour une culture de la non-symétrie', *Ecopolitique Now!*, 24, 1–16 (2016).

Stern, Nicholas, *The Economics of Climate Change: The Stern Review* (Cambridge: Cambridge University Press, 2007).

Stoekl, Allan, 'Stocks and Shares', *Radical Philosophy*, 200, 61–3 (2016).

Thompson, John B., 'Ideology and the Social Imaginary: An Appraisal of Castoriadis and Lefort', *Theory and Society*, 11:5, 659–81 (1982).

Tsing, Anna Lowenhaupt, 'On Nonscalability', *Common Knowledge*, 18:3, 505–24 (2012).

Tuck, Richard, *The Sleeping Sovereign: The Invention of Modern Democracy* (Cambridge: Cambridge University Press, 2016).

Turpin, Etienne (ed.), *Architecture in the Anthropocene: Encounters among Design, Deep Time, Science and Philosophy* (Ann Arbor: Open Humanities, 2013).

Valverde, Marianna, *Chronotopes of Law: Jurisdiction, Scale and Governance* (Abingdon: Routledge, 2015).

Veitch, Scott, 'Binding Precedent: Robert Louis Stevenson's *Strange Case of Dr Jekyll and Mr Hyde*', in Marco Wan (ed.), *Reading the Legal Case: Cross Currents between Law and the Humanities* (Abingdon: Routledge, 2012), pp. 217–30.

_____, 'The Sense of Obligation', *Jurisprudence*, 8:3, 415–34 (2017).

Veitch, Scott, Emilios Christodoulidis and Lindsay Farmer, *Jurisprudence: Themes and Concepts*, 2nd edn (Abingdon: Routledge, 2012).

Vidas, Davor, Jan Zalasiewicz and Mark Williams, 'What is the Anthropocene – And Why is it Relevant for International Law?', *Yearbook of International Environmental Law*, 25:1, 3–23 (2014).

Walker, Neil, 'The Idea of Constitutional Pluralism', *Modern Law Review*, 65, 317–59 (2002).

_____, *Intimations of Global Law* (Cambridge: Cambridge University Press, 2014).

_____, 'Late Sovereignty in the European Union', in Neil Walker (ed.), *Sovereignty in Transition: Essays in European Law* (Oxford: Hart, 2003), pp. 3–32.

_____, 'Postnational Constitutionalism and Postnational Public Law: A Tale of Two Neologisms', *Transnational Legal Theory*, 3:1, 61–85 (2012).

_____, 'The Sovereignty Surplus', *International Journal of Constitutional Law*, 18:2, 370–428 (2020).

_____ (ed.), *Sovereignty in Transition: Essays in European Law* (Oxford: Hart, 2003).

Walker, R. B. J., *After the Globe, Before the World* (Abingdon: Routledge, 2010).

Wallace-Wells, David, *The Uninhabitable Earth: A Story of the Future* (London: Allen Lane, 2019).

Watson, Irene, 'Sovereign Spaces, Caring for Country, and the Homeless Position of Aboriginal Peoples', *South Atlantic Quarterly*, 108:1, 27–51 (2009).

Weber, Max, *The City* (New York: Free Press, 1966).

Weil, Simone, 'Draft for a Statement of Human Obligations', in Sian Miles (ed.), *Simone Weil: An Anthology* (London: Penguin, 2005), pp. 221–30.

_____, 'Human Personality', in Sian Miles (ed.), *Simone Weil: An Anthology* (London: Penguin, 2005), pp. 69–98.

_____, *The Need for Roots* (Abingdon: Routledge, 2001).

Weizman, Eyal, *Hollow Land: Israel's Architecture of Occupation* (London: Verso, 2012).

Welzer, Harald, *Climate Wars: Why People Will be Killed in the 21st Century* (Cambridge: Polity, 2012).

Wendall Holmes, Oliver, *The Common Law* (Boston: Little, Brown, 1881).

Wolfe, Cary, *Before the Law: Humans and Other Animals in a Biopolitical Frame* (Chicago: University of Chicago Press, 2012).

Woodward, David (ed.), *The History of Cartography, Volume 3: Cartography in the European Renaissance* (Chicago: University of Chicago Press, 2007).

Worm, Boris, Edward B. Barbier, Nicola Beaumont et al., 'Impacts of Biodiversity Loss on Ocean Ecosystem Services', *Science*, 314:5800, 787–90 (2006).

Yack, Bernard, 'Popular Sovereignty and Nationalism', *Political Theory*, 29:4, 517–36 (2001).

Zalasiewicz, Jan, Colin N. Waters, Mark Williams et al., 'When Did the Anthropocene

Begin? A Mid-twentieth Century Boundary Level is Stratigraphically Optimal', *Quaternary International*, 383, 196–203 (2015).

Zalasiewicz, Jan, Mark Williams, Colin N. Waters et al., 'Scale and Diversity of the Physical Technosphere: A Geological Perspective', *The Anthropocene Review*, 4:1, 9–22 (2017).

Cases

Calvin's Case (1608) 7 Co Rep 1a, 77 ER 377.
Juliana v United States of America, et al. (2020) (US Court of Appeals, Ninth Circuit).
Mabo v Queensland (No 2) (1992) 175 CLR 1.
R (Miller) v Secretary of State for Existing the European Union [2017] UKSC 5.

Legislation

Te Awa Tupua (Whanganui River Claims Settlement) Act 2017.
The Constitution of the People's Republic of China (Adopted at the Fifth Session of the Fifth National People's Congress and promulgated for implementation by the Proclamation of the National People's Congress on December 4, 1982).
Native Title Act (1993) (Cth).
The Virginia Charter (1606).

Index

aesthesis, 8, 16, 47, 64–70, 85, 98, 117, 166–8

aesthetics
  of the Anthropocene, 36–7, 40–1, 47–8
  of popular sovereignty, 115–18, 136–8
  of scale, 140–1, 144, 145–7, 165–8
  of territory, 86–7, 88–9, 91–2
  of terrain, 97–8, 103–6
  see also aesthesis

affect, 8, 13, 47, 51–2, 57, 59, 64–8, 115, 117–18, 122, 125, 136–7, 146–7, 167
  affective geometry, 97, 104, 106

Agamben, G., 56, 58, 73, 123–4

Amin, A., 166–7

Anthropocene (definitions of), 6, 7, 21–34; *see also* Capitalocene

Arctic, 3, 49, 103–5
  Arctic Council, 104–5
  imaginary of, 104–5

Arendt, H., 49, 127

Arènes, A., 97

atmosphere
  as affective, 48, 65, 68
  as element of the earth system, 2, 6, 22, 34, 94, 98–100, 151, 164

attention, 14, 46–7, 126, 166, 168; see also Weil, S.

attachment, 12, 14, 19, 20–1, 41, 45, 70, 81, 84, 90–6, 104–6, 107

Australian bush fires (2019–20), 139–40

Azo of Bologna, 154, 158

Bagehot, W., 60, 73

Barber, B., 161–2

being-bound, 14, 20, 41, 47, 126, 136; *see also* earthbound

Benton, L., 60–2, 71

Berry, T., 37

biopolitics, 14, 55–7, 58–9, 69, 75, 114, 118, 123, 128, 170–1; *see also* sovereignty and biopolitics

Bodin, J., 54

Branch, J., 85–7, 88

Braudel, F., 153, 155–7

Brenner, N., 142–4, 162–4, 166–7

Brexit, 50–1, 105–6, 111, 144, 170

Brotton, J., 84

Brown, W., 63

Capitalocene, 23, 25, 28–8, 34; *see also,* Anthropocene (definitions of)

cartography, 74, 83–92, 115, 146; *see also,* maps
  cartographic ideal, 89–92

Castoriadis, C., 67–9

Chakrabarty, D., 30, 147–9, 150ʼ, 151

Chinese Communist Party (CCP), 110–11

Christoloudis, E., 44–7

Clark, T., 140

Coccia, E., 98

Coke, E., 44

colonialism, 23, 56, 88–92, 135; *see also* sovereignty and colonialism

Cormack, B., 18, 74–5, 87

Crutzen, P., 21–2

Davies, J., 25–7

Davies, M., 45–6

demogenesis, 111–12, 115, 122, 136–7

Derrida, J., 28, 73, 109, 119–120, 124–5, 134, 144–145

www.ingramcontent.com/pod-product-compliance
Lightning Source LLC
Jackson TN
JSHW011742100625
85897JS00004B/23